Mirror and Veil

The frontispiece reproduces the "Rainbow portrait" of Queen Elizabeth. Painted near the end of her reign, the portrait idealizes the queen's beauty by means of the "mask of youth" deriving from miniatures by Nicholas Hilliard. The rainbow symbolizes the peace of Elizabeth's reign, and the motto "Non sine Sole Iris" ("Not without the Sun comes the Rainbow") associates her with the sun. Elizabeth as the sun, a symbol used by both painters and poets, asserted the religious truth that shone upon England through her rule and the "common blessing" which her reign bestowed upon her subjects. The eyes, ears, and mouths on her cloak symbolize Fame, and the serpent on the left arm is Wisdom. The flowers of spring on her dress and sleeves may suggest the constant spring of the golden age that the royal Astraea restored to England. Reproduced by permission of the Marquess of Salisbury.

NON SINE SOLE
IRIS.

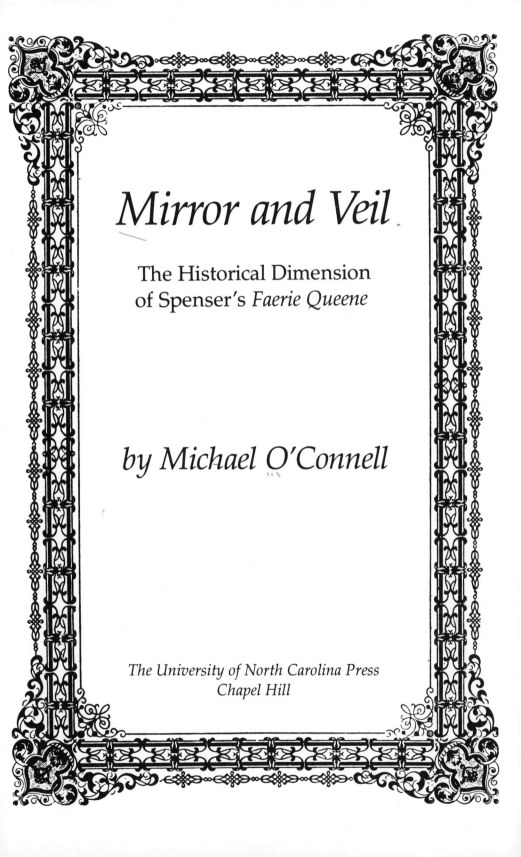

Mirror and Veil

The Historical Dimension
of Spenser's *Faerie Queene*

by Michael O'Connell

The University of North Carolina Press
Chapel Hill

Library of Congress Cataloging in Publication Data

O'Connell, Michael, 1943–
  Mirror and veil.

  Bibliography: p.
  Includes index.
    1.   Spenser, Edmund, 1552?–1599.   The faerie
queene.   I.   Title.
PR2358.025   821'.3   77-1733
ISBN 0-8078-1307-9

For Laura

✺ Contents

✿ Acknowledgments

Like several writers on Spenser and allegory in the past twenty years, I trace the source of my interest back to the Yale seminar of Professor John Pope. His seminar has proved a gentle nursery for the growth of a variety of ideas and critical approaches, and it is with a sense of following last in this daedal line that I express my gratitude to him. As a doctoral dissertation this study first took shape under his guidance and was fostered by his learning and wisdom.

Some debts go back even further. John Gleason of the University of San Francisco first opened to me the intellectual excitement of the Renaissance and its literature. At Yale Richard Sylvester taught me by precept and example the essential alliance of scholarship and criticism, and I suspect that whatever I have of scholarly sensibility is his molding.

Paul Alpers read the manuscript at two stages of its composition; I am grateful to him for shrewd criticism in both instances. Mark Rose, who also consented to a rereading, provided timely and valuable encouragement. Fred Nichols was a helpful reader of the original, and has given me effective support since then. Professors Jerry Leath Mills and Robert W. Hanning, readers for the press, made a number of useful suggestions. My colleagues Russell Astley, Norman Council, and Donald Guss have read chapters of the book and have made useful suggestions about specific points. I am particularly grateful to Richard Helgerson, who has patiently endured every revision and has never failed to provide me with the right criticism at the right time.

While I was revising sections of the book, the National Endowment for the Humanities granted me a year of pastoral otium in which to read classical literature. My understanding of Vergil, *inter alios*, was considerably extended by that reading, and I hope my discussions of Spenser's debt to Vergil may show the benefit of that year.

Chapter three appeared in a slightly different form as an article, "History and the Poet's Golden World: The Epic Catalogues in *The Faerie Queene*," in *English Literary Renaissance* 4 (1974).

I express my greatest debt in my dedicaton. My wife, Laura Stevenson O'Connell, has not only been a constant reader of draft after draft, but as a Tudor historian she has supplied me unfailingly with historical expertise and judgment. And this has been but a portion of her support to the author and his book.

Santa Barbara, California
February 1977

ᴊᴷ Explanatory Note

The text of Spenser quoted throughout is that of Edwin Greenlaw, C. G. Osgood, and F. M. Padelford, *The Works of Edmund Spenser: A Variorum Edition* (Baltimore: Johns Hopkins University Press, 1932–49), cited in the notes as *Variorum*. All citations of Scripture are to the Geneva Bible; I have quoted from the facsimile of the 1560 edition (Madison, Wis.: University of Wisconsin Press, 1969). For Vergil I have used both the text and the translation of the Loeb Classical Library, edited by H. Rushton Fairclough. Unless otherwise noted, translations are by the author. Quotations of sixteenth- and seventeenth-century texts are given in their original spelling and punctuation; contractions have been silently expanded.

There is a sizable body of scholarship identifying supposed historical allegories and allusions in *The Faerie Queene*, much of it quoted in the commentary and summarized in the appendices of the *Variorum* edition. I have not attempted to note my agreement or disagreement with all the various identifications, and my List of Works Cited should not be considered a bibliography of the scholarship on history in *The Faerie Queene*. As a convenience to the reader, I have generally cited the earlier criticism in the appendices of volumes of the *Variorum*, and I have not listed those works separately.

Mirror and Veil

✖ Introduction

Throughout his poetic career a significant portion of Spenser's attention was directed toward establishing a relationship between his poetry and political power. As a poet of moral vision, he recognized the importance of touching the mind of the ruler, for the ruler not only establishes national policy but also serves in some sense as the moral leader of a people. The poet whose voice is heard by those in power thus extends significantly his vatic power. It is, of course, an understatement to say that only rarely and with difficulty do poetic imagination and political power come into such a conjunction. From Old Testament times until the present, the more common relationship has been one of bitter opposition between prophet and king, poet and president. The modern sensibility supposes that opposition is inevitable, that being unacknowledged remains *the* occupational hazard of the poet as legislator. Only an age of buoyant optimism, we assume, would expect otherwise.

But Renaissance poets found the great archetype of the conjunction of poetic vision and political power in an age noted for political upheaval and pessimism: the relationship of Vergil and Augustus. The significant moment of that conjunction came in an incident that the Renaissance knew from the life of Vergil attributed to Donatus, a short biography deriving from Suetonius that was standard introductory fare in sixteenth-century editions of Vergil.[1] It was related that Vergil joined Octavian at Atella, where the latter, returning victorious from Actium, was delayed by a minor illness. For four days Vergil and Maecenas read to Octavian the recently completed *Georgics*. The leader who had emerged victorious from what was to prove the last battle of the civil wars was thus confronted with the poet's fervent and hopeful celebration of the arts of peace, a celebration punctuated with literal and symbolic reminders of the terrible costs of those wars. For once, then, and at a climactic moment in history, the man of power listened to the man of imagination. In the *Aeneid* Vergil would press his advantage and assume Augustus as a constant auditor of his poem.

3

There can be no doubt of the importance of Vergil's example to the poet who began his poetic career with *The Shepheardes Calender* and opened his own romance epic in imitation of the verses that stood at the beginning of the *Aeneid* in Renaissance editions. For sixteenth-century poets and critics Vergil crowned the summit of Parnassus, and a neoclassicist like Vida could advocate Vergil as the sole model for the aspiring poet:

> *Ergo ipsum ante alios animo venerare Maronem,*
> *Atque unum sequere; utque potes, vestigia serva.* [2]

Before all others, therefore, venerate the master Maro, and follow him alone; so far as you are able, keep even to his footsteps.

For Spenser, however, Vergil's importance was not so much as an exemplar of form as of moral stance. What Spenser found most attractive in Vergil was the poet who had judged and celebrated his nation and his age. The Roman poet had sensed the necessity of celebrating those elements of his culture that would stabilize a society torn by civil war. The explicit subjects of his epic became the traditional Roman strengths and virtues, the imperial destiny through which divergent peoples would unite, and a hero who finds his greatness in self-denial. But there emerges another voice in the *Aeneid*, one that judges the costs of Rome's arrival at unity and empire and is saddened by them. Vergil's own *lacrimae rerum* embrace the destruction of Carthage and the submergence of Italic cultures and traditions.[3] By no means do all of the points of contact between Aeneas and Augustus flatter the emperor. It is this dual purpose of celebration and moral judgment of a nation and an age that defines the most profound connection between Spenser and the Latin poet he emulated.

Although there are few explicit similarities between Vergil's Rome and Spenser's England, simply the word *Elizabethan* suggests to us a people arriving at a sense of national identity, a nation standing on the edge of empire. England's civil wars had been concluded a century earlier, but the religious turmoil of Mary's reign had left traumatic memories in the minds of Elizabeth's subjects. The continent, moreover, provided ready examples of the violence and bloodshed that England could expect if its monarch were not successful in leading the nation toward unity and an acceptable reformation of religion. Elizabeth's success, produced by her intelligence but reinforced by her own conscious decision of self-denial, gave England the forty-five-year period of peace and creativity that is named for her. It is this moral achievement—of Elizabeth and of the nation—that Spenser wished in part to celebrate in *The Faerie Queene*.

But any poet who chooses to write an allegorical poem for the moral instruction of his contemporaries (and explicitly includes his sovereign among his expected auditors) obviously does not find everything in his world unambiguously worthy of celebration. Indeed, even the choice of allegorical representation may suggest implicit doubt about contemporary deeds and events that might have been the subject of a more direct, straightforward mode of poetic treatment. In this regard the appropriate comparison is *The Lusiads* of Camoens. The Portuguese poet, writing two decades before Spenser, chose as his subject the actual deeds of actual men. As a result, the two national epics, so close in point of time and not greatly dissimilar in celebratory aims, differ considerably in their responses to those aims. Camoens celebrates Vasco da Gama's spread of the Portuguese empire to the East, and his patriotic poem seems almost of necessity to take on its frankly nationalistic character. Spenser's allegorical representation frees him from the necessity of treating actual events, and he is everywhere closer to myth than to history. Spenser's kind of allegory generally keeps the considerations of history within a framework of moral concern. *The Faerie Queene*, though undeniably patriotic, seems by its reticence toward specific historical deeds more skeptical—more Vergilian—than nationalistic.

The two motives of celebration and moral judgment describe accurately, I believe, the shape of Spenser's poetic meditation on his age. For the most part he prefers to separate them, almost as dialectical opposites, and often chooses different poetic modes for the expression of each.[4] *The Shepheardes Calender* provides us with a clear example of the way Spenser treats contemporary realities at the beginning of his career, and although he is seldom so schematic in *The Faerie Queene*, a brief look at his method in the early poem will serve to show some of the complexity I have postulated as his way of confronting contemporary political reality.

The two modes that Spenser employs in the *Calender* to consider this reality are the golden-age vision, deriving from Vergil's

Fourth Eclogue, and the satiric pastoral dialogue, deriving from Mantuan's eclogues of ecclesiastical satire. The *April* eclogue, which comes fourth in the *Calender,* celebrates Elizabeth and idealizes her virtuous rule. The three eclogues that deal with ecclesiastical affairs —*May, July,* and *September*—consider in an equally partial way some of the negative aspects of the rule of the actual Elizabeth. Both idealization and satire isolate elements of reality and treat them separately.

The *April* eclogue presents the hymn to Eliza as an idealization by setting it in a frame that contrasts the past and present states of Colin Clout's mind. Hobbinol explains that his own sadness arises from the alterations in Colin; earlier Colin had enjoyed a state of contentment and creativity, but now he has fallen into a destructive love melancholy. This melancholy becomes in the course of the *Calender* an effective metaphor for the fallen human condition. It is what makes Colin's life follow the seasons of the year, and it finally brings on his aging and death. In *June* Colin asserts that Hobbinol's contemplative equanimity has caused him to recover that paradise "whych Adam lost," but for Colin no such recovery is possible. His time of innocent enjoyment and celebration is past, except as it exists in song. Framed as it is by this sense of loss, the hymn to Eliza represents an ideal set not in an undefined future, as in Vergil, but in an undefined past. The first readers of the poem recognized that the actuality celebrated continued into the present, but this framing device emphasized the specifically ideal quality of the hymn.

The hymn itself is a static vision—the action it narrates is negligible—and one could easily imagine a painting of the scene. The figure of Eliza is in fact related to the actual queen through iconographic details. Eliza is "Yclad in Scarlot like a mayden Queene, / And Ermines white." An ermine was used to compliment the chastity of the queen, and as such it appears in one or her portraits.[5] The icon for the unification of the houses of Lancaster and York is deftly combined with the traditional imagery of the adored mistress of the sonneteers: "The Redde rose medled with the White yfere, / In either cheeke depeincten liuely chere." One icon in the vision links the poem to an important tradition of visual celebration of Elizabeth, a tradition employed in the woodcut to the *April* eclogue itself:[6]

I sawe Phoebus *thrust out his golden hedde,*
    vpon her to gaze;
But when he sawe, how broade her beames did spredde,
    it did him amaze.
He blusht to see another Sunne belowe,
Ne durst againe his fyrye face out showe:
    Let him, if he dare,
    His brightnesse compare
With hers, to haue the ouerthrowe.

[*April*, lines 73–81]

What the stanza depicts is the motif of a sun shining through a veil of clouds. The symbol suggests a comparison of the queen's present glory to the darkness and dangers of the past—an implicit comparison, perhaps, of Elizabeth's sunny reign to the dark clouds of the previous reign. As with the rose icon, the motif is given a hyperbolic amatory twist; political devotion becomes equivalent to the devotion of the lover. The bay branches of triumph and the olive crown complete the specifically political reference to the queen who had blessed England with a reign of peace. The idealization of Elizabeth in Eliza celebrates some specific realities: the queen is of the Tudor dynasty that ended the civil war and united the red rose and the white; as a rival of Phoebus, she has dispersed the dark clouds of the previous reign and the threats from the continent that attended her accession to the throne; and she has kept England both triumphant and peaceful.

The hymn to Eliza in *April* presents an idealized reciprocal relationship between poetry and political order. Like Tityrus in Vergil's first eclogue, Colin acknowledges the relation between his pastoral vision and the ruler who makes it possible: "Shee is my goddesse plaine, / And I her shepherds swayne, / Albee forswonck and forswatt I am." Colin says in effect, "*Dea* nobis haec otia fecit." The poet's song celebrates the order that makes song possible. The degree to which the actual Elizabeth falls short of the ideal Eliza is owing to the fallen human condition, and the reader understands this from the framing dialogue. But the duty of the artist, in terms of the celebratory motive in Spenser's poetry, is to show to men within the fallen state the points of connection between their actual ruler and the ideal of which she is merely the human participation.

England does not, of course, project the very image of the innocent golden age, but the degree to which it even approaches that ideal is its debt to a queen who has brought peace and security. Elizabeth resembles Eliza to the extent that England approaches the ideal of golden-age harmony. The duty of the poet is to celebrate such a proportion and provide the terms, here iconographic, that connect actual and ideal.

The satiric eclogues of the *Calender* delineate in pastoral terms the other side of the reality of contemporary England; *May, July,* and *September* explore the differences between that reality and the golden-age ideal. It is significant that none of the iconography of *April* alludes to the queen's role in establishing a religious settlement, and in these satiric eclogues Spenser shows himself to be far from satisfied with the state of the English church. He satirizes the comfortable complacency that he believes has arisen in the twenty years since the restoration of Protestantism. He expresses disapproval of the queen's intrusion into attempts to improve the level of clerical learning; in particular, he sympathizes with the plight of Edmund Grindal, the archbishop of Canterbury whose conscientious stand in support of such attempts in London led to his suspension by the queen. And most daringly, he charges in *September* that depredations of church livings by venal courtiers (with support in high places) were resulting in an erosion of religious life in the remote parts of the kingdom. The foreign threat to reformed religion was growing all the stronger because of official indifference to the effective preaching of the Gospel. The kingdom would be better served by competent bishops and educated clergy than by the "great hunt" for Catholic agents being carried on by the government. The total understanding of the contemporary church that emerges from the three eclogues represents some frank advice to the monarch in her role of supreme governor of the church.[7]

The satiric eclogues refer to the contemporary situation not by means of iconography but by names that allude to actual persons whom the poet identifies as representative of various values and attitudes. In Palinode of the *May* eclogue, for example, Spenser singles out Andrew Perne, the notorious master of Peterhouse, Cambridge, who had shifted his sails several times since Edward's reign to catch the changing winds of religious doctrine and had cruised comfortably under Catholic and Protestant monarchs. The perennial scorn of undergraduates for political pliancy had fastened upon Dr. Perne a number of amusing epithets, among them "old Father Palinode," one of the names he is known by in the Marprelate tracts.[8] Spenser is known to have disliked Perne from his Cambridge days, but in the eclogue he employs Palinode as an attack not so much on Perne himself as on the state of mind that sees compromise and accommodation as the answer to every problem. Such an attitude, the eclogue suggests, has fostered the dangerous complacency in the contemporary church. In the pastoral debate Palinode is opposed by Piers, whose name has been seen by critics to allude to John Piers, the hardworking and ascetic bishop of Salisbury. Piers insists that basic values, here the values of the Gospel, do not admit of compromise, that finally lines must be drawn and positions taken.

But when we recall the idealization of *April*, it is most noteworthy that Spenser actually implicates the queen in the satire of the *July* eclogue. Both *May* and *July* refer approvingly to the teaching of the shepherd Algrind (a name produced by reversing the syllables of Grindal), and in *July* the suspension of the Archbishop of Canterbury is afforded a curious pastoral guise. Asked who Algrind is, Thomalin replies:

> *He is a shepheard great in gree,*
>   *but hath bene longe ypent.*
> *One daye he sat vpon a hyll,*
>   *(as now thou wouldest me:*
> *But I am taught by* Algrins *ill,*
>   *to loue the lowe degree.)*
> *For sitting so with bared scalpe,*
>   *an Eagle sored hye,*
> *That weening hys whyte head was chalke,*
>   *a shell fish downe let flye:*
> *She weend the shell fishe to haue broake,*
>   *but therewith bruzd his brayne,*
> *So now astonied with the stroke,*
>   *he lyes in lingring payne.*

[*July*, lines 215–28]

The satire, of course, cannot with impunity touch the queen's suspension of Grindal too closely, but the comedy manages to express sympathy for Grindal and, by making the royal bird feminine, to suggest error in the queenly judgment. In the satiric part of the *Calender*, a nearsighted she-eagle replaces the shimmering Eliza as the fictive shadow of Elizabeth.

Because of the power of the eagle's prototype—the Puritan John Stubbs lost his right hand for daring to question her judgment —the pastoral satirist must pull his punch and content himself with such gentle taps. There is in the three satiric eclogues a tension, sometimes stated, between general moral satire and the satire that names names and points up specific abuses. The general moral satire, such as Piers's beast fable in *May*, is safe enough, but its weakness lies in its very generality; Palinode can borrow Piers's fable for the ignorant Sir John to use in a holiday sermon—in spite of the fact that it is precisely at the Sir Johns of the world that the fable is aimed. When in the *September* eclogue Diggon Davie decries with increasing clarity and bitterness the wretched state of the "shepherds" in his remote region, Hobbinol warns him:

> Nowe Diggon, I see thou speakest to plaine:
> Better it were, a little to feyne,
> And cleanly couer, that cannot be cured.
> Such il, as is forced, mought nedes be endured.
>
> [*September*, lines 136–39]

The satirist is treading on perilous ground as he points a finger at the official corruption that had despoiled the bishopric of Diggon's prototype.[9] This tension between generalized, safe (and probably ineffective) satire and specific, potentially dangerous satire points to a troubled and uncertain relation between poetry and the political order. Such a relation stands implicitly juxtaposed to the ideal reciprocity of poetry and the political order celebrated in *April*. If a goddess has granted pastoral otium to the poet, she can also hurl thunderbolts at him.

What is most impressive about the historical dimension of the *Calender* is the clear awareness it represents of the difficulties involved in confronting contemporary history poetically. As Vergil did in his *Eclogues*, Spenser wants to celebrate the potentiality of the present at the same time he portrays his own coming to poetic maturity. Spenser's political understanding, like Vergil's, includes the knowledge that the new order nevertheless still exists within a fallen world. Even in the golden-age eclogue Vergil speaks of "sceleris vestigia nostri" that yet remain, and in the first and ninth eclogues he poignantly adumbrates some of the human pain caused by Caesarian policies. Inclined to be more schematic, Spenser separates his celebration of the new order from his discussion of those "traces of our guilt," the results of man's fallen nature. His twofold vision of contemporary reality embraces both England's achievement of the ideals of peace and security, celebrated in the hymn to Eliza, and the subversion of Gospel ideals, satirized in *May, July,* and *September.* Both are parts of one reality, and both represent aspects of the actual ruler. The poet consequently must see his role as being twofold, and his relationship to political power must be characterized by motives of appreciative acceptance and critical judgment.

In *The Faerie Queene* Spenser confronts contemporary political realities in a less schematic way, but he shows himself equally aware of the necessity for a complex response to those realities. Understanding of his response by modern readers, however, has been obscured by the widespread use of the term "historical allegory" to describe what I prefer to call the historical dimension of *The Faerie Queene.* Although an eighteenth-century critic like John Upton could speak of "moral allegory with historical allusions,"[10] scholars in the latter half of the nineteenth and early twentieth centuries began to describe continued historical allegories that paralleled the moral allegory of the poem. Generally these historical allegories were more indebted to the fancy and learning of the critics than they were to Spenser's poem. A few critical demurrers were entered, notably by Edwin Greenlaw in 1932,[11] but the *Variorum* edition of Spenser enshrined most of the historical allegorizing of the earlier critics and further helped to keep the idea alive by including appendices entitled "Historical Allegory" to most of the volumes of *The Faerie Queene.* Although more theoretical sophistication among literary critics resulted, after the 1920s, in an end of such expeditions in search of historical allegory, the mere existence of these appendices appears to have convinced many later critics of the general validity of the term. It occurs from time to time, though generally without being seriously considered, in the rich outpouring of Spenser criticism in the 1960s. Recently, however, both the term and the critical assumptions behind it have enjoyed a revival in J. E. Hankins's *Source and Meaning in Spenser's Allegory*.[12]

The most evident difficulty with the idea that historical allegory informs much of *The Faerie Queene* lies in the very tenuous relation between nearly all of the supposed allegories and the poem itself. Furtive hints or allusions must be connected, and intervening non-allusive stretches of the poem must be brought under the control of the allegory. None of the various historical allegories fastened upon book 1, for instance, can actually be kept in mind while one is reading the poem attentively. (A. C. Hamilton proved this point when he constructed an allegory of the Russian Revolution to fit book 1; his allegory bore only slightly less relevance to that book than most of the allegories of the Reformation—Una as Anne Boleyn, Fradubio as Archbishop Cranmer—fashioned by the earlier critics.[13]) Both past and present critics who have sought out the historical allegories have seldom concerned themselves with basic questions: whether the narrative surface of the poem in fact gestures toward an historical reality beyond it or *how* the narrative makes such gestures. If we ask such questions of the poem, we discover that it generally points to the nonfictional world intermittently and then through special devices such as suggestive narrative rhetoric, allusive names, or iconography. The world of *The Faerie Queene* does indeed include prospects from which we catch sight of the historical world, but the poet does not insist that such views are constantly in sight; rather he leads us to viewpoints from time to time and generally affords us no more than a quick glimpse beyond the Faery landscape. The reader who becomes sensitive to this aspect of the poem understands that the historical world does not impinge constantly upon the allegory but rather that it is an impending presence, a presence that even when out of sight has a kind of pervasive relevance.

The most damaging result of the concept of historical allegory is that it has committed us to a poet representing history through a single celebratory mode. It has not permitted us to see him judging the same event or person from different perspectives, with differing assumptions about power and human history. In the *Shepheardes Calender*, as we have noted, the celebratory mode of *April* views the queen with assumptions about fallen human nature and the consequent value men place on the achievement of peace and tranquility. The satiric eclogues view man in a significantly different perspective; there the achievement of the Gospel values—justice, mercy, humility—takes precedence over a mere concern with social harmony. An overriding concern for harmony may in fact be harmful if it forces men to neglect or grow slack in their striving for those values. We have no reason to suppose that Spenser's way of considering power and history will have grown simpler in *The Faerie Queene*. The very fact that he is concerned to represent Elizabeth in a variety of images—including, as I hope to show, negative images of her rule—compels us to abandon the notion that historical allegory defines the nature of the poem's involvement with history.

This is not to say, however, that the term historical allegory never describes Spenser's means of representing contemporary history. In the second half of book 5, he constructs what can be properly described as historical allegory, for here historical events do indeed structure the allegory of the poem. It is significant, I believe, that readers have long felt that Spenser's vision at this point becomes disturbingly narrow, that the poem loses some of the moral complexity that characterizes the other books. Historical allegory, whether constructed by critic or poet, seems to require a certain singleness of purpose, and in book 5 the celebratory motive becomes apologetic and takes an unwonted precedence over the motive of moral judgment. I suspect that Spenser came to write historical allegory in book 5 because of a need he felt to confront history more fully and insistently than he had done earlier. Perhaps the need derived from the pressure of events in the 1590s, perhaps because Vergilian promises remained unfulfilled. In any case, an almost obsessive desire to celebrate and defend the policies of Elizabeth comes over the poem as the Legend of Justice moves toward its conclusion. Historical allegory is the result.

In the historical dimension of *The Faerie Queene*, I see not a static vision but a continuing meditation on the relation of poetry and political realities. On the evidence of the first three books of the poem, one may feel that Spenser is working toward a consistent vision of Tudor Britain. But we find in the later books a growing ambivalence toward history and political power, an ambivalence nowhere more evident than in the contrast between the final two completed books of the poem. When in the first book he considered the relation of personal holiness to what had been achieved historically in the English Reformation, he could not have anticipated, I believe, the skeptical direction his thoughts would take at the conclusion of the Legend of Courtesy. The satiric impulse evident in the *Shepheardes Calender* and *Mother Hubberds Tale* would not find more than intermittent expression in *The Faerie Queene*. What Thomas Edwards properly judged of *Colin Clouts Come Home Againe* applies equally well to the major poem: "for Spenser satire is an inadequate vehicle for the whole of Colin's experience." Elizabeth and her court were basically "a focus of positive commitments, an expressive synthesis of what was valuable in national life."[14] There remained, however, the sense of moral uneasiness that had originally kindled the satiric impulse, and this unease eventually was transmuted by the poet's experience into an impulse of imaginative withdrawal from the politic world. The energy that had earlier found expression in satire began at the end of Spenser's career to express itself in the creation of poetic moments more private and introspective, moments that are implicitly opposed to public celebration.

I see the development of *The Faerie Queene* as being increasingly concerned with the poet's own experience, especially his experience of Ireland, and in my last two chapters I argue, without apology, for the relevance of this experience to his epic vision. Spenser's life in Ireland surely acted upon his awareness of the complex and often uneasy relation of the imagination to political power and was finally decisive in motivating his imaginative withdrawal. The varying degrees and stages of this awareness, I believe, account for some of the most notable successes—and failings—of a poem that records a continued meditation on the moral nature of its age.

In the chapters that follow I shall not be attempting to provide a full and comprehensive reading of the poem. Recent criticism, though generally shy of Spenser's involvement with history, has provided us with satisfactory accounts of the artistry and moral concerns of the poem and its various books. While assuming that the reader has a general sense of *The Faerie Queene*, I shall offer readings of sections of the poem that represent Spenser's attempt to treat in epic terms of his contemporary world and of the moral potential of political power. What I hope to illuminate are the ways in which Spenser directs his moral themes toward his age and in turn uses the age to illustrate those themes. Though we no longer read *The Faerie Queene* as the detached dreamworld the romantics saw, we still need to achieve a better understanding of the ways in which its moral concerns are rooted in and directed toward contemporary realities. My aim is to restore some of the sense of Vergilian involvement with history, which I find a not inconsiderable part of the poem's appeal. An understanding of its serious concern for history can deepen, I believe, our growing sense of the poem's moral and psychological sophistication.

Chapter 1

The Method
of the Poet Historical

In the editorial material that accompanied the publication of the first three books of *The Faerie Queene*, Spenser fosters an air of mystery about the relation of his poem to the contemporary world. He provides a number of tantalizing hints that do not so much define the relation as pique the reader's curiosity about how—and to what extent—the poem will reflect contemporary reality. He speaks in the letter to Raleigh, for example, of a dual purpose in the character of Gloriana:

In that Faery Queene I meane glory in my generall intention, but in my particular I conceiue the most excellent and glorious person of our soueraine the Queene, and her kingdome in Faery land. And yet in some places els, I doe otherwise shadow her. For considering she beareth two persons, the one of a most royall Queene or Empresse, the other of a most vertuous and beautifull Lady, this latter part in some places I doe express in Belphoebe, fashioning her name according to your owne excellent conceipt of Cynthia, (Phoebe and Cynthia being both names of Diana.)

Since Spenser first suggests the double significance of Gloriana then explains that his representation of Elizabeth will not be limited to this character, we realize that we can expect no simple correspondence between fiction and reality. The poet is making distinctions about reality, and these distinctions are to be reflected in his fictional world. The very words he uses—"in some places els, I doe otherwise shadow her"—are a challenge to his reader's powers of perception and judgment. Where else is the queen represented, and what aspects of her person or rule are portrayed? The answer he seems to give in the mention of Belphoebe is really no more than a hint: "in some places" he has expressed the queen's private person in a certain character. But the reader is left to wonder whether these two characters are the limit of the poem's portrayal of the queen and in what sense her kingdom is to be understood in the fictional Faeryland.

Several of the dedicatory sonnets of this first installment of the poem play similarly, though less suggestively, with the idea that there is some subtle relation between the poem's fiction and matters contemporary or historical. In the sonnet to the earl of Oxford, Spenser asks him to defend the poem from "foule Enuies poisnous bit":

> *Which so to doe may thee right well besit,*
>   *Sith th'antique glory of thine auncestry*
>   *Vnder a shady vele is therein writ,*
>   *And eke thine owne long liuing memory,*
> *Succeeding them in true nobility.*

The veil is indeed shady, for if Spenser had any specific intention of celebrating Oxford or the Veres, it has not been discovered. Perhaps the claim is not specific, and Spenser merely wants to suggest that the English nobility is memorialized in the poem in a general sort of way. The sonnet to the earl of Essex is more cautious, for it makes no claim of present celebration (in 1590 there was little enough to celebrate) but holds out a promise for the future. The poet will "make more famous memory / Of thine Heroicke parts" when his muse is able to fly more boldly "to the last praises of this Faery Queene." Since dedicatory sonnets were, in part, the sixteenth century's equivalent of the publisher's puff, they are to be read not so much for a precise meaning as for the impression they seek to convey. These sonnets hint coyly that the queen's powerful servants will find much to interest them in this fictional veil of their political world.

But it is the stanzas that serve as proems to the first three books that most interestingly tantalize the reader with the suggestion that the poem shadows in some way the actual world. In these proems Spenser shifts his ground frequently and changes the terms by which he describes the relation of his fiction to contemporary reality. At the conclusion of the proem to book 1, he invokes the queen—in the company of Venus, Cupid, and Mars—as the muse of his poem:

> *And with them eke, O Goddesse heauenly bright,*
> *Mirrour of grace and Maiestie diuine,*
> *Great Lady of the greatest Isle, whose light*
> *Like* Phoebus *lampe throughout the world doth shine,*
> *Shed thy faire beames into my feeble eyne,*
> *And raise my thoughts too humble and too vile,*
> *To thinke of that true glorious type of thine,*
> *The argument of mine afflicted stile:*
> *The which to heare, vouchsafe, O dearest dred a-while.*

The subject of the poem is a "type" of the queen in its etymological sense of a figure or image. The adjective "glorious" seems to suggest Gloriana, but the actual argument of book 1 is the struggle and final victory of Una and the Redcross knight over the forces of Antichrist. Since the queen is both inspiration and subject of the poem, the poet may imply that this victory is in some sense a "type" of the queen's experience.

The proem to the second book pretends with a kind of Ariostan playfulness to answer an objection to the fabulous nature of this "history":

> *Right well I wote most mighty Soueraine,*
> *That all this famous antique history,*
> *Of some th' aboundance of an idle braine*
> *Will iudged be, and painted forgery,*
> *Rather then matter of iust memory,*
> *Sith none, that breatheth liuing aire, does know,*
> *Where is that happy land of Faery,*
> *Which I so much do vaunt, yet no where show,*
> *But vouch antiquities, which no body can know.*

But new regions are being discovered every day now, the poet objects, and the New World would have seemed just as fabulous to an earlier age. With a probable recollection of Astolfo's ascent to the moon in the *Orlando Furioso*, he asks what a skeptic would say if more worlds were discovered in "the Moones faire shining spheare" or in other stars: "He wonder would much more: yet such to some appeare." The last phrase suggests Ariosto specifically, but instead of stressing the similarity of Faeryland to Ariosto's world, the next stanza indicates the difference between them. The skeptical reader may be able to find Faeryland nearer at hand than Ariosto's fabulous world:

> *Of Faerie lond yet if he more inquire,*
>> *By certaine signes here set in sundry place*
>> *He may it find; ne let him then admire,*
>> *But yield his sence to be too blunt and bace,*
>> *That n'ote without an hound fine footing trace.*
>> *And thou, O fairest Princesse vnder sky,*
>> *In this faire mirrhour maist behold thy face,*
>> *And thine owne realmes in lond of Faery,*
> *And in this antique Image thy great auncestry.*

But the "explanation" is as much a cautionary warning as a direction. The image of the reader with leashed bloodhound following the poet's tracks is a comic touch designed to put us on our guard against supposing that the trail from Faeryland to the world of Elizabeth is well blazed or easily sniffed out. When the poet turns from the skeptical reader to the queen, he puts aside the playful and comic tone and commends the poem to her as a mirror. But the mirror of Renaissance art never returned an exact reflection, and this understanding of mirror is implicit in the pardon that he asks in the final stanza for enfolding "in couert vele" the glory of queen and realm.

In the proem to book 1, Spenser used one of Elizabeth's familiar cult icons when he asserted that the light of her glory "Like *Phoebus* lampe throughout the world doth shine."[1] In the proem to book 2, he insists that this light must be veiled and wrapped "in shadowes light" to enable the feeble eyes of men to look upon it. Spenser wishes to project a double—and paradoxical—understanding of the poet's role: the poet is the imitator who holds, as 'twere, the mirror up to nature, but he is also the hierophant who protects the sacred by revealing it only in veiled sense.[2] Thus the poem will "mirror" the queen's reality, but only to the initiated who can read the "certaine signes" and understand the shape of mysteries behind the veil. This paradoxical doubleness in the poet's role is similar to, but not quite the same as, the double stance of the poet in the *Shepheardes Calender;* there the poet is both Colin, the celebrant of the queen's glory, and the satirist who appears in Colin's absence to bewail the failings of the age. The suggestion of the hierophant does conform to the priestly, celebratory side of the pastoral Colin. But because satire will not generally be the poetic mode of *The Faerie Queene,* the "mirroring" of the poem will not exactly conform, as we might expect from Hamlet's formulation ("to show virtue her own feature, scorn her own image"), to the usual metaphor of the satiric moralist. The mirrors, as we shall see, are rather to be special precision instruments, prisms or parabolic reflectors, than straight looking glasses.

In the proem to book 3, Spenser compares himself to a painter to describe his method of representing the queen. Here portraiture becomes the equivalent of the mirror metaphor. Since he writes of chastity in this book, he asks, what need is there to "fetch from *Faery* / Forreine ensamples" of the virtue. It is enshrined in his sovereigne's breast, and one need only look at a portrait of her heart—"If pourtrayd it might be by any liuing art." This last point, of course, is the catch, and we expect the compliment to the queen which follows:

> But liuing art may not least part expresse,
>> Nor life-resembling pencill it can paint,
>> All were it Zeuxis or Praxiteles:
>> His daedale hand would faile, and greatly faint,
>> And her perfections with his error taint:
>> Ne Poets wit, that passeth Painter farre
>> In picturing the parts of beautie daint,
>> So hard a workmanship aduenture darre,
> For fear through want of words her excellence to marre.
>
> How then shall I, Apprentice of the skill,
>> That whylome in diuinest wits did raine,
>> Presume so high to stretch mine humble quill?
>> Yet now my lucklesse lot doth me constraine
>> Hereto perforce. But O dred Soueraine
>> Thus farre forth pardon, sith that choicest wit
>> Cannot your glorious pourtraict figure plaine
>> That I in colourd showes may shadow it,
> And antique praises vnto present persons fit.

Just as the brightness of the poet's subject prevented mirroring without a veil, so now the perfection of her virtue prevents portraiture. Since book 3 is the most Ariostan book of the poem, it may not be amiss to see in the reference to painting an implicit contrast to the art of contemporary representation in the *Orlando Furioso*. Many of Ariosto's references to his patrons and his contemporary world are contained in "prophetic" works of art described in the course of the narrative. These "art works"—frescoes, a sculptured fountain, tapestries—are all large in format. The "art" in each case is Ariosto's, and it is designed to portray, in a manner sometimes tinged with irony, the policies, deeds, and virtues of his d'Este patrons and their allies.[3] Ariosto paints with broad brush strokes on large surfaces; there is never any question about the identity of the portraits in the visual pageants he creates. If Spenser alludes to Ariosto's mode of portraying contemporary realities in the proem to book 3, then he implies a contrast between it and his own method of shadowing his patroness.

Specifically, of course, Spenser refers to Raleigh and his "portrait" of the queen in Cynthia. He insists that "liuing colours, and right hew" are to be found in Raleigh's portrait. In the final stanza of the proem, he defers to Raleigh and suggests that his own way of presenting the queen will be an alternative to portraiture:

> But let that same delitious Poet lend
> A little leaue vnto a rusticke Muse
> To sing his mistresse prayse, and let him mend,
> If ought amis her liking may abuse:
> Ne let his fairest Cynthia refuse,
> In mirrours more then one her selfe to see,
> But either Gloriana let her chuse,
> Or in Belphoebe fashioned to bee:
> In th'one her rule, in th'other her rare chastitee.

Though the poet's deprecatory reference to his "rusticke Muse," like the tone of the whole proem, strikes a pose of courtly humility, it is not hard to discern a sense of confidence that something more important than exact representation is going on in the fetching of "forrein ensamples" or the fitting of "antique praises" unto present persons. The phrase "mirrours more then one" reiterates the point made in the letter to Raleigh: distinctions about the reality of the queen are to be found in the poet's fiction. His "colourd shows" may be shadowing things too difficult to represent in mere portraiture. If we were to update Spenser's painting metaphor, we might see him opposing cubist perspective to representational portraiture. He protests that he cannot reproduce the queen's beauty, but his canvas will be analytic, will approach its subject from a variety of angles.

We must not neglect the possibility, perhaps even the likelihood, that the shifting metaphors of the various phrases Spenser applies to his art indicate a certain tentativeness about the relation of the fictional world to the actual world. The phrases gesture toward a relation, but they do not define it. Within the language of courtly compliment, I think we may sense something of the poet's problem in creating his romance epic. Part of his intention—the "general end," he writes to Raleigh—is ethical: "to fashion a gentleman or noble person in vertuous and gentle discipline." Another part of his intention is aesthetic: to emulate, in the sense of both to imitate and, if possible, to surpass the other "poets historicall," Homer, Vergil, Ariosto, and Tasso. A part of his intention visible in the proems, in the letter to Raleigh, and in some of the dedicatory sonnets is to write a poem celebrating his age and his nation. No doubt that aspect of the poet's intention I have called ethical was inseparably intertwined with this celebratory motive: a poem celebrating a nation and a ruler could in turn afford both a vision that would prove ennobling. The poem must be, as Milton was to phrase it in proposing genres and subjects to himself in the early 1640s, "doctrinal and exemplary to a nation."[4] In fact, ethical intent without such an imaginative vision of the age would risk the composition of a mere fictionalized behavior book. Certainly Spenser's overall intention was not to write such a book but to create *the* heroic poem for Elizabethan England. The central problem in creating a poem with both ethical and celebratory aims is that the two may be, if not in conflict, at least reconcilable only with difficulty. It is this problem that is considered, but not resolved, in the *October* eclogue of the *Shepheardes Calender*. With unperceived irony Piers there suggests that Cuddy abandon pastoral to sing heroically of "doubted Knights, whose woundlesse armour rusts, / And helmes vnbruzed wexen dayly browne." The eclogue asks how the poet can achieve heroic song in an age that is notably lacking in heroic exploits or heroic virtue. (One may suspect that "doubted" has its modern meaning lurking behind the archaism.) A secondary but related question is how the poet can write an epic poem whose implicit subject is not a king or military leader but a woman ruler. Hence the tentativeness conveyed by the various phrases Spenser uses to suggest the relation between the fictional and actual worlds makes me suppose that we are to see in them not only a desire to tantalize the reader with hints about the shifting nature of the relation but also the poet's own realization of the necessary difficulties in creating it.

i / "Antique Poets historicall": The Historical Dimension of the Aeneid

Since the problem of the reflection and celebration of Spenser's contemporary world in *The Faerie Queene* concerns us here, it would be well to inquire what possibilities were available to a European poet in the late sixteenth century. Italian literary criticism did not specifically take up the question of how an epic poet reflects contemporary national experience in his poem. The lack of specific discussion of this question derives in part no doubt from the political conditions of sixteenth-century Italy. The existence of so many states warring among themselves and the domination of most of these states by foreign powers effectively prevented, it would seem, poets and critics from conceiving of epic poetry in national terms. The political influences felt most strongly by a sixteenth-century Italian were those on the city-state in which he lived, and such influences, particularly after the 1520s, were rivalries between city-states and the pressures of invasion by French or Imperial forces. Since nearly all critical discussion in northern Europe derived from Italian criticism, the neglect of this dimension of epic proved nearly general until well into the seventeenth century.[5]

Nevertheless, it was recognized that Vergil had written an epic celebrating Augustan Rome, and whatever discussion one finds in the sixteenth century of the historical dimension of epic centers upon Vergil. Renaissance critics did not possess anything like a complete understanding of the historical dimension of the *Aeneid*. When poets and critics alike mention the relation of Vergil to Augustus, they generally refer to it as analogous to the relation of a court poet to his duke or prince; we often learn that Vergil included praises of Augustus in an attempt to win his favor and patronage. Even Ronsard, who tried to write a national epic, speaks of Vergil's conception of the *Aeneid* as a clever adaptation of legend to the acquisition of a patron.[6] Instead of a Vergil who creates the *Aeneid* with a complex vision of the history and responsibility of Imperial Rome, we generally find in the Renaissance a Vergil in search of a patron. The historical side of the *Aeneid* is most often regarded as such a digressive search or as ornamental. Giambattista Pigna appears to see the introduction of the historical as convenience and ornament; he suggests that the writer of romance take things from historians and vary "the places, the times, the persons, and other circumstances" in conveying them to his fiction. "This will lessen the difficulty of composition and give a reputation to the work." So too with contemporary allusions:

It will not be amiss if we hint at something that has occurred in our own times, in the way that Aeneas, confronting Dido in his departure, alludes to Augustus, who held his eyes fixed down before Cleopatra so that he not be inflamed by her. And Anchises, celebrated in death by funeral games held for him, alludes to Julius Caesar, who was celebrated with similar games. Venulus, snatched from his saddle by Tarchon [*Aeneid* 11. 740–58], also alludes to Caesar.[7]

As we shall see, the allusions Pigna notes in the *Aeneid* are not as eccentric as they might at first appear. But what is significant is that the thought of contemporary allusion in an heroic poem, though considered merely ornamental, immediately leads Pigna to Vergil.[8]

Giraldi Cintio, though he too fails to see an historical design in the *Aeneid*, believes the contemporary elements are more than ornamental. He understands Vergil's introduction of Roman and Italian rites into his epic as a function of the ethical side of poetry: since the poet is concerned with the improvement of men, he connects his poem to the present times by the introduction of the contemporary:

Whereas the historian ought to write only the facts and actions as they are, the poet shows not things as they are but as they ought to be for the ameliorizing of life.

This is the reason the poets, though they write of ancient things, nevertheless seek to fit them to the mores of their own age, bringing in things unlike those of ancient times but fitting for theirs. For example,

Vergil's Aeneas came from Troy where the forms of sacrificing, of celebrating funeral rites, and of arms were Asian rather than Italian; nevertheless the poet had the Trojans sacrifice, bury the dead, and fight according to the customs of Italy, not those before the founding of Rome but of the time of Octavian. Good poets have not only taken this license but have also given names to things of their own time and have written these as if they belonged in that earlier time, as is seen in Homer and Vergil.[9]

Both Giraldi Cintio and Tasso see the episode of Dido as introduced "to show in a poetic fiction that the Carthaginians were subjected to the Romans, were roused by them to rebel three times, and ultimately were destroyed."[10] But Tasso, characteristically, also suggests that the episode is feigned "to give occasion to mix in the pleasant subject of love amid the severity of the other materials."[11] Some of the historical and contemporary elements of the *Aeneid* are noticed, then, by sixteenth-century critics, but they are generally discussed as ornaments to the plot and often as devices introduced to win over or please Augustus. Perhaps Giraldi Cintio, though not precisely on target, comes closest to the mark by suggesting that anachronistic references to contemporary customs and events served the purpose of drawing the ethical meaning of a poem into the reader's own time.

Although they did not fully credit its importance, it is evident that Renaissance critics had nonetheless some awareness of the historical dimension of the *Aeneid*. The questions are whence such awareness derived and, more importantly, what a poet seriously interested in creating a national epic might have learned from the *Aeneid*. It is clear that Pigna's references to Vergil's supposed contemporary allusions come mostly from Servius's commentary on the *Aeneid*. Indeed, one may conclude that whatever knowledge of this dimension of the *Aeneid* a Renaissance reader possessed derived primarily from the scattered historical references he found in Servius. A reader who was especially interested in the *Aeneid* as a national epic would have found there a considerable amount of information—of varying degrees of utility, to be sure—on Vergil's use of history.

As the only complete commentary on Vergil to have come down from antiquity, Servius held a position of unique authority and honor in sixteenth-century editions of Vergil.[12] Indeed, his commentary was practically inescapable by Renaissance readers of

Vergil, for with his more recent followers, notably Badius Ascensius, Servius literally surrounded the text of Vergil; the grammatical, rhetorical, textual, mythological, and historical aids of the commentators typographically framed Vergil's verses on each page. Because of its authority, the Servian commentary inevitably appeared first in the list of scholia.

As a critic Servius has some obvious limitations. One looks in vain, for example, for any precise indication of the ways in which he felt Vergil used myth and legend in relation to history or the contemporary world. This is scarcely surprising, for Servius was writing four centuries after Vergil, in a world already very different in its literary and political conceptions.[13] In many cases Servius appears intent on handing down a tradition about a Vergilian passage but puzzled enough by the tradition to want to avoid further comment. One tantalizing example is his note on Vergil's final image of the dead Priam:

> *iacet ingens litore truncus,*
> *avolsumque umeris caput et sine nomine corpus.*

He lies a huge trunk upon the shore, a head severed from the shoulders, a nameless corpse.

(*Aeneid* 2. 557–58.)

Servius says simply, "This touches the story of Pompey."[14] He appears to mean that Vergil was thought to have alluded to the death of Pompey in Egypt. But the fascinating question what such an allusion would mean in this context is left unasked and unanswered. Indeed, Servius asks only the questions he can answer, and these generally concern basic problems of word usage and syntax.

But for all his literal-mindedness and tendency to explain what we know and not to explain what we find surprising, Servius adds a curious dimension to our understanding of the historical side of the *Aeneid*. He believes that history is pervasive in the poem, for he maintains that in a summary way Vergil celebrated all Roman history from the arrival of Aeneas in Latium up to his own times. "But it is concealed for the reason that the order is upset."[15] He asserts that for this reason the poem was called in earlier times the *Gesta Populi Romani*. But Servius also believes that the history incorporated into a poem must be somehow transformed. In a note to another passage, he says that Vergil touches history "per transitum" and explains that history, "because of the laws of poetic art," cannot appear openly. "Therefore Lucan does not belong among the poets because he is thought to have composed history, not a poem."[16] This idea that history is hidden leads him to find allusions to history, both past and contemporary, in places that may strike us as unexpected. Since Spenser, our "poet historicall," doubtlessly read Vergil in a Servian typographical frame, it is essential to see in more detail what Servius made of history in the *Aeneid*.

First of all, the note positing a hidden allusion to Pompey's death is scarcely unique. In every book of the poem, Servius sees several such arcane allusions. When, for example, in book 2 Sinon tells the Trojans how he escaped from being sacrificed and, hidden by sedge, lurked all night in a muddy marsh, Servius notes that Sinon "uses these circumstances to make the flight lifelike." But he continues, "It is indeed to be noted that Vergil relates the situations of well-known men under the characters of others, as he does here with Marius, and a little later with Pompey."[17] Apparently Servius believes, or is passing on the tradition, that Sinon's flight was somehow meant to recall Marius's flight from Rome to the marshes of Minturnae before Sulla's army. When the prodigious flame plays about the head of Ascanius at the fall of Troy (2. 683), Servius again sees Vergil covertly touching Roman history, for the same omen marked the infant Servius Tullius as a future king of Rome. One of the most cogent of Servius's suggested historical allusions occurs at the climax of book 10. In the fury of battle, Aeneas mocks and then slays the young Lausus, who has saved his father, Mezentius, from death. Servius says that Lausus's heroic deed is "from history" and sees it as deriving from the incident in the battle of Pydna in which Scipio Africanus the Younger, scarcely seventeen years old, defended his father in battle.[18] If Vergil's readers saw Lausus as a prophetic image of a well-known deed of Roman piety, they would have a further means of judging the *furor* that prevents Aeneas from recognizing this "patriae pietatis imago" until it is too late. And through Aeneas's blind fury Vergil in turn can comment upon the *nefas* of civil war in which even deeds of characteristically Roman piety and heroism fall victim to bloodthirsty rage. Since Servius notes these supposed allusions with no further comment, it is easy to see why Pigna—who mentions, among others, this last one—took them as merely ornamental. Some of the allusions Servius sees appear fanciful, but a number of them are at least suggestive and accord with what modern scholars have seen as Vergil's intention to direct his epic toward his contemporary world. Jackson Knight, for example, finds plausibility in the supposed allusion to Pompey and suggests that the unexpected reference to Priam's headless body was designed to evoke the tragic pathos of Pompey's death.[19] For our purposes, however, the interest lies not so much in the validity of the allusions as in the assertion by the only ancient commentary on Vergil that history and fiction are linked by such hidden and purely local allusions.

Most of Servius's attempts at historical elucidation are less puzzling and more obviously acceptable. Especially significant is his understanding of the relation of Aeneas to Augustus. Servius never gives a name to that relation, but it is possible that we shall be able to do so from his description of it. When in book 3 Aeneas and his ships make an unexpected landfall near Mount Leucata, they celebrate with games:

> *Ergo insperata tandem tellure potiti*
> *lustramurque Iovi votisque incendimus aras*
> *Actiaque Iliacis celebramus litora ludis.*

So having at last won land unhoped for, we offer to Jove dues of cleansing, kindle the altars with offerings, and throng the Actian shores in the games of Ilium.

[3. 278–80]

Servius provides geographical information and relates fiction to history:

Mount Leucata is the highest on the promontory of Epirus, near the city of Ambracia, which Augustus named Nicopolis after Antony and Cleopatra were conquered there. He founded a temple there to Actian Apollo and established the Actian games. Thus Vergil, in honor of Augustus, now gives an origin to those things that Augustus did. For Vergil says that Aeneas celebrated games there, and elsewhere has him promising a temple to Apollo, which it is known Augustus founded.[20]

The promise of the temple occurs in Aeneas's prayer before the grotto at Cumae (6. 60), and Servius again notes the link to Augustus: "As he is accustomed, Vergil mixes in history, for this temple was built by Augustus on the Palatine. But since Augustus was related to Julius Caesar, who traced his origin from Aeneas, Vergil means that Augustus fulfilled the vows of his ancestors."[21] But from Servius we get not just etiology and the fulfillment of prophecies in the relation of Aeneas and Augustus. He sees also certain pious acts of the fictional hero paralleling those of the actual emperor. Servius notes that the "divine honors" that Aeneas pays to Anchises with funeral games in book 5 derive from the obsequies that Augustus offered for Julius Caesar.[22] Thus the fiction imaginatively asserts that the savior of Rome has repeated an ancient piety of its founder. In his comment in this same book on the Troy game led by Ascanius, Servius reports the tradition that the helmets and twin spear shafts of each boy allude to those given by Augustus to the boys who rode in his Troy game.[23]

What we get from the scattered suggestions in the Servian commentary, I believe, is the sense of a relation that can without exaggeration be called typological. The analogy of course is to the interpretation of the Old Testament in relation to the Gospels, first by the evangelists themselves (preeminently St. Matthew) and then more systematically by the early church fathers. The life of Christ not only fulfills the ancient prophecies but symbolically recapitulates the history of Israel. This prophetic relation of Aeneas to Augustus (and with him contemporary Roman history)—although created in a fiction and not, as in the case of Scripture, imposed upon an already existent body of chronicle and poetry—can be fruitfully understood as typological, for typology does not insist upon a continual or rigorous allegory but allows a kind of intermittent symbolism. Though not employing the word typology, modern scholars of Vergil have seen in the *Aeneid* a fundamental relation to Augustus and contemporary history. Kenneth Quinn supposes that a contemporary reader of the poem would have taken it for granted that "somehow or other, Aeneas was Augustus": "Educated, by art even more than by literature, to a high degree of perceptivity in the recognition of symbols, he would quickly realize that the poem only made sense if, while seeming hardly to be about Augustus and the war at all, it was somehow about them all the time."[24] Although the fullness and complexity of this idea of the *Aeneid* was not available to the sixteenth century, the commentary of Servius allowed enough understanding of the historical dimension of the poem for a reader interested in this aspect of epic to grasp the implications of typology. One may be all the more confident of this because the understanding of Scripture that the Renaissance inherited from the Middle Ages fostered typology as a virtual habit of mind.

Several inferences about Vergil's technique in writing an epic that celebrates—and judges—the history of Rome can be drawn from Servius's commentary, inferences we can easily imagine would be drawn by an imitating poet ambitious to create a national epic. Prime among them would be that the epic poet can adumbrate history in a variety of ways. Besides the large-scale prophecies of history subsequent to the time of the epic fiction, historical events can be connected to the fiction as fulfillments of things begun in the fiction, as Aeneas's vows are actually "fulfilled" by Augustus, or rites and games supposedly founded by Aeneas are to "return" under Augustus. Connections can also be made in a similar, but more extensive, way by etiological fables within the fiction whose fulfillment will come in history, as Dido's tragedy is made fictional cause and symbolic shadowing of the tragedy of Carthage. Moments within the fiction can be made to suggest, merely by "coincidental" and surprising similarity, actual historical events, as Priam's headless trunk on the shore suddenly conveys the image of Pompey's on the sands of Egypt. Such allusions are fleeting and unexplained by the poet, left to be felt and understood by the reader. And most importantly, all of these means can carry a suggestion of typology, that persons and events of the fiction illuminate the present in a way that casts the light and shadow of moral perspective upon it. Aeneas bears the weight of a shield graven with scenes of Actium, and Augustus in turn bears the burden of a poem about a man forced to ground a civilization upon warring peoples.

What is particularly noteworthy for our understanding of Spenser is that Servius nowhere insists on an "historical allegory" in the *Aeneid*.[25] It should be evident from our look at several of his historical glosses that Servius sees connections between Vergil's fiction and contemporary reality in terms of momentary connections rather than of allegorical patterns. Even when the games that Aeneas celebrates for Anchises glance at those Augustus celebrated for Caesar, Servius avoids suggesting that Aeneas is an allegorical representation of Augustus. Indeed at several points he sees allusion to Augustus through names or circumstances unconnected with Aeneas.[26] This lack of insistence on allegory becomes all the more significant in that Servius does consider Vergil's *Eclogues* allegorical; there Vergil accomplishes his intent of favoring Augustus "per allegoriam" and represents various actual persons as fictional characters. With the *Aeneid* Servius instead uses such phrases as "this alludes to," "this is taken from history," "this touches the case of," and so forth. The momentary allusions may set up symbolic relations between fiction and reality, but he does not generally concern himself with the meaning of such relations: as a writer of scholia, he is not so much interested in critical interpretation as in simply pointing out the allusions he knows of. And perhaps because of his lack of any critical theory about history in the poem, Servius shows a considerable degree of flexibility. He does not limit himself to the obviously referential passages in the prophecies of Augustan Rome, for he understands that the fiction itself must also bear the weight in a poem in which history is so pervasive.

ii / Italian "Poets historical":
Ariosto and Tasso

Of all the influences upon the decidedly eclectic Spenser, only that of the *Orlando Furioso* is such that we could scarcely imagine *The Faerie Queene* without it. In a number of important ways, Spenser discovered in Ariosto the kind of poet he was to be. To a lesser but still significant extent, Tasso too left an indelible imprint upon *The Faerie Queene*; with Tasso the influence was more for indispensible specific elements than for structural principles. We may find it somewhat surprising, therefore, to realize that Spenser drew comparatively little from these poets for the historical dimension of his romance epic. This is in part because neither Italian poem can be called in any real sense a national epic. For the same reasons that Italian critics were not concerned to discuss theoretically the historical dimensions of epic poetry, Ariosto and Tasso did not write poems that express national experience. This is not to say that they are unconcerned with history or the contemporary world; Ariosto in particular stands in judgment of the politics of his world, nor does he swerve from expressing his outrage at the suffering inflicted upon Italy by the princes of Europe. But Ariosto was the court poet of the Duke of Ferrara. In the *Orlando Furioso* the political direction taken in a particular celebration of the Este family reflects the pressures on Ferrara at the time of composition. Ariosto exhibits a complex and sometimes independent attitude toward his patrons, but one finds no national vision of political realities in Italy.[27] His political world was indeed too fragmented and too variable to admit the possibility of any such vision.

Primarily in the means by which Ariosto directs his poem toward the contemporary world can we see the significant difference from what Spenser attempts. This is perhaps nowhere more evident than at the one point where Spenser found in Ariosto a useful solution to a problem of historical celebration. In Bradamante, fictional ancestress of the Este family, Spenser saw a model for his Britomart, fictional ancestress of Queen Elizabeth, and thereby a partial response to the problem inherent in celebrating a woman ruler in an epic context. But Britomart also becomes, as Bradamante had not been, a fictional *type* of the patroness, and her actions within the fiction sometimes serve to shadow the rule of Elizabeth. In addition, Spenser creates other characters, Una, Belphoebe, Mercilla, whose actions shadow or allude to some aspect of the actual queen. Ariosto's characters, however, have a certain freedom from history, and even the fictional forebears of the Este line appear essentially independent of their descendants.

Ariosto may from time to time allow ironic sallies upon the contemporary in his fiction. But such points, one feels, are rare and invariably satiric, never part of a serious design of historical judgment. For in the main Ariosto restricts history to two entrances into the poem. One of these is through the sections clearly marked as prophecies. These "prophecies" of the contemporary world are introduced as revelations of the future by one of the characters skilled in magic, or they are portrayed in one of the magic art works. Extended genealogies of the Este family, for example, are the substance of Melissa's prophecies in cantos 3 and 8 and in the tapestry that is the nuptial pavilion of Ruggiero and Bradamante in the final canto. Similarly, Merlin's fountain in canto 26 figures an extended allegory of the defeat of cupidity by the contemporary princes of Europe. The second way contemporary matters are allowed entrance into the poem is through the narrator's asides or addresses to his audience. These asides range in tone from the humorous comparison of Ruggiero's strength to Alfonso d'Este's two cannons, to the poet's bitter lament for the suffering of Italy at the beginning of canto 34.

Ariosto makes this latter method possible by maintaining a narrative voice that can turn easily from the fiction to the audience he is addressing. At the beginning of the canto that describes the fictional battle for Paris, the narrator, for example, intrudes mention of Alfonso's historical victory at Ravenna:

> *Ebbon vittorie così sanguinose,*
> *che lor poco avanzò di che allegrarsi.*
> *E se alle antique le moderne cose,*
> *invitto Alfonso, denno assimigliarsi;*
> *la gran vittoria, onde alle virtuose*
> *opere vostre può la gloria darsi,*
> *di ch'aver sempre lacrimose ciglia*
> *Ravenna debbe, a queste s'assimiglia.*

> *So bloody was the price of victory,*
> *Small ground was left them triumphs to prepare;*
> *And if, unconquered Duke Alphonso, we*
> *May modern things with ancient deeds compare,*
> *The battle, whose illustrious palm may be*
> *Well worthily assigned to you to wear,*
> *At whose remembrance sad Ravenna trembles,*
> *And aye shall weep her loss, this field resembles.*

[14. 2][28]

The next seven stanzas recall the battle at Ravenna in a far from wholly favorable manner, and Ariosto clearly states the outrages suffered by Ravenna at the hands of Alfonso's French allies. The context of comparison with the fictional assault upon Paris by the Saracens also qualifies "la gran vittoria" of Alfonso. But the relation of the historical event to the fiction is that of a simile within a narrative: the sack of Ravenna is presented as an extended simile, one in which the simile is qualified by the fiction as well as the reverse. As in a simile, the object or event to which the fiction is being compared is kept, except for the points of comparison, logically separate from the fiction. The result is a relation at once clearer but less suggestive than Vergil's unstated, but always implicit, metaphor.

The devices of prophecy and prophetic art also serve the purpose of basically separating historical references from the narrative fiction, for Ariosto's prophetic passages, unlike Vergil's, impinge minimally upon the fiction. Melissa's grave admonition to Ruggiero in canto 7 (60–64) to think of his glorious descendants if his own honor does not keep him from misbehaving is not without its comic side. Among those not to be born if Ruggiero continues unregenerate are Ippolito and Alfonso d'Este, of whose reality the reader is well aware. History makes Ruggiero ashamed and silent for about a stanza, then the magic ring takes his and the reader's attention, and we are left more amused than alarmed at the notion that Ruggiero's dalliance with Alcina might have forestalled Ariosto's patrons. As a dimension of the poem, history remains the prerogative of the narrating poet; as such it is suffused with the irony we associate with him and his relation with the fiction.

Ariosto nevertheless found a Servius to detail his supposed contemporary allusions in Simon Fornari, who published a commentary on the *Orlando Furioso* in 1549.[29] In a chapter entitled "Allusions to be seen in the *Orlando Furioso* to many things which have occurred in our own or earlier times," Fornari suggests a series of about two dozen passages in the poem that appear to him allusive: Norandino's tournament at Damascus (canto 17), for example, he sees as shadowing a Florentine tournament given by the Medici, and the funeral of Brandimart as allusive to that of Ippolito d'Este. Few, if any, of Fornari's suggested allusions are convincing in themselves, and they appear all the more unlikely in view of Ariosto's readiness to establish explicitly stated connections between poem and contemporary world. Toward the end of his chapter, however, Fornari seems to give the game away when he suggests that in the siege of Paris the poet shadows the siege of Ferrara by the Venetians, "as Vergil in recounting the battles between the Latins and the Trojans gave a likeness of the battles fought in Gaul by Julius Caesar." Fornari clearly has one eye on Servius, and commentator imitates commentator more obviously than poet imitates poet. Nevertheless, though Fornari tells us little that is useful about Ariosto's method of treating history, he unwittingly tells us something about the way Vergil was read through Servian spectacles. Since Ariosto imitated Vergil, he must also have imitated, Fornari implies, Vergil's mode of shadowing history.

A peculiarity of the *Gerusalemme Liberata* is that Tasso chose a subject so seemingly fruitful for historical celebration and yet appears so very reticent about contemporary history. As an epic treatment of the first crusade, the poem, one feels, must bear some relation to what may be seen as the last crusade, the battle of Lepanto, which took place during its composition. The poem appears as if it should implicitly exhort Tasso's Este patrons to take a leading part in the protection of Christendom from the Turk (absurd though it might be for the duke of Ferrara to assume such a role). In fact, however, one looks in vain for any sense of historical immediacy in the poem. The one prophecy that touches the court of Ferrara does so only in the most general terms. In two stanzas that stand at the very center of the poem, Pietro the hermit predicts that the offspring of Rinaldo will achieve memorable deeds in the protection of the church from tyrants and rebels. Thus "l'aquilla estense," the eagle of Este (which Fairfax rendered "This bird of east"), will fly as far as the paths of the sun:

> *E dritto è ben che, se'l ver mira e'l lume,*
> *ministri a Pietro i folgori mortali.*
> *U' per Cristo si pugni, ivi le piume*
> *spiegar dee sempre invitte e trionfali;*
> *ché ciò per suo nativo alto costume*
> *dièlle il Cielo e per leggi a lei fatali.*

> *Her eyes behold the truth and purest light,*
> *And thunders down in Peter's aid she brings,*
> *And where for Christ and Christian faith men fight,*
> *There forth she spreadeth her victorious wings;*
> *This virtue Nature gives her and this might.*

[10. 77][30]

The use of the heraldic eagle as a metonymy for the family relieves the poet of the necessity of being specific about persons or deeds. Curiously enough, Tasso avoids the actual projection of his patron into the poem by prophecy that not only Ariosto but Vergil as well had sanctioned. The only mention of history at all modern is the uncontroversial prophecy by Fortune in canto 15 that Columbus will discover the New World.

The peculiar lack of an important historical dimension in the *Gerusalemme Liberata*, a lack all the more striking because of the way the poem's subject seems to suggest the great contemporary victory, derives no doubt from the poet's personal anxiety as well as from the lack of freedom of political and religious expression that the Counter-Reformation bred in Italy. The danger in which Tasso felt himself to be from the Inquisition indicates why the promise of an historical dimension held out by the story of the first crusade remains so unfulfilled. The sensibility of its creator and the political uncertainties of Counter-Reformation Italy appear to force the *Gerusalemme Liberata,* exquisitely delicate poem that it is, to retreat from history.

Spenser's debt to the Italian poets for characters, episodes, and the romance structure of his poem is well known, but studies of his imitation of Vergil have not fully considered his debt to the Roman poet for the historical dimension of *The Faerie Queene.*[31] The common poetic ground that Vergil and Spenser share is their position as poets confronting the complex experience of nations that had emerged from the darkness of civil war into a period of peace and creativity. Of the three poems that exerted the most influence on Spenser's imagination as he composed *The Faerie Queene,* only from the *Aeneid* could he have derived his feeling that the epic should achieve a serious historical dimension. The *Aeneid,* moreover, seen through Servius's annotations becomes a model of flexibility in the treatment of history. It considers history explicitly in the extended prophecies of Roman imperial destiny, and within the fiction it gestures allusively toward contemporary and historical figures in a way we can understand as typological. Though Spenser wrote historical allegory in book 5 of *The Faerie Queene,* he did not, I believe, begin with such an idea. Rather he began with the sense that history should enter the poem in a variety of ways: through the creation of "types" as well as "ancestors" of the queen, through allusive adumbrations of contemporary history, through the interweaving of myth and history in the British chronicles of books 2 and 3. When Spenser does come to fashion historical allegory, he does so in response to the feeling that his poem must engage history even more explicitly. And here, of course, he does not follow the *Aeneid.* But this should not keep us from seeing that his previous attempts at the creation of an historical dimension elude the definition of historical allegory and are finally most comprehensible as imitation of Vergilian epic designed to celebrate and judge his own age.

It is incontrovertible that Spenser's poem is in the end a less successful fusion of myth, history, geographical evocation, and symbolic comment upon the contemporary. Vergil's achievement of a complexly historical epic remains unique. But one can also see that Spenser's task was made more difficult by the eclecticism that is such an important element of his imagination. The legend that forms the basis of the *Aeneid* was already connected with the history of Rome. But the multiplicity of Spenser's sources and the variety of his concerns complicated the creation of an historical dimension in *The Faerie Queene*. If Arthurian sources deriving from Geoffrey of Monmouth and his successors seemed a promising beginning for epic consideration of history, other elements of that tradition would pull the poet in other directions. Arthurian material had become associated with romance and chivalry, and this side of the tradition centered upon such ahistorical concerns as love and the marvelous. Ariosto, Tasso, and Malory would work in Spenser's imagination to develop this side of his Arthurian sources. And Renaissance mythography and the traditions of iconography would add further complexity to his intentions.

But the Vergilian nature of both Spenser's methods and motives toward history remain clearly visible in the poem. He had begun with Vergil's example in the *Shepheardes Calender*, and would continue to hold it before him in *The Faerie Queene*. Indeed, it would be in terms of Vergil that the following century would praise his poetic accomplishment. In the historical dimension of *The Faerie Queene*, realized with varying degrees of success, we can recognize Spenser's most profound imitation of Vergil.

Chapter 2

Holiness
and Historical Fulfillment

In book 1 of *The Faerie Queene*, Vergil's influence is more insistent than in any other book of the poem. Certain episodes, the Cave of Mammon in book 2, for example, may strike us as more Vergilian in tone than the whole of book 1, but no other book contains so many imitations in single lines, in motifs, or in whole episodes. It is evident that Spenser had the tradition of Vergilian epic very much in mind as he composed book 1. It should not seem surprising, then, that in the Legend of Holiness the poem should most successfully and most complexly achieve its historical dimension. In his provocative attempt to reopen the question of history in book 1, Frank Kermode has drawn attention to the Vergilian analogue of Spenser's accomplishment. Taking exception to the archetypal approach to *The Faerie Queene*, Kermode noted that Spenser used an apocalyptic pattern not so much for its value as archetypal myth but for its specific application to "now and England":

The achievement of Spenser in that heroic First Book is not to have dived into the archetypes, but to have given them a context of Virgilian security —to have used them in the expression of an actual, unique, critical moment of a nation's culture and history. He looks backward only to achieve ways of registering the density of the central situation: the reign of Elizabeth. *Iam redit et Virgo.* He does not convert event into myth, but myth into event. His mood is acceptance; he welcomes history, not seeking to lose his own time in some transhistorical pattern. Such patterns of course exist; but only the unique and present moment can validate them. . . . Spenser celebrates the Elizabethan *renovatio* with something of Virgil's sober exaltation.[1]

We could not expect, however, that a poet would turn myth into event without to a certain extent absorbing event into myth. By creating mythic typologies for the present, Spenser insures that the interchange of myth and present event will be a two-way process: the present may be comprehended through myth, but since the myth will not be locked to that present or exhausted by it, present event cannot but become an adjunct of the myth.

The acceptance of history in book 1 is genuinely Vergilian, but Spenser does not use his specific imitations of Vergil as the medium of his contemplation of history. The Legend of Holiness required a prophetic vision of a sacred rather than secular cast. As a myth to mediate the claims of history upon holiness, Spenser had the daring to employ the book of Revelation. Revelation, because of the hyperbolic mode of its symbolism, has always carried with it perilous seeds of excess; only its association with St. John assured it admittance into the canon of Scripture.[2] But it possesses a special character among the books of the New Testament in its concern for communal salvation, for its prophecy of the endurance through time of the Christian church. The utility of Revelation to Spenser was augmented by the Reformers' historical interpretation of it.[3] That interpretation remains familiar enough: the symbolic seven-headed beast and the whore of Babylon, through which the original writer had shadowed Rome and its persecutions of the early church, were seen as the Roman church and the papacy, whose eventual overthrow was felt to be assured by the prophecies of the final five chapters. In England this interpretation was well known through the glosses of the Geneva Bible and the comprehensive new understanding of ecclesiastical history contained in Foxe's *Actes and Monuments*. By employing this historical interpretation, Spenser advances the claim that the England he celebrates is playing a part in the fulfillment of the sacred history prophesied in Revelation.

Though the content of his historical vision in book 1 is essentially different from Vergil's, Spenser makes us sense the Vergilian nature of what he accomplishes there in the technique by which he subtly gestures toward history. He delineates an historical dimension by means which never seem far removed from the shadowy, allusive technique of Vergil.[4] The Vergilian nature of book 1, in fact, extends to its way of suggesting that the actual world stands just beyond the fictional world but that the former can be comprehended only momentarily and in allusions which do not break the integrity of the fictional world. It is because of the insistent allusiveness of book 1 that critics have long felt the need to give some comprehensive form to the history it considers.[5] But because it is allusive, no comprehensive allegorical structure has ever seemed quite true to our reading of the Legend of Holiness. Rather, the relationship that emerges through the allusions is typological. In its suggestiveness, the fiction projects figures and events from history, not constantly but in moments of special significance. Like all his literate contemporaries, Spenser knew typology from the interpretation of the Old Testament in the light of the New. But Vergil had been the first to create typology in a fiction that, through the allusive symbolism peculiar to him, "prophesies" the present—and in that prophecy interprets and judges the contemporary world.

The Faerie Queene is first and foremost a moral allegory, and one must ask how history fits into the poem's moral scheme. In the Legend of Holiness, the question poses itself in a particularly acute form. As allegory, book 1 is about the achievement of holiness as a moral and psychological state. What part can history have in the achievement of a state that is finally so individual? Historical consciousness would appear in any age to be the least important component of personal sanctity. With other Renaissance Englishmen, however, and in common with Old Testament prophets, Spenser thought otherwise. A full answer to the question must be deferred until we have described the historical dimension in greater detail. But one can discern a pattern that suggests the importance of that dimension relative to the moral and spiritual allegory. In the moments of greatest spiritual testing in the book—the episode in the cave of Despair, for example, or the climactic dragon fight in canto 11—we feel comparatively little pressure from the historical dimension. But when the pressure of the moral allegory is relaxed and the issue of spiritual or psychological import is resolved, historical allusion unexpectedly broadens our range of vision from the realm of the individual psyche to the arena where historical forces have fought analogous battles. This pattern suggests that the individual is to find relevance to his own moral state in historical patterns, perhaps even that the individual soul is a microcosm where the events of the macrocosm of history are played out anew.

i / Heavenly and Earthly Cities

The position of human history in Spenser's conception of holiness is most clearly indicated in the vision that the Hermit of Contemplation grants to the Redcross knight in canto 10. Holiness, the reader there comes to realize, is not a mere yearning for otherworldly perfection but a commitment to what is most ennobling in human history. The hermit shows to the knight a city the description of which corresponds to the city in Revelation 21: "Whose wals and towres were builded high and strong / Of perle and precious stone" (stanza 55). When the knight asks what city this is, the hermit replies that it is the New Jerusalem, in which will dwell the people redeemed by "that vnspotted lam." Curiously, the vision makes Redcross think of another city, one that is now eclipsed in his estimation by the New Jerusalem:

> *Till now, said then the knight, I weened well,*
> *That great* Cleopolis, *where I haue beene,*
> *In which that fairest* Faerie Queene *doth dwell,*
> *The fairest Citie was, that might be seene;*
> *And that bright towre all built of christall cleene,*
> Panthea, *seemd the brightest thing, that was:*
> *But now by proofe all otherwise I weene;*
> *For this great Citie that does far surpas,*
> *And this bright Angels towre quite dims that towre of glas.*
>
> [1. 10. 58]

Cleopolis is the "city of glory" and as the capital of the Faery Queen is to be taken as the focus of the noblest human activity. Insofar as the Faery Queen herself is a type of Spenser's sovereign, Cleopolis becomes a type of London, her capital. But it is significant that the description of the earthly city partakes of the scriptural description of the New Jerusalem. Carried in the spirit "to a great and an hie mountaine," St. John saw a city "that was pure golde like vnto cleare glasse" (Rev. 21:18–20). Dimmer though it is, the transparency of the Faery Queen's crystal tower affords us a glimpse of the crystal New Jerusalem beyond. Because of his sharpened vision of spiritual perfection, Redcross is inclined to reject the earthly sharer in the beauty of the celestial city, to abandon the pursuit of merely mortal glory. But the hermit warns against an ascetic scorning of the earthly participant of the heavenly city:

> *Yet is* Cleopolis *for earthly frame,*
> *The fairest peece, that eye beholden can:*
> *And well beseemes all knights of noble name,*
> *That couet in th'immortall booke of fame*
> *To be eternized, that same to haunt,*
> *And doen their seruice to that soueraigne Dame,*
> *That glorie does to them for guerdon graunt:*
> *For she is heauenly borne, and heauen may iustly vaunt.*
>
> [1. 10. 59]

Significantly, the hermit's gaze is not so firmly fixed upon the eternal and transcendent as we first expect when Mercie leads Redcross to his hill. His vision is not simply teleological, for he knows the knight's origins as well. Along with Redcross's view of the heavenly city comes knowledge of his earthly nation; though the knight has been "accompted Elfins sonne," he is actually "sprong out from English race." The hermit had first addressed him etymologically as "thou man of earth" (stanza 52); now he tells him he is of a specific land, that he will be not simply Γεωργός but "Saint *George* of mery England." In the fulfillment of the prophecy, the actual land will take the place of the fictional type. As "frend and Patrone" of that actual nation, Redcross will become a link between the New Jerusalem and its earthly sharer, and the cross of St. George will become in both physical and spiritual battle "the signe of victoree."

Redcross is so overcome by this knowledge and by the vision that it is not until after the hermit has told him that he must return to the world that he is struck by the revelation of his origin and inquires how this can be. The hermit's reply makes one suspect that Spenser has taken in hand an etiological matter that was only partially completed in what we have of *The Faerie Queene*. Redcross is told he is of an "ancient race of Saxon kings," that he is a changeling. We recall from canto 9 that Arthur too does not know his origin; assured by Merlin only that he is the son and heir of a king, he knows that he was brought up by a Faery knight in Wales. In the castle of Alma in book 2, Arthur will learn the history of the British kings down to Uther Pendragon, whom the reader is expected to identify as Arthur's father. Arthur does not learn even then of his origin because of a lacuna in Eumnestes' manuscript. Spenser's plans doubtless called for Arthur to discover his British origin at some climactic moment, perhaps at the same time he discovers his mission to restore the Briton nation, now subject to the Saxons. Hence the "fast friendship," sealed with sacred gifts, that Redcross and Arthur pledge in canto 9, was undoubtedly intended to be recalled later and become the etiology of the uniting of Saxon and Briton peoples (like Vergil's prophecy of "aeterna gentis in pace futuras," *Aeneid* 12, 504) in the modern British nation. Faeryland, whose queen they are both to serve, becomes the ideal and typological prefigurement of this nation.

It may strike us as strange that in the knight's vision of eternal things and a transcendent city of perfection so much should be made of his earthly origins and a mortal city. But in effect the typological dimension of the Legend of Holiness serves precisely to connect the two realms. The direction of Spenser's thought can perhaps be most readily appreciated by reference to the gloss in the Geneva Bible to the concluding description of the New Jerusalem: "And the people which are saued, shal walke in the light of it: and the Kings of the earth shal bring their glorie and honour vnto it" (Rev. 21:24). "Here we see as in infinite other places," the gloss declares, "that the Kings & Princes (contrary to that wicked opinion of ye Anabaptists) are partakers of the heauenlie glorie, if they rule in ye feare of the Lord." Service of such a God-fearing prince, of course, becomes sacred because of this partaking. But Spenser goes beyond this commonplace doctrine. By gesturing toward events in the recent past through the medium of allusion to the book of Revelation, he suggests that Britain's history has itself become a partaking of sacred myth. By his reticence in detailing (or allegorizing) specific events, he avoids limiting that sacred myth to fulfillment here and now; other godly princes and other history, past or future, may equally partake of sacred myth. But Elizabethan Englishmen should sense the ways in which their own age and nation have shared in those sacred, transcendent patterns.

It is in the role that Spenser implies for himself and for poetry that we can discern something of his daring in suggesting these things. Right before Redcross's vision in the passage just considered, the hermit leads the knight to "the highest Mount" (like St. John's "great and an hie mountain"), from which the vision is to be seen. The parallel to the mountain of Revelation is evident from the context, but Spenser provides an extended simile that compares the hermit's mountain to Sinai, where Moses dwelt forty days before receiving the Law. The simile continues another stanza to a startling conclusion:

> *Or like that sacred hill, whose head full hie,*
> *Adornd with fruitfull Oliues all arownd,*
> *Is, as it were for endlesse memory*
> *Of that deare Lord, who oft thereon was fownd,*
> *For euer with a flowring girlond crownd:*
> *Or like that pleasaunt Mount, that is for ay*
> *Through famous Poets verse each where renownd,*
> *On which the thrise three learned Ladies play*
> *Their heauenly notes, and make full many a louely lay.*

[1. 10. 54]

This surprising parallel between Parnassus and mountains of sacred prophecy, Sinai, Olivet, and the mount of apocalypse in Revelation, means that poetry too achieves a prophetic function. The poet who "meditates the muse" is implicitly connected with Moses, whose meditation preceded his teaching of the chosen people, and with Christ, whose meditation accompanied the teaching of the new law. The "heauenly notes" of the muses should be seen as a claim for the poet's song equivalent to the assertion of the heavenly origin of the Faery Queen five stanzas later: as the queen and her city are given a participation in the New Jerusalem, the poet may claim a participation in prophetic visions. His poem likewise claims a sharing in the patterns of sacred myth. Queen and city, poet and poem are here-and-now participants of what is known to be eternal and transcendent. In the next stanza the narrating poet seems to qualify this implicit vaunt of the prophetic role of poetry by insisting that the vision of the New Jerusalem is "too high a ditty for my simple song." The disclaimer may take him out of competition with the poet of Revelation, but it scarcely cancels his prophetic vaunt; his poem is "only" a partaking of such sacred vision.

ii / "A sunshine in the shadie place"

At the center of the celebration of historical accomplishment in book 1 stands the figure of Una. The name itself makes initially evident Una's polysemous nature. The headnote to canto 2 tells us that the enchanter parts "the Redcross Knight from Truth," and it is commonplace that "truth is one." We learn in the course of the narrative that Una also symbolizes the true church that guides the Christian soul; the Nicene Creed, translated in the *Book of Common Prayer*, expresses belief in a church that is "*unam*, sanctam, catholicam." What is less well known is that Una was also used as a cult epithet of Queen Elizabeth. In her important study "Queen Elizabeth as Astraea," Frances Yates demonstrates that the "one" theme was always strong in the worship of the queen. A version of the queen's motto *semper eadem*, for example, was the subject of Latin verses presented to her at Cambridge during her progress to Audley End in 1578:

In ἀποφθεγμα *Sereniss.*
Principis Elizabethae
SEMPER VNA.
VNA quod es SEMPER, quod semper es Optima Princeps,
Quam bene conveniunt haec duo verba tibi:
Quod pia, quod prudens, quod casta, quod innuba Virgo
Semper es, hoc etiam SEMPER es VNA modo.
Et Populum quod ames, Populo quod amata vicissim
Semper es, hic constans SEMPER et VNA manes.
O utinam quoniam sic SEMPER es, VNA liceret,
VNA te nobis SEMPER, Eliza, frui. [6]

On the apothegm "Always One"
Of the Most glorious Princess Elizabeth

Because you are always one, because you are always the best of sovereigns, how well do these two words fit you! Because you are always pious, prudent, chaste, because you are ever an unwed virgin, even thus are you always one. And because you love your people and are loved by them in return, you remain unchangeable and one. O since you are ever thus, one and only Eliza, may we be ever permitted to enjoy you alone.

As Yates has made evident, the veneration of Elizabeth as the unique phoenix was part of a complex cult of Virgo-Astraea. At the most literal level Elizabeth was One because she was, as we would say, "single." She was unmarried and would have no descendants. But the *renovatio temporum* implied in both phoenix and Astraea also symbolized complex political and religious ideas on which the claims of the English church rested.[7] The apologists of the Elizabethan church based the claims of the church to apostolic authority on the supposed pre-Augustinian beginnings of Christianity in England. Foxe asserts that the Gospel was received by the British in the first century, either through the agency of Joseph of Arimathea or through other disciples.[8] Only later, when Pope Gregory sent Augustine at the end of the sixth century, did Roman influence begin to be felt in the British church, and not until the end of the following century did Rome begin to usurp authority in Britain.[9] The freeing of the church from domination by Rome thus represents not innovation but a restoration of the primitive British church as it existed in its earliest centuries. In the reign of Elizabeth, "semper una," the unique phoenix is reborn and the virgin Astraea returns to the earth to restore truth. To attempt to weave together some of the strands spun by the name Una, we might say that Spenser envisions the return of the truth of a single apostolic church through the person of a unique royal virgin.

A complementary claim of the Elizabethan church expressed by the symbols of *renovatio* concerns imperial authority over the church. Most important to our understanding of Tudor royal symbolism, as Yates has shown, is the fact that the doctrine of the divine right of kings to rule over both church and state was "a derivation from the claims of Roman Emperors to be represented in the councils of the Church."[10] Foxe continually notes the deference of early bishops of Rome to the emperor, and he relates how Constantine burned the complaints of bishops against one another. Since kings succeeded to the imperial power of the Roman emperors, they were therefore alleged to have a share in this authority before it was gradually usurped by the popes. Based on this historical interpretation, Elizabeth's title of supreme governor of the church is actually the restoration of imperial ecclesiastical authority to the state that existed in the early British church before the usurpation of primacy by Rome. It is this claim to imperial power that Spenser acknowledges in his dedication of *The Faerie Queene* to "the Most High, Mightie, And Magnificent Empresse."

In Gloriana Spenser intended to shadow the rule and governing of his queen, presumably in the never-to-be-written book in which she was to appear. The use of the cult name Una suggests that the poem may typologically "prophesy" the role of the unique queen as supreme governor in restoring a pure and primitive Christianity to her realm. When we are first introduced to Una, for example, the poet embodies the claim to imperial authority in her heritage:

> *So pure an innocent, as that same lambe,*
> *She was in life and euery vertuous lore,*
> *And by descent from Royall lynage came*
> *Of ancient Kings and Queenes, that had of yore*
> *Their scepters stretcht from East to Westerne shore,*
> *And all the world in their subiection held;*
> *Till that infernall feend with foule vprore*
> *Forwasted all their land, and them expeld:*
> *Whom to auenge, she had this Knight from far compeld.*
>
> [1. 1. 5]

Duessa, in her disguise as Fidessa, uses a false version of the same claim; she, however, alleges descent from only the western half of the empire and rests her claim on the authority of Rome rather than on that of the universal church. She maintains that she was "Borne the sole daughter of an Emperour, / He that the wide West vnder his rule has, / And high hath set his throne, where *Tiberis* doth pas" (1. 2. 22). Her claims to be "sole daughter" are paralleled by her sentimentalized version of Christ's death. Instead of a living Christ she seeks the body of dead Christ. Her story is the one St. Matthew says the Roman soldiers were bribed to spread and was commonly reported by the unbelieving "until this day" (Matt. 28:11–15). But Una's imperial claim and her gospel are not specifically Roman, and the realm stretching "from East to Western shore" suggests both the universality of the empire and church from which she descends and the direction of the spread of the true Gospel.

At two significant moments in book 1, Spenser makes us aware of this cult image of the queen in Una by associating her with the important royal icon he used in the *April* eclogue: the sun bursting through a veil of clouds.[11] The first of these iconographical allusions to the queen comes when Una is wandering alone in the wilderness after Redcross has deserted her:

> *One day nigh wearie of the yrkesome way,*
> *From her vnhastie beast she did alight,*
> *And on the grasse her daintie limbes did lay*
> *In secret shadow, farre from all mens sight:*
> *From her faire head her fillet she vndight,*

And laid her stole aside. Her angels face
As the great eye of heauen shyned bright,
And made a sunshine in the shadie place;
Did neuer mortall eye behold such heauenly grace.

[1. 3. 4]

In his addresses to the queen, Spenser so often associates her with the radiance of the sun (in the proem to this book, for instance) that I think here too one feels the pressure of royal symbolism in the sun that breaks through the shady gloom. But because of the importance of the book of Revelation in the Legend of Holiness, we should understand that the sunlike radiance of Una's face alludes in a primary way to the woman clothed with the sun who flees into the wilderness. The Geneva Bible interpreted the woman as the church and her sojourn in the wilderness as the time of persecution by Antichrist. Spenser appears here to personalize the sorrows of Una to make his readers see more deeply into the human pathos of the suffering of the church.

There is, as we shall see, some independent contemporary support for this suggestion of iconographical allusion, but we should ask what Spenser may mean by associating his queen with the radiant woman of Revelation who flees, like Una, into the wilderness. Other historical allusions of cantos 3 and 4 refer to the reign of Mary Tudor, and I believe Spenser is creating a typological "prophecy" of Elizabeth's figurative sojourn in the wilderness at this time, a sojourn that involved suffering and undoubted danger to her life. This does not mean anything like an allegorization of the events of Mary's reign, of course, or that we must find fictional correspondences for Cardinal Pole or Stephen Gardiner. What I suggest is that Spenser's historical location of the prophecies of Revelation involves allusions to the career of the woman who brought the English fulfillment of those prophecies. That this fulfillment came through Princess Elizabeth's patient sufferance of humiliation and physical danger no reader of the *Actes and Monuments* would have doubted. Foxe tells the story of Elizabeth's being taken from a sickbed and conveyed under guard to Westminster after Wyatt's rebellion, of her confinement in the Tower, and of her virtual imprisonment at Woodstock. Foxe is insistent about the dangers that surround the princess as the representatives of papal and Spanish

Antichrist plot against her life. Only the grace of God, working through her loyal servants and the love and sympathy of common Englishmen, preserves her from her foreign enemies.[12]

Foxe's *Actes and Monuments* was chained beside the Bible in Elizabethan cathedral churches, and it is in the spirit of the association of the two books, I believe, that the sorrows of the royal virgin are associated with the woman clothed with the sun who flees into the wilderness.[13] The narrative rhetoric of the opening stanzas of canto 3 appears to look beyond the fiction momentarily, and an age nurtured on Foxe's famous accounts of the Marian years could scarcely have helped feeling in the narrating poet's sorrow for Una the historical sorrows of another royal virgin. The poet feels his heart "perst with so great agonie":

> And now it is empassioned so deepe,
>> For fairest Vnaes sake, of whom I sing,
>> That my fraile eyes these lines with teares do steepe,
>> To thinke how she through guilefull handeling,
>> Though true as touch, though daughter of a king,
>> Though faire as euer liuing wight was faire,
>> Though nor in word nor deede ill meriting,
>> Is from her knight diuorced in despaire
> And her due loues deriu'd to that vile witches share.

[1. 3. 2]

John Dixon, a sixteenth-century reader of *The Faerie Queene* who appreciated and noted the references to the book of Revelation, penned "Eliza" in the margin of his copy opposite Una's name.[14] Dixon obviously felt that the narrative pity for this "daughter of a king" extended to his own queen in the nadir of her career. This reaction of a contemporary, the earliest on record, provides significant support for the suggestion of an iconographic allusion, for it is a stanza later that Una removes her veil and creates "a sunshine in the shadie place." At this initial moment of vision in the poem, Spenser wants us to see into Una and understand that besides being "forsaken truth," she is also a figure of sacred myth and an actual queen who has in some sense historically recapitulated that myth.

The historical suggestiveness continues in canto 3 and gradually grows more explicit. A "ramping Lyon" rushes forth to attack

Una. But if the lion will not touch the true prince, neither will it harm the true princess, and it becomes instead a submissive and faithful guardian of the desolate maiden. The "ramping" lion initially suggests the crown of England. But Una's apostrophe to the absent Redcross makes us see that detail as in fact ironic, for she has been left desolate by the lion who should be her protector: "But he my Lyon, and my noble Lord, / How does he find in cruell hart to hate / Her that him lou'd . . . ?" Spenser has given a religious dimension to the romance motif of the lion who recognizes and protects the true heir to the throne. As a surrogate for the alienated Redcross, the lion suggests God's grace working through the natural world to substitute for human faithlessness. It is not necessary, I think, to see the lion as a more specific allusion than this, though to Elizabethans he might have suggested the faithful witnesses to Protestantism or the protection of Elizabeth which Foxe found in loyal Englishmen. But the lion appears in the episode a more general symbol of grace working to accomplish divine ends. His purpose will be to protect Una from the powerful malevolence of Kirkrapine.

In the completion of the episode, Spenser is predominantly interested in delineating the strengths of Protestantism, even in a powerless disestablished state, in relation to Catholicism. Una's quiet dignity is made to contrast to the fearful, compulsive religiosity of Corceca and the frantic threatening of Kirkrapine. This is developed through a series of details that build up to a typological prophecy of the Marian years. Una and the lion first encounter a damsel carrying a pot of water who does not respond to Una's questions because "She could not heare, nor speake, nor vnderstand." This is later amplified when we learn that her name is Abessa, which besides abbess also suggests *abesse*, to be absent. Corceca's incessant *Pater nosters* and *Aves* indicate papistry and suggest that Abessa's absence is to be seen as an alien, Roman religiosity. Together they represent a parody of religious asceticism, an almost willful deafness and blindness to the needs of others. We learn their names, in fact, when Kirkrapine arrives and completes the tableau of allusion to physically powerful but spiritually impotent Catholicism. Described as a burglar of churches, he becomes the most vivid and threatening of the three; he preys upon the poor box and the "ornaments" of the church:

The holy Saints of their rich vestiments
He did disrobe, when all men carelesse slept,
And spoild the Priests of their habiliments,
Whiles none the holy things in safety kept;
Then he by cunning sleights in at the window crept.

[1. 3. 17]

Once again a reference to Revelation mediates the allusion. In the account of the pouring out of the vials of wrath in chapter 16, the church is admonished: "Blessed is he that watcheth, & kepeth his garments, lest he walke naked, and men se his filthines." In the Geneva Bible "garments" are glossed as "of righteousness and holines, wherewith we are cled through Iesus Christ." And the bride of the Lamb is said to be clothed in pure linen, "for fine linen is the righteousness of Sainctes" (Rev. 19:8). Kirkrapine is a powerful thief of the spiritual "ornaments" of the church. Spenser has taken the Protestant charge, traditional since the Lollards, that Rome has fleeced the English faithful and by allusion to the symbolism of Revelation has given it a spiritual dimension. The thievery is not merely material; more significantly, it is a stripping away of the "rich vestiments" of holiness and redemption and a despoiling of the "habiliments" of the priests, whose real glory is the preaching of the Gospel. At the beginning of the episode, papistry appears in Abessa and Corceca only an ineffectual sort of blind, deaf, and dumb piety, scarcely threatening when confronted by its Protestant antithesis. But it is maintained by the fearsome strength of Kirkrapine, who has the power to destroy what the Reformation has accomplished in England unless he is checked by other power. When Una's lion slays Kirkrapine, we are to understand this as proleptic of Redcross's final victory—a promise that even in the dark moments of history God's grace works toward final victory. At the conclusion of the episode, Una again becomes the focus of the narrative as Abessa and Corceca pursue her "that was the flowre of faith and chastity" with insults and railing. This appears to point toward the campaign of slander waged against Elizabeth by the agents of the Catholic powers. Corceca's final malediction in stanza 23—"That plagues, and mischiefs, and long misery / Might fall on her"—may even glance at the excommunication that would be pronounced against Elizabeth in 1572.

iii / *Antithesis:*
"Phoebus *fairest childe*"

Una is the consistent locus of allusions through which Spenser celebrates his queen's role in England's partial fulfillment of the prophecies of Revelation. But the next canto, the fourth, contains a glancing allusion that appears to hint at a possible negative element in the royal character. Without qualifying his celebration of Elizabeth's accomplishment of reform, Spenser injects a moment of doubt that, I believe, serves as a warning of human weakness. We should recall again the gloss of the Geneva Bible to the passage describing the glory of the New Jerusalem but this time emphasize the admonitory clause with which it concludes: "Here we see as in infinite other places, that Kings & Princes . . . are partakers of the heauenlie glorie, *if they rule in y*ᵉ *feare of the Lord.*" Insofar as they do not, they are partakers of merely human glory, which is pride. From Redcross's adventures in cantos 4 and 5, the reader is to understand the insufficiency of human glory and human heroism. Such human glory, if it rests merely in a trust in human abilities and strengths, becomes a malevolent and corrupting pride. The world in which Redcross should learn this lesson—but does not— is presided over by a lady who is first described in this curious stanza:

> *High aboue all a cloth of State was spred,*
>   *And a rich throne, as bright as sunny day,*
>   *On which there sate most braue embellished*
>   *With royall robes and gorgeous array,*
>   *A mayden Queene, that shone as* Titans *ray,*
>   *In glistring gold, and peerelesse pretious stone:*
>   *Yet her bright blazing beautie did assay*
>   *To dim the brightnesse of her glorious throne,*
> *As enuying her selfe, that too exceeding shone.*

[1. 4. 8]

We have not yet learned the lady's name, only that she lives in an impressive (though imperfectly constructed) palace, where she is surrounded by "a noble crew of Lordes and Ladies" who much beautify the chamber by their presence. Spenser follows his usual technique of creating a scene whose significance the reader must guess before the characters are named and their moral natures clarified. In this stanza the seemingly pointed description of the lady as "a mayden Queene," the possible royal symbolism of her shining "as *Titans* ray," and the emphasis on her "bright blazing beautie" could cause a reader attentive to such details to wonder for a moment if the lady might be yet another image of an actual maiden queen. The final line, with the tip-off phrase "too exceeding," steers one away from the identification, but if the actual maiden queen herself momentarily wondered, Spenser's purpose was fulfilled. These details are, I think, a purposeful attempt to insinuate a question about godly rule, and seen as such, they imply that Elizabeth must be aware of her own temptations to pride. To the degree that she and her court might resemble what Redcross sees, she would be a queen who partakes of human pride, which is antithetical to rule "in the feare of the Lord." Elizabeth, we know well enough, was not immune to a certain vanity about her person and about her court, and it is this, I expect, that Spenser hints at in the momentary ambiguity. One is reminded not only of the nearsighted eagle of the *July* eclogue of *The Shepheardes Calender* but also of the court satire of *Mother Hubberds Tale* and *Colin Clouts Come Home Againe*.

In the next stanza the image of the sun is given an ironic twist: this queen is not really like Phoebus but "like *Phoebus* fairest childe"—Phaeton, the emblem of foolish pride and ambition. We learn that she rules her realm not with laws "but pollicie." Lucifera is not a rightful queen "But did vsurpe with wrong and tyrannie" the scepter she holds. A reader now realizes that this maiden queen cannot be the queen celebrated in Una. But the discomfort induced by the previous stanza appears real, and perhaps Spenser means to imply that whatever resemblance Elizabeth bears to Lucifera is a kind of usurpation of her true nature as a godly queen. The moment is designed not so much as satire as exhortation, a reminder of human failing.

This warning about the danger of a ruler's taking pride in merely human strengths returns with more insistence at the end of the next canto. Redcross learns who fills the dungeon of the House of Pride, and the roll call of that dungeon produces a four-stanza list of exempla of pride—all princes or great leaders. And lest queens feel themselves exempt, the poet concludes the list with feminine examples: "Amongst these mighty men were wemen mixt, / Proud wemen, vaine, forgetfull of their yoke" (1. 5. 50). Not surprisingly, all the feminine exempla turn out to be queens.

The moral opposition of book 1 is not just between Una and Duessa, between reformed religion and papistry. As in other books of the poem, feminine figures stand at the various moral poles, and this can scarcely be an accident in a poem not only dedicated to a queen but written in an age and political context in which Elizabeth and Mary Stuart were viewed as actual moral and psychological poles. The historical dimension of the poem sets up a complex of oppositions. The opposed histories of Una and Duessa advance the claim of the English church to derive from primitive Christianity against Rome's charges of innovation. As this primitive Christianity, Una contrasts in her sober dignity to the dotage of Corceca and the debility of Abessa. Through the allusions in Una to the queen who brought the fulfillment of reform in England, the reigns of Elizabeth and her sister Mary are starkly opposed. The contrast of the maiden queen Lucifera to Una projects the opposition between two ideas of queenship as it applies to spiritual realities: the queen who prides herself on a brilliant court and trusts in her own wit and power is set against the humble *ancilla domini* who accepts suffering and betrayal as the price of final spiritual victory. There is also, of course, significant opposition between the works of Lucifera's House of Pride and the merciful works of Dame Celia's house, and this polarity too was to be grasped by the royal reader of the poem. The weight of the Legend of Holiness falls on the side of historical celebration, but Spenser does not abandon the responsibility implicit in his prophetic role to judge and exhort his ruler.

iv / *"Cruel malice and strong tyranny"*

Spenser's most complete adumbration of England's national religious experience comes in the cantos that narrate Redcross's deception by Duessa and his captivity by Orgoglio. As the future patron of England and the bearer of the cross on England's banner, Redcross has been generally assumed to have a symbolic relation to the English nation in addition to his significance as Everyman achieving Christian holiness. His deception and captivity therefore refer to England's submission to the yoke of papal authority, either during the Middle Ages or during Mary's reign. Both periods seem meant in a general way, but the 1550s are more consistently relevant to the allusive elements of the poem. When John Dixon saw historical relevance in book 1, he located it in the reign of Mary and Philip.

Nevertheless, at least one detail of Redcross's deception— Archimago's role as necromancer and representative of papal power —indicates that the reader is to understand generally the Middle Ages as well.[15] Foxe alleges that Sylvester II, pope in the year 1000 (an important date in the historical interpretation of Revelation), obtained the papacy by sorcery.[16] Foxe asserts that Benedict IX, "practicing enchantments and conjurations in woods, after a horibble manner," also aspired to the papacy by magic. Prominent among Benedict's companions was Hildebrand—"a sorcerer most notable, and a necromancer," who as Gregory VII was also responsible of course for advancing the power of the papacy over that of the emperor.[17] Spenser uses this Protestant tradition of papal sorcery to transmute the usual romance wizard (Ariosto's Atlante, for example) into an agent of Antichrist as well.

When we encounter Redcross for the first time after he has left Una, he is about to acquire Duessa in the combat with Sansfoy. Duessa is endowed with the iconography of the papal whore of Babylon: she is dressed in scarlet, covered with jewels, and crowned with a *"Persian* mitre," the tiara.[18] The allusion is general and refers to no particular pope or period of English history. Although readers of Foxe might associate it with medieval English deference to the papacy, every contemporary reader would also recall that England had deferred to the papacy more recently.

At two points in Redcross's alienation from Una, in his capture by Orgoglio (canto 7) and his rescue by Arthur (canto 8), Spenser directs his fiction toward a typological prophecy of England's recent history. Orgoglio first appears as a terrifying and swift consequence of Redcross's sojourn in the House of Pride and his dalliance with Duessa. Like the nymph from whose fountain he drinks, the knight has sat down "in middest of the race." He has forgotten Una, and his escape from Lucifera's dungeons appears merely fortuitous. From this point of view, Orgoglio seems a monstrous objectification of the knight's pride, of his trust in his own strength and powers of perception. But Orgoglio quickly becomes much more than an external image of Redcross's interior state. Here, in fact, we can observe one of those points at which the poem pivots from concern for the individual consciousness to awareness of an analogous pattern in history. We learn that Orgoglio has "arrogant delight" in his descent and "through presumption of his match-lesse might" scorns "all other powres and knighthood" (stanza 10). At the moment that the giant is about to slay Redcross, Duessa first calls Orgoglio by his name and offers to be his "Leman" if he will spare Redcross to be his "eternall bondslaue." As the knight is thrown into a dungeon, we get a complex of iconographic and scriptural details that project the political dimension:

> *From that day forth* Duessa *was his deare,*
> *And highly honourd in his haughtie eye,*
> *He gaue her gold and purple pall to weare,*
> *And triple crowne set on her head full hye,*
> *And her endowd with royall maiestye:*
> *Then for to make her dreaded more of men,*
> *And peoples harts with awfull terrour tye,*
> *A monstrous beast ybred in filthy fen*
> *He chose, which he had kept long time in darksome den.*
>
> [1. 7. 16]

In its multiplicity of heads, the beast resembles the Hydra Hercules slew:

> *But this same Monster much more vgly was;*
> *For seuen great heads out of his body grew,*
> *An yron brest, and backe of scaly bras,*
> *All embrewd in bloud, his eyes did shine as glas.*
>
> *His tayle was stretched out in wondrous length,*
> *That to the house of heauenly gods it raught,*
> *And with extorted powre, and borrow'd strength,*
> *The euer-burning lamps from thence it brought,*
> *And prowdly threw to ground, as things of nought;*
> *And vnderneath his filthy feet did tread*
> *The sacred things, and holy heasts foretaught.*
> *Vpon this dreadful Beast with seuenfold head*
> *He set the false* Duessa, *for more aw and dread.*
>
> [1. 7. 17–18]

The stanza depicts, of course, the whore of Babylon riding upon the seven-headed beast of Revelation (17:1–7; 12:4). The Geneva Bible glosses these texts historically: "The beast signifieth ye ancient Rome: ye woman that sitteth thereon, the newe Rome which is the Papistrie, whose crueltie and blood shedding is declared by skarlat." Orgoglio's position in this scheme is that of the "kings of the earth" who have "committed fornication" with the woman (Rev. 17:2; 18:3). In Spenser's formulation Orgoglio is also responsible for setting the woman on the beast and giving her the rich ornaments she wears; he implies that the power of the papacy rests entirely upon the "kings of the earth" and their military might. In Redcross's captivity we recognize a typological prophesy of England's subjection to Rome and the power of Spain. Some readers have asserted that Orgoglio's liaison with Duessa figures the marriage of Philip and Mary, but the passage does not seem to bear so specific an interpretation.[19] The image of the beast vividly projects the horror and violence that eternally occur when the *superbia* of the individual is projected into the arena of history. Earlier, while the mode of the narrative veered toward the classical in the underworld episode of canto 5, the melancholy story of Aesculapius portrayed a seemingly benign version of individual pride, the almost excusable pride of the healer. In his healing Aesculapius lost sight of the source of life, and in so doing he too threatened the heavens. Now in Orgoglio we see a horrible magnification—or parody perhaps—of that heaven-threatening pride. Because the beast is "all embrewd with blood," it represents the ultimate affront to heaven, for in a reversal of Aesculapius's offense, it destroys God-given life. Among the "holy heasts" trampled on by the Counter-Reformation is "Thou shalt not kill."

Canto 8 follows the same pattern, in which concern for spiritual and moral understanding is succeeded by emphasis on an understanding of history. During Arthur's battle with Orgoglio, the symbolic emphasis remains on the spiritual meaning: the narrative rhetoric and figurative language emphasize Arthur's role as an instrument of divine providence and suggest that Orgoglio's destruction is encompassed by a Nature horrified at the unnatural. When the veil falls from Arthur's shield, it happens "by chaunce" to indicate the way God's grace appears to man. The shield blinds the beast, and Orgoglio collapses like a punctured dirigible; even the most formidable mortal power falls to nothing before that grace. When the battle is ended, allusions again point to a political dimension. Ignaro is discovered within the castle, a blind old man whose white beard and bunch of keys suggest an icon of the papacy. In place of the pompous image of Duessa with tiara, gold, and jewels, Orgoglio's collapse reveals just an ignorant old man with his head reversed (viewing the Old rather than the New Covenant?) who cannot even use the rusty keys he carries. The icon implies that a lack of political support reveals the papacy to be just such an image of senility. Arthur honors "his reuerend haires and holy grauitie" but cannot get an answer to the simplest questions. The keys open every room but the crucial one in which Redcross is locked. We have in a sense returned, in terms of Spenser's historical analysis, to the point at which Una encountered the deaf and dumb Abessa before Kirkrapine's arrival.

But Orgoglio is a much more terrifying image of political power than Kirkrapine, and the narrative now fixes our gaze on the dreadful effects of that power. The contrast between the previous image of papal splendor in Duessa's appearance on the beast and this image of "doted ignorance" in Ignaro is repeated by the more sinister contrast within the locked rooms:

> *There all within full rich arayd he found,*
> *With royall arras and resplendent gold,*
> *And did with store of euery thing abound,*
> *That greatest Princes presence might behold.*
> *But all the floore (too filthy to be told)*
> *With bloud of guiltlesse babes, and innocents trew,*
> *Which there were slaine,* as sheepe out of the fold,
> *Defiled was, that dreadfull was to vew,*
> *And sacred ashes ouer it was strowed new.*

> [1. 8. 35; emphasis added]

The reference to the innocents slain as if they were strayed sheep brings us historically to the end of Mary's reign. The next stanza associates these martyrs with the tradition of the historical interpretation of Rev. 6:9: "I saw under the altar the soules of them that were killed for the worde of God, and for the testimony which they mainteined."

And there beside of marble stone was built
An Altare, caru'd with cunning imagery,
On which true Christians bloud was often spilt,
And holy Martyrs often doen to dye,
With cruell malice and strong tyranny:
Whose blessed sprites from vnderneath the stone
To God for vengeance cryde continually,
And with great griefe were often heard to grone,
That hardest heart would bleede, to heare their piteous mone.

[1. 8. 36]

The deaths of "true Christians" becomes the most damning charge brought against the representatives of Antichrist. The allusion to the slain witnesses of Protestantism reminds a generation nourished by Foxe's accounts of terrible cruelty and heroic suffering how great were the costs of the Marian years.

Such memory cuts in two directions, however, for it recalls not only the cruelty of the forces of Antichrist but also the infidelity of the majority of Englishmen who were not martyrs or exiles. Significantly, the allusion to the Protestant martyrs occurs at the physical and spiritual nadir of Redcross. Arthur hears only his "hollow, dreary, murmuring voyce" calling for death:

O who is that, which brings me happy choyce
Of death, that here lye dying euery stound,
Yet liue perforce in baleful darkenesse bound

[1. 8. 38]

Redcross's despair and desire for death echo the despair expressed in Revelation when the plague of locusts (glossed as "false teachers") descends at the fifth blast of the trumpet: "Therefore in those daies shal men seke death, and shal not finde it, and shal desire to dye, and death shal flee from them" (9:6). The spilling of the blood of the martyrs—and through his faithlessness Redcross's complicity in it—induces a despair in human strength and human history. As a spiritual and psychological state, despair is vividly portrayed in the next canto, but here the emphasis remains on its cause. Arthur enters into Redcross's prison cell and finds it an abyss, "all a deepe descent, as darke as hell." We can understand now Spenser's reason for allowing Orgoglio to be both a monstrous image of

Redcross's own faithless pride and a figure of the arrogant powers of Catholic Europe. Only the faithlessness of individual Englishmen had made possible England's captivity by the forces of Antichrist. Through the reign of Mary, the majority of Englishmen had, at least outwardly, conformed their religious belief and practice to Catholicism. The importance and visibility of the martyrs and exiles notwithstanding, it is obvious that Mary could never have gone as far as she did in returning England to Catholicism without the help and at least silent acquiescence of most Englishmen. These painful memories remained generally unspoken until the religious controversies of the 1570s and 1580s began pointing to old scars and reflecting on who had inflicted them. Many of Elizabeth's churchmen, in fact, had had their fling with Duessa in the 1550s. But the Legend of Holiness intends to heal: its adumbration of painful history is directed toward an understanding of common human frailty. Una's question of the cause of Redcross's collapse does not stay for an answer before she welcomes him back with implicit forgiveness. Arthur in fact cautions against the renewal of specific memories and offers what could be an Elizabethan's epitaph for those years: "But th'onely good, that growes of passed fear, / Is to be wise, and ware of like agein" (1. 8. 44).

v / "By signes to vnderstand"

We have already noted how Redcross's despair is healed by the vision of spiritual perfection in canto 10, a vision that paradoxically requires an understanding of earthly origins and commands commitment to human history. In the final canto, after the spiritually conclusive battle with the dragon, allusive elements again return the historical dimension to the reader's consciousness and knit together the spiritual and psychological allegory with the poem's sense of history. Since these allusions depend upon that aspect of Una that shadows the queen, it is interesting to discover how John Dixon glossed the verse headnote to the canto:

> *Faire Vna to the Redcrosse knight*
> *betrouthed is with ioy:*
> *Though false Duessa it to barre*
> *her false sleights doe imploy.*

"A fiction of our Queene Eliz:" noted Dixon, "the maintainer of the gospell of Christe, to be by god himselfe betrouthed unto Christe, though by k:p: and rc: for: 6: yeares it was debared."[20] (King Philip and Roman Catholics, it would seem, are intended in the abbreviations.) Dixon's associating the reign of Mary with the six years Redcross must defer marriage to Una to serve the Faery Queen is somewhat inconsistent in view of his note at the end of the canto that "the daye of the Crownation of *our* bleesed princess Eliz" is shadowed in the betrothal of Una to Redcross.[21] Nevertheless, the linking of this betrothal to Elizabeth's coronation is significant, especially in regard to Dixon's notations that the marriage of the Lamb is also signified in the betrothal. We know that Elizabeth herself spoke of her coronation as her marriage to England as early as 1559 when the Commons pressed her about marriage. Camden described the famous incident in which she drew off her coronation ring and declared, "Yea, to satisfie you, I haue already ioyned my selfe in marriage to an husband, namely, the Kingdome of England. And behold (said she, which I marvaile ye haue forgotten,) the pledge of this my wedlocke and marriage with my kingdome."[22] This "marriage" between the queen and her kingdom was also the subject of at least one popular ballad, "A Songe betwene the Queene's Majestie and Englande," in which "Bessy" and her lover "England" exchange stanzas in dialogue fashion.[23] Una, of course, is not exclusively a symbol of the queen, but in view of her earlier association with Elizabeth as princess and Dixon's contemporary assertion that "a fiction of our Queene Eliz" is somehow a part of the canto, we can understand how a typological prophecy of Elizabeth's mystical marriage to England is allusively suggested. The victory procession from the castle, for example, may have recalled the famous scenes of the young queen's coronation procession through London, in which children's pageants had greeted her at every juncture:[24]

> And them before, the fry of children young
> Their wanton sports and childish mirth did play,
> And to the Maydens sounding tymbrels sung
> In well attuned notes, a ioyous lay,
> And made delightfull musicke all the way,
> Vntill they came, where that faire virgin stood;

> *As faire* Diana *in fresh sommers day,*
> *Beholds her Nymphes, enraung'd in shadie wood,*
> *Some wrestle, some do run, some bathe in christall flood.*
>
> *So she beheld those maydens meriment*
>   *With chearefull vew; who when to her they came,*
>   *Themselues to ground with gratious humblesse bent,*
>   *And her ador'd by honorable name,*
>   *Lifting to heauen her euerlasting fame:*
>   *Then on her head they set a girland greene,*
>   *And crowned her twixt earnest and twixt game;*
>   *Who in her selfe-resemblance well beseene,*
> *Did seeme such, as she was, a goodly maiden Queene.*
>
>   [1. 12. 7–8]

The curious crowning "twixt earnest and twixt game" leads to the assertion in the final line that Una not only seems but in fact *is* a maiden queen. In the fiction, of course, she should still be a princess, for her father is king and marshalls the victory celebration. But he is symbolically the Old Adam now redeemed from bondage. Indeed, the poet himself seems "twixt earnest and twixt game" as he plays with his own fashioning of symbols in a phrase like "selfe-resemblance well beseene." And in the Diana simile he playfully advances another of the queen's mythic images. At this point the betrothal prophesies the mystic betrothal of another "goodly maiden queen."

In stanzas 22 and 23 the allusions to Revelation fuse the figure of the woman clothed with the sun with the bride of the Lamb, both symbols for the church. Una casts aside "her mournefull stole" and the "widow-like sad wimple" that had covered her head and now wears a garment "all lilly white, withoutten spot, or pride." Once again the sun comes from behind the clouds, but now it dazzles Redcross himself:

> *The blazing brightnesse of her beauties beame,*
> *And glorious light of her sunshyny face*
> *To tell, were as to striue against the streame.*
> *My ragged rimes are all too rude and bace,*
> *Her heauenly lineaments for to enchace.*
> *Ne wonder; for her owne deare loued knight,*
> *All were she dayly with himselfe in place,*

> *Did wonder much at her celestiall sight:*
> *Oft had he seene her faire, but neuer so faire dight.*
>
> [1. 12. 23]

But at this moment Duessa's false claim to betrothal with Redcross provides another allusion that underscores the association of marriage with assuming a throne and adds unmistakeably the suggestion of an historical dimension. A messenger, who turns out to be Archimago, bursts in and delivers a letter from "Fidessa," "The wofull daughter, and forsaken heire / Of that great Emperour of all the West." She claims Redcross has "already plighted his right hand / Vnto another loue, and to another land" (stanza 26). Dixon had no doubt that the claims of another queen were alluded to in Duessa's letter: "A fiction of a Challenge by Q: of: s: that the religion by hir maintained to be the truth."[25] Presumably her claim upon Redcross represents as well the claim of the queen of Scots to the throne of England in 1559, a claim that extended to her quartering the arms of England on her coat of arms.[26] Duessa's signing herself "thy neither friend, nor foe, *Fidessa*" predictably cast no dust in Dixon's eyes, for he wrote alongside, "more foe than frend ma:". Duessa's threat that her cause "shall find friends, if need required soe" is of course an accurate reflection of the peril in which England and Elizabeth stood from the forces of Catholic Europe at her accession. Una uncovers the trick of the forces of Antichrist by unmasking Archimago in the messenger.

Before the final knitting up of the fiction in Redcross's return to the Faery Queen, Spenser associates the conclusion of Revelation with the conclusion of his Legend of Holiness; the betrothal of Una and Redcross conflates history and sacred myth, the accession of Elizabeth and the mystic marriage of the Lamb. Characteristically, both earthly and heavenly music accompany the betrothal—as if the music, like Spenser's understanding of the myth of Revelation, exists both in time and beyond time. Someone sings "a song of loue and iollity" while "a heauenly noise" is heard like the sound of "many an Angels voice":

> *Yet wist no creature, whence that heauenly sweet*
> *Proceeded, yet eachone felt secretly*
> *Himselfe thereby reft of his sences meet,*
> *And rauished with rare impression in his sprite.*
>
> [1. 12. 39]

The heavenly noise is the voice of the multitude in Revelation, rejoicing at the marriage of the Lamb (19:6–7). But here the rejoicing is also earthly, and in poetry it may be understood only "by signes" expressing usual joys of a wedding celebration:

> *Great ioy was made that day of young and old,*
> *And solemne feast proclaimd throughout the land,*
> *That their exceeding merth may not be told:*
> *Suffice it heare by signes to vnderstand*
> *The vsuall ioyes at knitting of loues band.*
> *Thrise happy man the knight himself did hold,*
> *Possessed of his Ladies hart and hand,*
> *And euer, when his eye did her behold,*
> *His heart did seeme to melt in pleasures manifold.*

[1. 12. 40]

Dixon understood the signs to mean "the daye of the Crownation of our bleesed princess Eliz"—even though the day that in fact became a solemn feast throughout England, with increased fervor after the Armada, was the anniversary of Elizabeth's accession rather than her coronation.[27] In any case, Dixon sees in the betrothal of Una to Redcross an allusion to Elizabeth's coming to the throne of England, an event the queen herself had called her marriage. In thus understanding the conclusion of book 1, Dixon sees a historical dimension woven into Spenser's recasting of the mythic climax of the book of Revelation, the marriage of the Lamb.

The assertions of this contemporary reader of *The Faerie Queene* accord with what we have spoken of as a cult image of Elizabeth expressed allusively in Una, most evidently in her name, in the sun imagery, and in her associations with imperial descent. Dixon's appreciation of the historical dimension is rendered all the more significant by his almost unfailing sensitivity to the pattern of allusion to the book of Revelation. Dixon appears to move back and forth very easily between the scriptural and the historical: indeed at times it would be more accurate to say that he sees them as identical. Just a few stanzas before he associates the betrothal feast with Elizabeth's coronation, he identifies her reign with the visionary conclusion of Revelation: "The Church and the Lambe Christe united by god himsellfe, a happy knotte wherby peace hath beine Continewed 39 year: the holy citie ore temple of god are Light with the glory of god; which is the Lambe."[28] The thirty-nine years of peace indicate that Dixon was reading the poem around 1597. For him Una, the church, and Elizabeth all become identical; the betrothal of the poem unites sacred prophecy and history.

Spenser's association of scriptural and historical allusions, to which Dixon is so sensitive, suggests an English fulfillment of the book of Revelation, that the Protestant historical interpretation of Revelation had found a further realization in the England of Elizabeth. History had followed the patterns of sacred myth, and the prophetic function of the poet lay in using that myth to make known the correspondences. Spenser sees the religious peace that England had experienced (in sharp contrast to the Continent) for over three decades as beginning with the accession of Elizabeth. Antichrist had been dealt a decisive blow by the queen who was primarily responsible for these thirty years of peace, and the defeat of the Armada seemed conclusive. Human responsibility appeared to have cooperated with divine grace for the achievement of Christ's church, so human analogues for the woman clothed with the sun and the bride of the Lamb suggest themselves to the poet who sees his role as prophetic. In England the victory was achieved by the English people, who, though they had fallen into the captivity of Antichrist, suffered through their martyrs and returned to the reformed church, and by their queen, who had cooperated with God's grace to lead them back to the primitive English church.

From this association of the scriptural and the historical, we can begin to answer, I believe, the question that posed itself at the outset: how does the historical dimension of the poem relate to the moral and spiritual allegory? what part does history play in the individual's achievement of holiness as a moral and psychological state? In the climactic dragon fight of canto 11, we see the moral and spiritual allegory temporarily isolated from the historical dimension. In canto 12, as we have seen, allusions again suggest the relevance of history. The relationship of these two cantos suggests, I think, the relation of the moral allegory to the historical dimension. Both cantos allude insistently to Scripture, but the emphasis in each canto falls on different sections of the New Testament, sections that themselves differ in theological emphasis.

In the battle with the dragon, the stress is Pauline, and the allegory portrays Everyman's achievement of an *imitatio Christi* in overcoming death and the elements of human nature that draw one toward death. As Rosemond Tuve has insisted, Redcross is not a "Christ figure" or a "type" of Christ but the man who "takes on" and becomes Christ in a Pauline sense.[29] The process that Paul everywhere insists on is a profound psychological identification with Christ; the external events of Christ's life—especially Crucifixion, death, and Resurrection—must take place again internally in the psyche of the individual. The dragon is portrayed (especially in the narrative rhetoric of stanzas 12 and 13) as mortality itself; like the term *death* in Pauline theology, the dragon is both physical death and the spiritual state that death figures.[30] Redcross must reach full identification with Christ in order to defeat the dragon. Paradoxically (in regard to the battle metaphor) but properly (in regard to Christian theology) this full sense of identification involves passive receptivity, and Redcross's two falls shadow the psychological recapitulation of the focal event of the life of Christ, his death. Critics have often felt that in the well of life and the stream of balm Spenser allegorizes the two sacraments of the Protestant churches, baptism and Holy Communion. But in fact he creates different symbols for the spiritual events of which the sacraments are themselves symbols. Paul speaks of baptism as a death: "Knowe ye not, that all we which haue bene baptized into Iesus Christ, haue bene baptized into his death?" (Rom. 6:3). Because the knight's fall images this death, the dragon claps his "yron wings" and supposes himself victor. But the greater strength of Redcross on the second day enables him, even though pierced with the sting of the dragon's tail, to cut off that sting (recalling 1 Cor. 15:55, "O death, where is thy sting?"). When Redcross is again thrown down, this time into the "streame of Balme" that flows from the Tree of Life, a second death is figured, a dying into the crucified Christ. The power of death ends, and the knight slays the dragon with the first stroke just as day begins to dawn on the third day. The "triumphant Trompets" may derive from the traditional liturgical transition from Tenebrae to Easter morning, but in the allegory they celebrate a victory of the individual self. The episode portrays allegorically the progression to be made by the individual Christian from his natural, unredeemed state to full acceptance of and identification with the sacrifice of Christ.

It is only after the complete symbolic expression of this necessary development within the individual that the fiction opens out to an historical dimension as well. It does so in canto 12, as elsewhere in book 1, by allusion to the scriptural book that is concerned not so much with personal as with communal salvation; the book of Revelation promises the endurance of the Christian community through time and its eventual victory over the evil that threatens it. Like the relationship of Revelation to St. Paul, the final canto broadens our vision from the arena of the individual psyche to the greater realms of time and space where a Christian people are engaged in spiritual conflict; Redcross becomes not simply Everyman but a people who become faithless, suffer despair, face death, and are finally saved by God's grace. We move from the microcosm of the individual to the macrocosm of a Christian society. Redcross becomes the England whose faith was weak but who finally imitated Christ many times over in the fires of Smithfield, the England that was finally reunited with the reformed church in its betrothal to a virgin queen. The progression of the individual expands to become the progression of the nation from seduction and captivity by the forces of Antichrist to an identification with Christ in its martyrs.

We have noted that the poem adverts to history when the pressure of the moral allegory is comparatively relaxed. Characteristically this turning also coincides with moments of vision within the fiction—when Una's dark veil is laid aside, when Orgoglio's castle is opened, when Redcross experiences his vision of the New Jerusalem from the mount of Contemplation, when Una's face is revealed to him. To apply a critical term suggested by Angus Fletcher, these are "prophetic moments"—moments at a critical juncture "when the prophetic order of history is revealed."[31] Like the characters in the fiction who see more clearly and more fully at such moments, the reader sees into the historical context of the achievement of holiness. He is made to feel that the accomplishment of the individual fits into the larger pattern of accomplishment by the nation elected for the completion of reform.

Because history reveals a "prophetic order"—patterns that recapitulate a sacred archetype—one realizes that there exists a reciprocal relationship between the individual and that history. On the one hand, history must be "read" as Scripture is read if one is to understand the patterns and discover meaning. (Here again one thinks of Foxe's great "reading" of England's ecclesiastical history chained beside the Bible.) Just as Scripture is not the record of unconnected marvels, so history is not a series of discrete, unrelated events. But in both the individual must search and compare to discover order and meaning. On the other hand, history itself depends upon the actions of individuals. The reading of Scripture or of history is not an end in itself but a preparation for moral action. Liberation from Antichrist, as Foxe made clear, came only because individual Englishmen, from bishops to apprentices, witnessed for the reformed church. And Spenser does not confuse the peace of Elizabeth's reign with the end of the need for reformation, for the court satire of Lucifera's palace (as well as the satire of the *Shepheardes Calender*) indicates a poet far from complacent about what had been and what was yet to be achieved. History would continue to depend upon the strength of individual Englishmen, those gentlemen or noble persons to be fashioned "in vertuous and gentle discipline." Together they will comprise, as Milton would express it in *Areopagitica*, "a knowing people, a nation of prophets, of sages, and of worthies." For this accomplishment history remains to the individual both an impetus and a context.

Spenser implies this reciprocal relationship between the development of the individual self and the history of the nation by the way he relates the moral allegory to history. We should not say flatly that the moral and spiritual allegory is "more important" and that the historical dimension is "merely" allusive. Rather the moral allegory is necessarily *prior*; the reader must see into himself before he is prepared to see into history. He must, for example, recognize in himself Orgoglio's trust in merely earthly power before he is allowed to see it in the Roman Church. To proceed in the other direction would breed chauvinism and complacency. (Spenser illustrates this by having Redcross confidently defeat the Dragon of Error, with its vomit of papist tracts, just before he is deceived and falls into real error.) History, adumbrated typologically in the "prophetic moments" of the poem, comes as confirmation of what has been experienced in the self. It comes also as implicit challenge. The visionary moments truly suggest another dimension of human experience, one that is a necessary complement to individual moral responsibility. For Spenser the New Jerusalem remains transcendent, the spiritual goal of the individual self; but through the active strength of men, the earthly participant of its glory could be achieved, however imperfectly, in England's green and pleasant land.

Chapter 3

History
and the Poet's Golden World

In Spenser's allegorization of the human body in the castle of Alma (book 2, canto 9), Arthur and Guyon encounter a vivid personification of what we recognize as man's cultural memory. He is Eumnestes, an old man whose name means "well remembering." His chamber comes third in Alma's guided tour, after Phantastes' chamber of pure imagination and the chamber of reason or judgment, and it is the only one of the three chambers in which the knights linger. Both chamber and proprietor are curious mixtures of apparent debility and actual strength. The room seems "ruinous and old," but the walls are actually firm and strong. The old man himself is "halfe blind" and decrepit of body; yet he is vigorous of mind and "of infinite remembrance." His memory, in fact, goes back beyond Methuselah, but he must prod it with the continual reading of the books and manuscripts that line the walls. Eumnestes allows nothing done in the past "to perish through long eld," but his parchment rolls and books are "all worme-eaten, and full of canker holes." Similarly, his constant tossing and turning of pages, his apparently compulsive searching for information, defeats any attempt to keep his library in order, for he needs an assistant, the boy Anamnestes, to find the things that are "lost or laid amis." The image of Eumnestes toiling incessantly in his timeworn library depicts the constant activity of man's cultural memory, a memory in which nothing is ever really lost altogether but in which continual searching and comparison and restoration are necessary for true understanding.

The books that Arthur and Guyon read in Eumnestes' chamber represent such a search to establish part of a cultural memory. To Arthur and Guyon the books are history; to the reader they are a blending of myth and history. In book 3 two more "historical" catalogues fuse myth and history in a similar way: Merlin's prophecy to Britomart in canto 3 makes her aware of an historical destiny, and her questioning of Paridell in canto 9 about the Trojan past gives her a sense of the temporal extent of that destiny. But in book 4 Spenser presents another catalogue, which seems, although in several ways parallel to the historical catalogues, a different approach to the question of cultural memory. The marriage of the Thames and the Medway (canto 11) fuses geography with myth, but this time the myth is largely the creation of the poet. Spenser has in a sense brought things from Phantastes' chamber to be enrolled in the cultural memory of Eumnestes' library. In this last catalogue Spenser asserts the role of the poet as the augmentor, as well as the custodian, of cultural memory.

Michael Murrin has written of what he calls the "memorial role" of allegorical poetry in society; poetry was to civilize men by making them aware of their past, by developing their collective memory.[1] In the historical catalogues of books 2 and 3, Spenser would appear to have this goal specifically in mind. The common attitude toward history in the sixteenth century was that the past provides lessons for the present.[2] All ages, of course, have held this view of history, either explicitly or implicitly, in one form or another. But it is the specificity of the lessons to be found in history which characterized the Renaissance. One expects to find this attitude toward the "lessons of history" in the historical catalogues of *The Faerie Queene*. Instead we find that poetry stands between history and the present. A nation's cultural memory is not just the store of what happened in the past; it also includes the legends formed about the past and the poetry that by its feigning continues legends and myth. Spenser appears to suggest initially a relationship between history and the poet's feigning, a relationship that benefits the consciousness of the present age. When he comes back to the question in the river catalogue of book 4, he broadens his claims for the poet's vision. Understanding of this relationship—and of the way Spenser develops it in book 4—requires a closer look at Spenser's fusion of history, legend, and geography within the catalogues.

i / *Earthly and Heavenly Lineage*

The three passages in books 2 and 3 that unite history and legend from chronicle sources have different functions within the books, but taken together they form a summary narrative of British "history" from the mythical founding of the nation by Brutus up to Elizabeth's reign. This narrative, of course, is not presented in anything like chronological order, and the way it unfolds becomes as important as the content of the narrative. We ought first of all to note the Vergilian precedent for tracing a summary of national history and legend in the epic. Servius asserts that Vergil celebrated in summary all of Roman history "from the arrival of Aeneas up to his own times," not chronologically, but with the order upset.[3] In Britomart's questioning of Paridell (3. 9. 38–51), Spenser treats the mythical arrival of Brutus in Albion. When Arthur reads the *Briton moniments* chronicle in Eumnestes' chamber (2. 10), he learns the legendary history of the period from Brutus's reign to Uther Pendragon, who is, though Arthur is unaware of it, Arthur's father. Merlin's prophecy (3. 3. 29–49) opens to Britomart the future of the Britons from the time of Conan, whom the fiction represents as her son, until their defeat by the Saxons; then in a more shadowy summary it predicts the Danish and Norman invasions and the "return" of British rule in the Tudors. In addition, the Faery chronicle that Guyon reads shadows an idealized pattern of Tudor rule to contrast with the British chronicle that Arthur reads. It seems clear, then, that Spenser, imitating Vergil, is uniting legend and history in a narrative that is not chronologically ordered, but that taken as a whole forms a summary of the national past. In this he differs from Ariosto, who ends each of his genealogical excurses with a clear celebration of his patrons. Like Vergil (and again unlike Ariosto) Spenser becomes increasingly less detailed and explicit about history that is closer to his own present time, closer to *history* in the modern sense of the word. The Norman invasion, for example, is sketched very generally in one stanza (3. 3. 47), with no kings or battles actually named, while the wars of the Britons and the Saxons are covered in greater detail. The most remote "event," the arrival of Brutus, is treated in two narratives, at the beginning of Arthur's chronicle and in greater detail in the last historical section, Paridell's account of Troy.

The chronicle history passages in books 2 and 3 represent for the characters concerned a search for the past. This is another reason why Spenser is intent that the narrative not be an orderly, chronological progression. Until he reads Eumnestes' book, Arthur seems to know nothing of the history he finds there. When he has read of the past, his new-found knowledge affects him strongly, "And wonder of antiquitie long stopt his speach":

> *At last quite rauisht with delight, to heare*
> *The royall Ofspring of his natiue land,*
> *Cryde out, Deare countrey, O how dearely deare*
> *Ought thy remembraunce, and perpetuall band*
> *Be to thy foster Childe, that from thy hand*
> *Did commun breath and nouriture receaue?*
> *How brutish is it not to vnderstand,*
> *How much to her we owe, that all vs gaue,*
> *That gaue vnto vs all, what euer good we haue.*

[2. 10. 69]

From the reader's point of view, there may be further implications to this stanza—implications I shall suggest below—but surely its primary purpose is to convey Arthur's excitement with his new sense of the past of his nation. A similar excitement is evident when Britomart hears Paridell's own rather trivial story of Troy from the point of view of Paris's descendants. She is not satisfied to leave the story where Paridell at first concludes but insists that Aeneas's story be told as well. She then picks up the thread and tells of the "third kingdome" that arose from the Trojan remnant. In Merlin's prophecy future history becomes Britomart's destiny; the importance of this destiny is emphasized by Merlin's insistence that knowledge of it will strengthen her in the quest for Artegall. As "historical" Britons and ancestors of a nation, Arthur and Britomart have a responsibility to history; between them they share Aeneas's role in their consciousness of history and destiny. In this sense, then, the historical catalogues are an important part of the characterization of the figures whom we are to consider historical.

The question that remains, however, is how these catalogues are to affect the reader, who is to some extent already conscious of the past. Spenser's general concern, it seems to me, is to evoke this consciousness of history in the reader, to do with history what a simple allusion to a classic myth does to evoke a consciousness of the whole myth and its implications. Rather than present a unified historical pageant, Spenser seems intent on emphasizing the variety of the chronicle sources. Carrie A. Harper's study of the sources of these historical catalogues concluded that Spenser's manner of composing them suggests a picture of the poet similar to his own image of Eumnestes, who sits in a chamber "hangd about with rolles, / And old records from auncient times deriu'd":[4]

> *Amidst them all he in a chaire was set,*
> *Tossing and turning them withouten end.*
>
> [2. 9. 58]

One suspects that if Spenser did not actually assume that his devoted readers would pore over these sections of his poem with reference books in hand, he at least expected them to be in mental possession of a good deal of the history from Geoffrey of Monmouth or some other general source.

This of course is not to defend the historical catalogues as effective poetry or to suggest that modern readers must steep themselves in the old records from ancient times derived in order to understand Spenser's strategy here. But perhaps some understanding can be gleaned from noting one's reaction to the catalogues. If asked what they recall from these passages, most readers, I think, would reply that the Lear story is their most (perhaps *only*) striking memory. (More devoted readers of Elizabethan drama will reply that the Gorboduc story is also to be found there.) The most noteworthy thing about the Lear story is its difference from the one we know: with Cordelia's help Lear manages to regain his kingdom and rules for a number of years before he dies; the sons of Goneril and Regan avenge their parents against Cordelia, who hangs herself in prison. What the poem has done is to evoke our knowledge of the Lear story, knowledge that makes our most salient memory of Spenser's version its difference from Shakespeare's. If more of the history and legend were as familiar and vital to us, Spenser's summaries would engage us as immediately as one imagines they engaged the Elizabethan readers who bought up chronicles and abridgments as fast as they could be brought out.[5]

What Spenser intends, I believe, is to use our consciousness of history as a foil for the specifically idealized terrains of his poetic world—to contrast our sense of the past to his created ideal. His reason for doing so is best illuminated by Sidney's familiar comparison of the poet's fiction to the historian's "truth." In asserting that the poet delivers a golden world in contrast to the "brasen" world of nature, Sidney contends that it is not "too sawcie a comparison to ballance the highest poynt of mans wit with the efficacie of Nature." But since the fall of Adam, "our erected wit maketh vs know what perfection is, and yet our infected will keepeth vs from reaching vnto it."[6] This comparison between what should be and what is is echoed in his comparison of the moral values of poetry and history:

> Nowe, to that which commonly is attributed to the prayse of histories, in respect of the notable learning is gotten by marking the successe, as though therein a man should see vertue exalted and vice punished. Truely that commendation is peculiar to Poetrie, and farre of from History. For indeede Poetrie euer setteth vertue so out in her best cullours, making Fortune her wel-wayting hand-mayd, that one must needs be enamoured of her. Well may you see *Vlisses* in a storme, and in other hard plights; but they are but exercises of patience and magnanimitie, to make them shine the more in the neere-following prosperitie. And of the contrarie part, if euil men come to the stage, they euer goe out (as the Tragedie Writer answered to one that misliked the shew of such persons) so manacled as they little animate folkes to followe them. But the Historian, beeing captiued to the trueth of a foolish world, is many times a terror from well dooing, and an incouragement to vnbrideled wickednes.[7]

Sidney goes on to emphasize the amoral quality of many of the "lessons of History":

> For see wee not valiant *Milciades* rot in his fetters? The iust *Phocion* and the accomplished *Socrates* put to death like Traytors? The cruell *Seuerus* liue prosperously? The excellent *Seuerus* miserably murthered? *Sylla* and *Marius* dying in theyr beddes?

One must be aware of history certainly, but Sidney implies that a man must not trust his moral understanding to the "lessons of history."

In the introductory stanzas to the first of the historical catalogues, Spenser dwells on the vertical movement necessary if his poetry is to celebrate properly the lineage of his queen. The movement implicitly suggests the distance between "erected wit" and "infected will":

Who now shal giue vnto me words and sound,
    Equall vnto this haughtie enterprise?
    Or who shall lend me wings, with which from ground
    My lowly verse may loftily arise,
    And lift it selfe vnto the highest skies?
    More ample spirit, then hitherto was wount,
    Here needes me, whiles the famous auncestries
    Of my most dreaded Soueraigne I recount,
By which all earthly Princes she doth farre surmount.

Ne vnder Sunne, that shines so wide and faire,
    Whence all that liues, does borrow life and light,
    Liues ought, that to her linage may compaire,
    Which though from earth it be deriued right
    Yet doth it selfe stretch forth to heauens hight,
    And all the world with wonder ouerspred;
    A labour huge, exceeding farre my might:
    How shall fraile pen, with feare disparaged,
Conceiue such soueraine glory, and great bountihed?

                                    [2. 10. 1–2]

The poet feels the need to raise his verse "from ground" unto "the highest skies" in order to recount the parallel movement of the queen's ancestry "from earth" to "heauens hight." The canto that follows is the poet's answer to the question he asks himself in the final two lines. The queen's genealogy derives quite literally from the earth and ends with the heavenly ideal expressed in the Faery chronicle.

In the early part of the canto, we find a decided interest in the land and its acquisition of names. The chronicle evokes a sense of the contrast between what the land was and what it is now:

The land, which warlike Britons now possesse,
    And therein haue their mightie empire raysd,
    In antique times was saluage wildernesse,
    Vnpeopled, vnmanurd, vnprou'd, vnpraysd,
    Ne was it Island then, ne was it paysd
    Amid the Ocean *waues, ne was it sought*
    Of marchants farre, for profits therein praysd,

> But was all desolate, and of some thought
> By sea to haue bene from the Celticke mayn-land brought.

[2. 10. 5]

At that time the land did not "deserue a name to haue," but a name comes from the land itself when the first mariner sees the white cliffs. It is only a tentative name, for the land is still "vnpeopled." From the mingling of land with people, sometimes the quite literal physical fusion of land and heroes, other place names will come. The race of giants that inhabit the island become actual personifications of the land; born of the earth's "owne natiue slime," they will return to the earth when subdued by Brutus's heroic troop. The giants are malevolent counterparts of Vergil's fauns and nymphs who spring from the trees in Evander's account of ancient Latium:

> *Haec nemora indigenae Fauni Nymphaeque tenebant*
> *gensque virum truncis et duro robore nata,*
> *quis neque mos neque cultus erat, nec iungere tauros*
> *aut componere opes norant aut parcere parto*
> *sed rami atque asper victu venatus alebat.*

In these woodlands the native Fauns and Nymphs once dwelt, and a race of men sprung from trunks of trees and hardy oak, who had no rule nor art of life, and knew not how to yoke the ox or to lay up stores, or to husband their gains; but tree-branches nurtured them and the huntsman's savage fare.

[*Aeneid* 8. 314–18]

When Saturn comes as an exile, gathers them together, and civilizes them with law, he then gives a name to the land: "Latiumque vocari maluit, his quoniam latuisset tutus in oris." Evander tells how other names were given or were changed in response to this early history.

Spenser was certainly aware of the Vergilian precedent as he brought etymologies into the poem, but one cannot help supposing that deep-rooted psychological motives are also touched by such stories of the simultaneous subduing and naming of land. The giant whom Corineus conquers becomes the "western Hogh" at Plymouth, and more mysteriously Debon and Canute also contribute to the landscape in overcoming giants (stanza 11).[8] From these remote and legendary victories the poet derives more familiar names; etiology becomes etymology:

> In meed of these great conquests by them got,
>   Corineus had the Prouince vtmost west,
>   To him assigned for his worthy lot,
>   Which of his name and memorable gest
>   He called Cornewaile, yet so called best:
>   And Debons shayre was, that is Deuonshyre:
>   But Canute had his portion from the rest,
>   The which he cald Canutium, for his hyre;
> Now Cantium, which Kent we commenly inquire.
>
> [2. 10. 12]

Nature seems to be stamped—but indifferently—by history in the heroic age; victory and shame both leave names on the land. Cambria and Albania are named for heroes, but an enemy chieftain gives his name to the Humber, and a "sad virgin innocent of all" names the Severne in her death. Spenser's playing with names, languages, and geography reaches its height in the stanza describing the victories of the "second *Brute*," Brutus Greenshield, in Hainaut:

> Let Scaldis tell, and let tell Hania,
>   And let the marsh of Estham bruges tell,
>   What colour were their waters that same day,
>   And all the moore twixt Eluersham and Dell,
>   With bloud of Henalois, which therein fell.
>   How oft that day did sad Brunchildis see
>   That greene shield dyde in dolorous vermell?
>   That not Scuith guiridh it mote seeme to bee,
> But rather y Scuith gogh, signe of sad crueltee.
>
> [2. 10. 24]

Germanic, French, and Welsh words seem in conflict, conflict analogous to that of peoples. Part of the significance of the chronicle of legendary history is that the names do indeed "tell" of conflicts of which they are the only remaining evidence.

When we come to the end of the strife-filled account of Brutus's "sacred progeny," we almost suspect irony in the poet's assertion that they bore the scepter seven hundred years "With high renowme, and great felicitie" (stanza 36). But it is more likely that such conflict is to be considered renowned and felicitous in an age of legendary heroes. The irony comes in the final lines of this stanza when the poet asserts "That in the end was left no moniment / Of Brutus, nor of Britons glory auncient." This is rather like Aeneas's lament for Palinurus: "nudus in ignota, Palinure, iacebis harena" (5. 871). For the chief monument of Brutus, as Spenser expected his readers would know from Geoffrey, is the very name of the Britons.[9] The names of shires (which Spenser etymologizes, incorrectly, from share), of rivers, of hills and forests, and especially of cities are monuments to Brutus's progeny. Land and history seem fused in this early period, and the names that remain embody the fusion.

The second historical period, as Harry Berger points out, is one in which emphasis falls on law and civility.[10] Human problems of war and orderly succession remain, but the attempt to impose order is emphasized. The first king of this period is Donwallo, who unites the divided kingdom, defeats its enemies, and brings "ciuill gouernance" through law. Called the "gracious *Numa* of great *Britainie*," he seems almost a prefigurement of Henry VII. It is significant that the first etymology Spenser gives in this section concerns law; he derives the Mertian laws from "Dame Mertia," wife of Donwallo's great-grandson Guitheline. But the frustrations and defeats possible in an age of law are significantly demonstrated by the tragic story of a woman ruler, Bunduca, which Spenser interpolates at a convenient place in the narrative.[11] When the Romans subdue the weak parts of the kingdom, Bunduca rises against them and battles them with less success than she deserves, and is finally betrayed by her own men. After regrouping her army and attacking again, she is decisively defeated and kills herself. Spenser devotes a stanza to her praise; later Bunduca will be held up to Britomart as a model of the woman warrior (3. 3. 54). The relevance of the Bunduca story is not, I think, that she represents an inadequate sort of temperance, as Berger suggested,[12] but that even though she is a worthy type of feminine heroism, she fails to achieve her end. What seems to defeat her is simply the bad fortune that history so often records. This is the sort of harsh reality repeatedly encountered in the last two periods of which Arthur reads; even the good kings (Cassiblane, Kimbeline, Lucius) fall prey to treachery or die without sons to succeed them.

In Arthur's chronicle Spenser traces the queen's lineage "from earth"—indeed literally at times as he records how history and geography fuse in early legends—then through the beginnings of civil government and law to Arthur himself, the greatest of Britons. Politically Spenser is doing nothing more complicated than using what was a commonplace of Tudor propaganda and what one supposes he saw as little more than a convenient myth: that the Tudors were the true descendants of King Arthur and the ancient Briton kings.[13] But as Vergil had done, he uses the commonplace political myth of origins merely as a starting point. His real intent is to evoke early legends and history and to associate them with the kingdom he is celebrating. This association extends specifically into the language that is the medium of his celebration: etymologies, both the ones specifically mentioned and the ones only implied, suggest that even language preserves some of this history too remote to be more than legend. As Spenser evokes a consciousness of the past, he associates its conflicts and turmoil, its failures as well as its accomplishments, with the land and the names men have for its features. This association makes the past more vivid (there is something inherently fascinating about etiological fables and etymology), but at the same time consciousness of the past makes the reader more aware of its bitter realities and the uncertainties of human endeavor. The queen's lineage "from earth" is not a story of unmixed glory. Arthur's exclamation is not, I think, to be seen as wholly optimistic by the reader:

> *Deare countrey, O how dearely deare*
> *Ought thy remembraunce, and perpetuall band*
> *Be to thy foster Childe, that from thy hand*
> *Did commun breath and nouriture receaue?*

[2. 10. 69]

Remembrance that is "dearely deare" would appear to include some sense of "costly" as well as "precious."

It is to this bitter reality of conflict and turmoil that the Faery chronicle is meant to contrast.[14] Instead of internecine warfare, treason, and childless kings, the chronicle Guyon reads records orderly conquest, construction, and succession. Many of the motifs are similar to what Arthur reads in *Briton moniments*—battles with foreign enemies, giant slaying, city building, etc.—but with the significant difference that everything succeeds:

> *His sonne was* Elfinell, *who ouercame*
> *The wicked* Gobbelines *in bloudy field:*
> *But* Elfant *was of most renowmed fame,*
> *Who all of Christall did* Panthea *build:*
> *Then* Elfar, *who two brethren gyants kild,*
> *The one of which had two heads, th'other three:*
> *Then* Elfinor, *who was in Magick skild;*
> *He built by art vpon the glassy See*
> *A bridge of bras, whose sound heauens thunder seem'd to bee.*
>
> *He left three sonnes, the which in order raynd,*
> *And all their Ofspring, in their dew descents,*
> *Euen seuen hundred Princes, which maintaynd*
> *With mightie deedes their sundry gouernments;*
> *That were too long their infinite contents*
> *Here to record, ne much materiall:*
> *Yet should they be most famous moniments,*
> *And braue ensample, both of martiall,*
> *And ciuill rule to kings and states imperiall.*

[2. 10. 73–74]

Spenser proceeds to the Elfin shadowing of Tudor rule, with Henry VII, Prince Arthur, Henry VIII, and Elizabeth represented in the names Elficleos, Elferon, Oberon, and Tanaquill. Certainly this Elfin idealization of the Tudors achieves as much meaning in what it pointedly excludes as in what it includes. The circumstances under which Henry VII came to the throne more closely resemble Arthur's chronicle than Guyon's. The Faery chronicle does include the untimely death of Elferon but is tactfully silent about the marital difficulties that occurred after Oberon's prototype, Henry VIII, doubly supplied his brother's place "in spousall, and dominion." It is also silent about the two unhappy reigns that less idealized history would place before Tanaquill's prototype.

The important thing about the Faery chronicle is that it *is* idealization—not flattery, but conscious and poetic idealization. As the Platonic idea that the actual only imperfectly embodies, the Faery chronicle traces that part of the queen's "auncestry" that "doth it selfe stretch forth to heauens hight." Like the celebration of Eliza in the *April* eclogue, the Faery chronicle has a hortative function in that it implicitly encourages the further realization of the ideals of peace and order. Insofar as Tudor rule approaches the Faery ideal of order, it fulfills the promise of its "heauenly" genealogy.

The Faery chronicle is as obviously a created world as it is an ideal one. The story of Prometheus's creation of Elfe from animal parts and fire stolen from heaven is an evident mythologizing of the biblical creation stories. The important thing about the Faery version is not its differences from the biblical, I think, but that it is so evidently "made up"—a fusion by the poet himself of Christian and classical stories. When we learn that Elfe discovers the woman Fay in "the gardins of *Adonis*," we are aware that we are undoubtedly back again in the world of *The Faerie Queene* after the side trip into legendary British history. The etymologies parallel those in Arthur's chronicle, but I think that their point is again that they are fictional. Prometheus calls the man he created Elfe, "to weet / Quick," and the man calls the "goodly creature" who is woman "Fay" *because* he deems her "either Spright / Or Angell." The unsolved puzzle in the first and the playful tautology in the second might convince us that we should cease attempting to solve a riddle and allow Spenser his whimsy. The significance of the contrast of the *Briton moniments* to the Faery chronicle is not just the contrast of the uncertainty of the actual to the orderliness of the ideal but also that the ideal is embodied in a fictional world. Fiction amends the actual and thereby makes it ideal.

The Sidneian distinction between historiographer and poet stands behind Spenser's juxtaposition of Arthur's and Guyon's chronicles. Faeryland is not a simple shadowing of Tudor rule but an idealization of it. *Briton moniments* illustrates the moral ambiguities of history, and what is left out of the Faery idealization implies that moral ambiguity and imperfection continue into the present. Faeryland, as the poet's golden world, can present a moral vision in a way that history's brazen world cannot. But such an idealization risks becoming remote, and it is for this reason also, I feel, that the evocation of history is important to Spenser. Faeryland, the creation of man's heavenly, erected wit, must be placed in the context of a world in which earthly, infected will is still very active.

ii / *"Eternal union shall be made"*

Each of the other two historical catalogues is likewise succeeded by a fictional image of what the catalogue has evoked historically. In Merlin's prophecy to Britomart (3. 3. 25–49), the most important theme to emerge is the paradoxical achievement of concord and harmony from the discord and moral ambiguity of history. In the early part of the prophecy, victories are succeeded by defeats and nothing permanent is ever accomplished. History becomes ethically more complicated by the conversion of the Britons' enemies, the Saxons, to Christianity.[15] The Saxons massacre the Briton monks of Bangor, and four stanzas later the Briton Cadwallin crowns "with martyrdome" the sacred head of the godly Saxon king, Oswald. In a state of moral shame, the Britons will lose their rule. Merlin gives ambivalent reasons for their defeat. His first explanation seems classical and epic: since the "full time prefixt by destiny" has expired, "heauen it selfe shall their successe enuy." Yet when Cadwallader, Cadwallin's son, survives the plagues that afflict the Britons and intends to avenge their defeat, he is persuaded by a vision that heaven has willed the Britons' decline "for their sinnes dew punishment." Both are attempts to explain why the Britons are finally and decisively driven from rule, but neither answer resolves the moral ambiguities that increasingly surround the prophecy. What is unambiguous is the suffering and caprice of history:

> Then woe, and woe, and euerlasting woe,
> Be to the Briton babe, that shalbe borne,
> To liue in thraldome of his fathers foe;
> Late King, now captiue, late Lord, now forlorne,
> The worlds reproch, the cruell victours scorne,
> Banisht from Princely bowre to wastful wood:
> O who shall helpe me to lament, and mourne
> The royall seed, the antique Troian blood,
> Whose Empire lenger here, then euer any stood.

[3. 3. 42]

Spenser actually seems to have made more conclusive and final the account of the Britons' end—almost as if to diminish their glory.[16] In spite of the fact that Merlin's prophecy concludes with the "return" of Briton rule in the Welsh Tudors, Spenser is not concerned with whitewashing the early Britons or with attributing their fall simply to bad luck. Nor are the Saxons, in spite of the saintly Oswald, any improvement. Their rule was ill won and becomes worse; after two hundred years they in turn will be overrun by the Danes. Then the Danes too will be supplanted by the Normans. The animal imagery in stanza 47 emphasizes the continued absence of moral progress in this last invasion. It is a seesaw world suggested by the traditional image of fortune's wheel.

But when "the terme is full accomplished," concord comes as suddenly as Cambina in book 4 to resolve conflict and to restore the Briton blood to the throne. The emphasis is on the Vergilian theme of assimilation of peoples rather than on the more obviously political matter of "return." The Wars of the Roses are implicitly included in the centuries of conflict resolved in the union:

> *Thenceforth eternall vnion shall be made*
> *Betweene the nations different afore,*
> *And sacred Peace shall louingly perswade*
> *The warlike minds to learne her goodly lore,*
> *And ciuile armes to exercise no more.*
>
> [3. 3. 49]

This eternal union will be personified in a "royall virgin" who will stretch her power as far as "the Belgicke shore." Though Britomart does not, the reader of course knows the identity of this unnamed royal virgin who resolves the discord of previously warring peoples.

Merlin's prophecy breaks off at this point, and the narrative returns to the fictional virgin whose marriage to Arthegall will begin the descent. Britomart becomes in the fiction an image of the resolution of which she has just learned—a prefiguring of the royal virgin who will represent the true *discordia concors*. Britomart is a Briton, and whatever else her name signifies, it surely reminds us of her race. Her nurse Glauce, however, in suggesting that Britomart become a martial maid, adduces the example of "a Saxon virgin":

> *Faire Angela (quoth she) men do her call,*
> *No whit lesse faire, then terrible in fight:*
> *She hath the leading of a Martiall*
> *And mighty people, dreaded more then all*
> *The other Saxons, which do for her sake*
> *And loue, themselues of her name Angles call.*

> *Therefore faire Infant her ensample make*
> *Vnto thy self, and equall courage to thee take.*

[3. 3. 56]

Not only does Britomart take Angela's example, she also takes her armor. She appropriates a captured suit of Angela's armor that King Ryence displayed as a war souvenir. Armor in Spenser is rarely just armor, and its being put on or taken off is seldom without symbolic import. As a Briton maid dressed in the armor of a Saxon maid (especially a Saxon maid who *names* her people), Britomart becomes herself an image or type of the resolution that, as Merlin prophesies, must be the end of centuries of conflict.[17] In the armor she appears a fusion of the two dominant peoples whose conflict occupies Merlin's prophecy. Moreover, the spear made by Bladud links her to the earlier legendary history which had concerned Arthur (2. 10. 25–26). At the beginning of the conflict of Britons and Saxons, Britomart is a prophetic image of its final resolution in the queen whose fictional ancestor she is. Both Britomart and Elizabeth are embodiments of *discordia concors*: Britomart early, fictional, and prophetic; Elizabeth present, actual, and fulfilling.

The final consideration of legendary history is the discussion by Britomart and Paridell of the succession of ruling cities: Troy, Rome, Troynovant, and their fictional counterpart, Cleopolis. The attitudes that Britomart and Paridell each display toward this succession become the actual focus of the episode. Because she now knows of her historic role, Britomart is eager to know of the past; her role impels her curiosity but does not seem to arouse necessary expectations. Paridell, on the other hand, knows just enough of the past to give a tolerable sort of summary; he is not particularly concerned to know more, and what he does know is strictly in the service of the present. He is proud of his ability as a raconteur, and his version of the Trojan story is designed for the very practical use of winning Hellenore's pity. To him the point of the story of Troy is quite simply its pathos: once great, Troy is now no more than "an idle name."

> *What boots it boast thy glorious descent,*
> *And fetch from heauen thy great Genealogie,*
> *Sith all thy worthy prayses being blent,*
> *Their of-spring hath embaste, and later glory shent.*

[3. 9. 33]

It is all very sad. Paridell seems at this point quite ignorant of Troy's progeny: when questioned later, he admits to knowing something of Troy's offspring, but here all that would spoil the effect of the story.

Paridell is also a revisionist; he claims that the most famous worthy of Troy was Paris and that Helen was his "meed of worthinesse." Helen is praised for being what the war was fought over; for her so many "carcases of noble warrioures" strewed the plain. Helen, however, has little to do with Paridell's lineage, for his race derives from Paris's sowing of wild oats ten years before the siege of Troy. Paris's son, named Parius after him, becomes a kind of small-time Aeneas who "Gathred the *Troian* reliques sau'd from flame, / And with them sayling thence, to th'Isle of *Paros* came." Paridell descends from this noble line, but he has left his native soil to seek adventures "for faire Ladies loue, and glories gaine." What is striking in Paridell's story, of course, is its variance from the usual literary tradition of Paris as the effeminate and dissolute cause of the Trojan War and of Helen as a mindless beauty, oblivious of the suffering she has caused. To Paridell the Trojan War is simply a picturesque setting for his ancestry. The purpose of his recounting the story is simply to impress a new Helen; history, suitably revised, is at the service of the moment.

To Paridell's casual use of history, Spenser opposes Britomart's earnest search for the past. She mistakenly supposes that Paridell actually feels the historical pathos of Troy, that he understands the fall of the city as a national tragedy and the beginning of new destinies. She eagerly asks him to go back and tell what happened to the more important conveyor of the Trojan fates. It develops that Paridell really does know the more significant story of the "*Troian* reliques"; it had simply not suited his purpose to mention it earlier since it makes the story of Paris's line look rather paltry by comparison. Paridell's account of Aeneas is a comically brief and flat retelling of the *Aeneid*: two stanzas give the epic story (one stanza for each six books!), and another stanza the subsequent history until the founding of Rome. (As Thomas Roche has noted, Paridell leaves out the story of Dido, the one event in the *Aeneid* that might reflect unfavorably on him.[18]) In contrast, Britomart takes up the story enthusiastically and asserts the existence of "a third kingdome" that will dare to equal both "first and second *Troy*."

> *It* Troynouant *is hight, that with the waues*
> *Of wealthy* Thamis *washed is along,*
> *Vpon whose stubborne neck, whereat he raues*
> *With roring rage, and sore him selfe does throng,*
> *That all men feare to tempt his billowes strong,*
> *She fastned hath her foot, which standes so hy,*
> *That it a wonder of the world is song*
> *In forreine landes, and all which passen by,*
> *Beholding it from far, do thinke it threates the skye.*

> [3. 9. 45]

The vigorous image of London Bridge as the city's foot fastened on the river's neck contrasts sharply with Paridell's languid rhetoric and offhand summaries. Britomart is interested in details, where Brutus built the city gates and what the boundaries of the city were. Asking pardon for having forgotten about the third Trojan kingdom—"for my wits bene light"—Paridell remembers that he does know the story of Brutus's accidental killing of his father, Silvius, and his wanderings that led to his arrival in Britain. His conclusion brings us back to the point at which *Briton moniments* began in book 2.

But the very end of Paridell's recital reminds us once again of the fictional counterpart of Troynovant and therefore of the fictional world of the poem. Brutus, he says, founded both Troynovant and Lincoln,

> *both renowmed far away,*
> *That who from East to West will endlong seeke,*
> *Cannot two fairer Cities find this day,*
> *Except* Cleopolis: *so heard I say*
> *Old* Mnemon.

> [3. 9. 51]

The recollection that the city of the Faery Queene is fairer than mere historical cities brings us back to the specific world of the poem. In this world Paridell is a scatterbrained, false version of Aeneas, who understands history not as an indication of destiny but as something that may be conveniently rearranged for the sake of the present moment. Britomart, on the other hand, is a true imaginative descendant of Aeneas; she has an historical responsibility and accordingly searches the past for an understanding of her role.

Spenser does not make Britomart and Arthur find in the past (or prophesied future) a mirror for magistrates or a treasury of political wisdom. Paridell's historiography may in fact parody the way the past is distorted when it is put into the immediate service of the present as "lesson." From the viewpoint of the poet and the reader, who know that legend is a part of the historical catalogues, the fusion of legend and history suggests that the resultant mythic patterns may be just as important to national consciousness as the undeniably historical facts. Myth in this sense is a version of history in which facts have lost their primacy. In his selection and arrangement of details from his chronicle sources, Spenser is rarely concerned with "facts" as such. What does concern him are the patterns that show the complexity, conflict, and uncertainty of human endeavor. Thus whatever general "lessons" can be implied are more often than not negative, and the nation's past is "dear" in the sense of costly as well as precious. Perhaps the most accurate general description of the history presented in the catalogues is that it is an image of *discordia* as yet unresolved in time.

And yet history, with all its uncertainties, is also a context for human sexuality, and here we have one of the central themes of book 3. In what came to be called the Legend of Chastity but might have been as aptly titled the Legend of Love, Spenser is concerned to establish a morality of human love, especially for its sexual expression. To do so, he needs to clarify the contexts and purposes of love between the sexes. One such context, of course, is the great regenerative cycle of nature, and it is a vision of this cycle that we find at the very center of the book in the Garden of Adonis. Because Nature ordained human love as an element of this regenerative process, we can see why the frivolous toying with love and sex at Malacasta's castle and the even more sinister and perverse ideas of love at Busirane's house reflect an inadequate understanding. To both Malacasta and Busirane fertility would be an embarrassment rather than the acknowledged end of sexual love, and at neither house can lovers be seen as cooperating in the eternal processes of the Garden of Adonis. For Britomart history is another context of love. Her love for Artegall impels her toward history; their marriage will forge a link in an historical chain running from the Trojan past to the Tudor present. Her quest for Artegall represents her responsibility to her nation and its history. And because heroic love has this historical context, we can see more fully the inadequacy of Paridell. His cavalier attitude toward history accords perfectly with his cavalier treatment of Hellenore, for he accepts responsibility for neither. By wandering about seeking adventures and love affairs, he takes himself out of history and out of responsibility for the future. Perhaps it is the very fragility of historical progress that demands Britomart's commitment and responsibility. So often the chronicles narrate failings of human love—and of human fertility —and wars and suffering are the result. In this sense Britomart is a version of the Elizabeth who might have been, the Elizabeth upon whom the duty of marriage was so often urged in the first half of her reign. Perhaps an unstated contemporary context for this theme in book 3 are the notably unhappy royal marriages in the Tudor dynasty. No contemporary would have needed to be reminded of what Spenser had pointedly excluded from the Elfin shadowing of Henry VIII's reign or of the marriages of Mary Tudor and Mary Stuart. And though the idea of Elizabeth's marrying was of necessity abandoned in the early 1580s, surely Spenser's conception of the purposeful, historically committed Britomart had much to do with this earlier hope. The inclusion of Belphoebe adjusted the poem to the historical reality of the late 1580s, but Spenser still centered book 3 on Britomart in part because her active, questing love is a corrective to the Petrarchism of the loves of Belphoebe and Amoret, but also because his idea is essentially true that human love demands commitment to past and to future.

Because each of the historical sections of books 2 and 3 concludes with a fictional equivalent of what the history has evoked, Spenser balances the claim for the poet's golden world against the necessary realities of history's brazen world. Each of these claims for the importance of the poet's vision relates to his version of Tudor rule: the Faery chronicle asserts the ideal of peace and harmony as an element of that rule; Britomart, as ancestress and type of Elizabeth, is a prophetic image of ethnic *discordia concors*; Cleopolis, though its outlines remain hazy and incomplete, was to be an ideal of London. Spenser is not, of course, claiming that all the centuries of discord were definitively resolved in his own age and in his queen. This is why fictional ideal, not contemporary fact, embodies the resolution. The fictional world stands between a past that is so in need of resolution and the possibilities, the potential, of the present. As ideals, the fictional images of concord look back to the past, then turn hortatively toward the present.

iii / "The seas abundant progeny"

The second half of *The Faerie Queene* exhibits a significant alteration in the poet's attitude toward history. On the one hand he feels the need to confront history, particularly contemporary history, more directly, and he is consequently less insistent about the distinction between the morally brazen world of history and the poet's golden world. This impulse we shall examine in more detail when we consider book 5. On the other hand, Spenser suggests the value of withdrawal from the arena of history into a more private poetic world. The central location of this second impulse is in Calidore's glimpsing of Colin's vision in his retreat into the pastoral world in book 6. The poet characterizes this second impulse by the self-consciously poetic nature of the passages that embody it. But not only does the poetry call attention to its own fonts, it also implies that its vision is sufficient, that there is no longer any need for that vision to be explicitly balanced against the claims of history.

The geographical celebration of Britain in the marriage of the Thames and the Medway (4. 11) embodies this second impulse in a particularly impressive way. Spenser is broadening his claim for the importance of his own poetic world. His strategy is to unite the geography and mythology of the classic world with English and Irish geography and the poet's own newly created mythology. His vision embraces "great Ganges, and immortal Euphrates" and the humble Churne and Charwell. We seem to be near the Ovidian world of etiological metamorphosis even as information about the latest explorations of South America is advanced. Quite exact characterizations of little-known English and Irish streams lead to the abstraction of the parade of Greek sea nymphs, who are simply exotic words. The poet's knowledge of actual rivers merges with his delight in creating poetry from such disparate material as "the goodly Barow, which doth hoord / Great heapes of Salmons in his deepe bosome" and "snowy necked *Doris*, and milke white *Gala-*

thea." Spenserian eclecticism has been raised to a higher power to emphasize his mythopoeic claims.

There are indications in the canto that we are to see the river procession as a parallel to the historical catalogues of books 2 and 3. The poet assumes the stance of the epic bard faced with the task of beginning a catalogue of forces, but his "forces" are the gods and nymphs of the oceans, rivers, and brooks:

> *All which not if an hundred tongues to tell,*
> *And hundred mouthes, and voice of brasse I had,*
> *And endlesse memorie, that mote excell,*
> *In order as they came, could I recount them well.*

> *Helpe therefore, O thou sacred imp of* Ioue,
> *The noursling of Dame* Memorie *his deare,*
> *To whom those rolles, layd vp in heauen aboue,*
> *And records of antiquitie appeare,*
> *To which no wit of man may comen neare;*
> *Helpe me to tell the names of all those floods,*
> *And all those Nymphes, which then assembled were*
> *To that great banquet of the watry Gods,*
> *And all their sundry kinds, and all their hid abodes.*

[4. 11. 9–10]

The invocation of Clio parallels the similar invocation in book 3 before Merlin's prophecy. The reference to rolls and "records of antiquitie" reminds us of Eumnestes' chamber, but hitherto these records have not been available to Eumnestes. With the supposed aid of the muse of history, the wit of the poet will enroll them in man's cultural memory. In the first four lines Spenser is imitating a line that occurs twice in Vergil. The more apposite Vergilian context is the introduction to the second *Georgic*, in which the poet protests to Maecenas that his verses cannot embrace all facets of a vast subject. Spenser's allusion to Vergil suggests a good deal about the catalogue that is to follow, for the second *Georgic* is Vergil's splendid celebration of the beauty and fruitfulness of the Italian earth. Vergil's catalogues there are not epic roll calls of warriors but a georgic honoring of trees, fruits, and especially vines. With his loving enumeration of place names—rivers, lakes, mountains, towns, regions—Vergil evokes and memorializes an Italy, as yet more hope than reality, thriving in the arts of peace. Spenser's procession of rivers is likewise to be a georgic catalogue. The fields are filled with flowing water instead of warriors; the dominant note will be concord rather than conflict.

The river marriage, like the historical catalogues, is concerned with the extent of the nation. In the historical catalogues the reader feels the temporal extent of Britain; the nation's past extends so far back in time that its origins can be expressed only in myth—myth that makes Britain the offspring of Troy and coeval with Rome. In the river-marriage pageant the reader senses the spatial extent of Britain. One is impressed by the size and variety of the regions that together comprise the realm. There can be little doubt that Spenser's imagination, like Shakespeare's, is more stimulated by the sense of temporal extent, but in the celebration of Britain's rivers, one becomes aware of some of the imaginative interest in spatial extent that would characterize poets like Drayton, Donne, and later Milton.

Part of the strategy of the canto is to change the way the reader views natural change, personified, we come to realize, by Proteus. In the first stanza the poet elicits our sympathy for the detained Florimell. "Vnlouely *Proteus*" has thrown her into a dungeon and "cruelly" binds her with chains. The sea, as part of Proteus's means of imprisonment, "rag'd and ror'd" about the walls that enclose her, and "ten thousand monsters foule abhor'd" swim about in it. Kathleen Williams has suggested that Florimell's seven-month imprisonment appears a Proserpina-like death that in part symbolizes winter in the annual cycle of nature.[19] Even Florimell's name suggests a connection with the most beautiful part of the vegetable world. Proteus is as cruel to Florimell as winter is to that world. But then our perspective on Proteus begins to alter gradually. We find that it is in Proteus's house that the marriage of the Thames and the Medway is to be celebrated. This, of course, describes the literal fact that the two rivers do not meet until they reach the sea; the Medway flows into the Thames estuary. But the procession of rivers coming to Proteus's house seems to shadow as well the vernal change of rivers loosened from winter ice and flowing amply to the sea. Spenser's mythopoeia turns Proteus into a personification of seasonal change.[20] The beauty of the procession of rivers alters the way we view Proteus, just as the coming of spring causes us to forgive the natural processes that brought winter. The strategy here anticipates that of the *Mutabilitie Cantos;* Mutability grows more beautiful as her threatening claims to dominance become feebler.

The pageant of sea and river gods and nymphs is neither an exact attempt to express actual aspects of bodies of water through personification nor an abstract listing of purely literary creations. The procession of the classic sea gods suggests that they represent aspects of the sea but that they embody as well man's play of mind regarding natural phenomena. Neptune makes the seas rise and fall, and accordingly he wears a "Diademe imperiall" to show his power. Amphitrite, his queen, represents the beauty of the sea, and she is fancied wearing pearls in her hair. Triton "becomes" the sound the sea makes, and the poet pictures him as a trumpeter "that made the rockes to roar." The list of sea gods in stanzas 13 and 14 is a mixture of classic personifications of the sea and legends associated with it. That the mythic founders of nations are sons of Neptune seems to express the importance of the sea to a civilization, but Spenser focuses the interest on the names themselves (in some cases on their meaning) and on their legendary associations. It is evident that "aged *Ocean*" represents the primordiality of the sea. But Nereus, though a sea god, is an example of more complex mythopoeia, and Spenser brings together traditions found in Hesiod, Homer, and Horace.[21] Natalis Comes said that Nereus represents skill in seamanship and navigation, and this skill he further allegorizes as the moral understanding and trust possessed by the wise man on the sea of life. Basically Spenser appears to be taking the sea gods and other sea-connected legendary figures as he found them in classical literature and the Renaissance handbooks of mythology. The play of mind that created these figures ranges from simple personification to elaborate myth, and it is the wide extent of such mythmaking that interests the poet. The result is a rich context of mythologized nature in which a vision of Britain's geography may become myth.

The procession of British rivers duplicates the extent of the classic mythopoeia. The Thames's "mother," the Ouze "whom men doe Isis rightly name," is, for example, a simple personification of a very winding river: "Full weake and crooked creature seemed shee, / And almost blind through eld, that scarce her way could see" (4. 11. 24). Tributaries therefore become "two smal grooms" who try to sustain her. With the Thame, the "father" of the Thames, personification becomes slightly more complex. His hoary head and gray beard at first seem to characterize the river's waters, but the next stanza pictures him with his back bowed in carrying Oxford. His ancient gravity seems to slide over into the university that is his burden.

The personification of the Thames itself is more extensive still and becomes more elaborately symbolic:

> But he their sonne full fresh and iolly was,
>> All decked in a robe of watchet hew,
>> On which the waues, glittering like Christall glas,
>> So cunningly enwouen were, that few
>> Could weenen, whether they were false or trew.
>> And on his head like to a Coronet
>> He wore, that seemed strange to common vew,
>> In which were many towres and castels set,
> That it encompast round as with a golden fret.
>
> Like as the mother of the Gods, they say,
>> In her great iron charet wonts to ride,
>> When to Ioues pallace she doth take her way:
>> Old Cybele, arayd with pompous pride,
>> Wearing a Diademe embattild wide
>> With hundred turrets, like a Turribant,
>> With such an one was Thamis beautifide;
>> That was to weet the famous Troynouant,
> In which her kingdomes throne is chiefly resiant.

$$[4. 11. 27-28]$$

The playful doubt whether the waves are true or false calls attention to the art of the representation, and this attention makes us aware of the movement from the river god's robe of watchet hue to a symbolic representation of the capital of the kingdom in his turreted crown. In the course of the two stanzas, the vision of the Thames seems to become an image of a vigorous maritime nation. Roche suggests how the simile of Cybele adds to the feeling that the Thames becomes an image of more than a personified river, becomes in fact symbolic of the continuity of civilization:

Cybele is a symbol of ancient civilization and fertility, of which Troynouant is the latest example. Spenser is going beyond the patriotic zeal of the antiquarian poets to show that his nation partakes of the ancient order of civilization, that its youthful fertility, symbolized by the Thames, is the inheritance of the beginning of civilization, of Troy and Rome, and thus generalizes the Trojan imagery woven into the third and fourth books. This brief simile implies his belief in the destiny of Britain and its ultimate roots in the glories of the past.[22]

If the Thames with his turreted crown connects Britain with the ancient order of civilization, the Medway personifies the fresh beauty of the land itself. Her flowing locks are "with flowres bescattered" and spread about her shoulders "as a new spring." She is crowned with a "chapelet of sundry flowers" from which the morning dew falls. The symbolic marriage of the Thames and the Medway imaginatively resolves several strands of the national and celebratory dimensions of the poem. It suggests the joining of ancient civilization with the vigor of a modern nation. And it becomes as well a vision of the union of the man-made beauty of the city with the natural beauty of the land.

The device of having all the English and Irish rivers come to the marriage of the Thames and the Medway, of course, allows Spenser to encompass the whole geography of Britain in the twenty-four stanzas that contain the procession. But more importantly, it allows him scope to play with language and to invent fables to add to the ones that were the basic material of the historical catalogues. The Wylibourne "with passage slye" takes his name "of his wylinesse." The Stoure hints at Spenser's general use of the word as the river takes its place in the procession "with terrible aspect." The Mole, "like a nousling Mole," runs underground until he overtakes the Thames. And again Spenser wants to suggest a multiplicity of linguistic origins. He proposes a French etymology for the River Trent, which has "Both thirty sorts of fish, and thirty sundry streames." Along the banks of the Tyne, the Emperor Severus built a wall to hold out the Picts, "which yet thereof Gualseuer" they call in the Briton tongue.

Spenser invents several etiological fables to expand the traditions of the historical catalogues. To the legend of Locrinus and Humber mentioned in Arthur's chronicle (2. 10. 16), he adds his own tale of the metamorphosis of "six sad brethren" slain by Humber into six rivers in Yorkshire. More ingenious is the myth he invents to account for the origin of three Irish rivers, "the gentle Shure," "the stubborne Newre," and "the goodly Barow."

> *And there the three renowmed brethren were,*
> *Which that great Gyant* Blomius *begot,*
> *Of the faire Nimph* Rheusa *wandring there,*
> *One day, as she to shunne the season whot,*
> *Vnder Slewbloome in shady groue was got,*
> *This Gyant found her, and by force deflowr'd,*
> *Whereof conceiuing, she in time forth brought*
> *These three faire sons, which being thence forth powrd*
> *In three great riuers ran, and many contreis scowrd.*
>
> [4. 11. 42]

P. W. Joyce shows that the etiological fable is designed to shadow the natural phenomena that in fact produce the rivers. Blomius is the Slieve Bloom range of mountains, and Rheusa—the feminine participle of the Greek verb *rheo*, to flow—personifies the rain.[23] The rivers have their source where the mountain range "by force" causes the rain to fall. Along with these invented legends, the poet also recalls his fable in *Colin Clouts Come Home Againe* of "Mulla mine, whose waues I whilom taught to weep."

The procession ends with the fifty Nereids following the Medway. The poet says the Nereids "haue the sea in charge to them assinde," and they seem to represent various benign aspects of the sea. But as they are listed, they are simply Greek words woven together for the sake of their sound. Some of the nymphs are accompanied by etymological epithets, but all the epithets together produce a ground base of English over which the Greek plays a kind of light descant. I have called the list of the Nereids almost abstract in quality because the sound of the catalogue seems its chief poetic aim. In a sense the counterpointed Greek and English words become an epitome of the whole vision. The rivers of Britain have been honored by their counterpoints from the classical world, and the mythopoeia of the English poet has complemented the mythology of classical literature. Vergil accomplished something very like this in the second *Georgic*, and we can now understand more of the reason why Spenser recalled that poem at the outset: Vergil wove the geography (and the fruits and wines) of Italy into a poetic tapestry that included the geography and flora of Greek literature. He sings "Hesiodic song through Roman towns"—or perhaps sings Roman towns into Hesiodic song. Britain's rivers, even the humblest streams, have taken their place with the Scamander and Tiber in the imagination. In the list of the Nereids, the English language, augmented in the river procession, we sense, by the "Briton tongue," French, and Gaelic, moves in concert with the Greek. The image of *discordia concors* that the marriage pageant represents has become linguistic as well.

The vision of English and Irish rivers, then, with simple personifications, more elaborate symbolic personifications, etiological fables, and playful etymologies, duplicates and complements the poetic world of classic mythology. Like that poetic world, the vision of the English *vates* mythologizes—and therefore humanizes—an actual landscape. Human play of mind anthropomorphizes the land and civilizes it. If the etiologies of the historical catalogues seemed fables of the taming and cultivation of the land, the self-consciously poetic personification and created myths of the marriage procession draw the land into the more thoroughly refining realm of poetry.

The most surprising facet of the river-marriage vision—and noteworthy because it is part of a general tendency in the last three books of the poem—is the personal note that the poet introduces. Like the Renaissance painter who includes an unobtrusive self-portrait among the lateral figures of his masterwork, Spenser makes reserved reference to his own life. In charting the course of the Ouse, he first lists its tributaries, then adds his own association with it. The group of rivers flows by Huntington and Cambridge,

> *My mother Cambridge, whom as with a Crowne*
> *He doth adorne, and is adorn'd of it*
> *With many a gentle Muse, and many a learned wit.*

[4. 11. 34]

The river beautifies Cambridge, but it is in these very verses that a gentle muse adorns the river. The poet surprises us by this reference to his *alma mater*, for it is the first time in the narrative of the poem that he has interrupted the anonymity imposed on him by the role of epic bard to refer to his actual life. Seven stanzas later he recalls his etiological fable in *Colin Clouts Come Home Againe* for the stream near his own Irish estate. Less personal, but still a reference to something that occurred in Ireland during Spenser's service there, is the characterization of the "Balefull Oure" (the Avonbeg of Glenmalure) as "late staind with English blood." It is curious that these personal associations should find a place in the geographical celebration of Britain, but it is characteristic of Spenser's later poetry to introduce such associations at visionary moments. The vision of the *Prothalamion* encompasses the poet's experience of London as his "most kyndly Nurse" as well as a place of disappointment and "olde woes." The fable of Molanna and Fanchin inserts an etiology of the poet's own landscape near Kilcolman into the great vision of mutability. And we should recall the fourth grace for whom Colin pipes on Mount Acidale in book 6; at the center of his vision of inspiration dances "a countrey lasse" who fills the role once filled by Eliza in the *April* eclogue. Moments of vision coincide with assertions of the relevance of the poet's actual experience to such moments. Spenser seems increasingly concerned to present the figure of the poet as a part of each vision. Indeed the figure of the poet presides over the visions as Eumnestes presided over the historical catalogues. The reader now stands in the role of Arthur or Britomart as the one whose consciousness is extended by the visionary moments.

The canto itself is a poetic tour de force in which diverse materials are fused in a vision of harmony. The blending of nature with art makes us feel that the harmony belongs to, indeed characterizes, nature but that the vision of such harmony is proper to the mythopoeic powers of poetry. Spenser often sums up the burden of a canto in the narrative introduction to the next, and the first two stanzas of canto 12 seem to encapsule the relationship between the poet's vision and nature's fertile harmony:

> *O what an endlesse worke haue I hand,*
> *To count the seas abundant progeny*
> *Whose fruitfull seede farre passeth those in land,*
> *And also those which wonne in th'azure sky?*
> *For much more eath to tell the starres on hy,*
> *Albe they endlesse seeme in estimation,*
> *Then to recount the Seas posterity:*
> *So fertile be the flouds in generation,*
> *So huge their numbers, and so numberlesse their nation.*
>
> *Therefore the antique wisards well inuented,*
> *That* Venus *of the fomy sea was bred;*

For that the seas by her are most augmented.
Witnesse th'exceeding fry, which there are fed,
And wondrous sholes, which may of none be red.
Then blame me not, if I haue err'd in count
Of Gods, of Nymphs, or riuers yet vnred:
For though their numbers do much more surmount,
Yet all those same were there, which erst I did recount.

The poet's wonder at what he is doing—and in some measure has accomplished—is balanced against his realization of how incomplete it will finally seem. "Therefore" poets have invented myths to express what can never be enumerated. Poetic myth mediates what otherwise cannot be spoken of. Spenser concludes with an assertion of the "truth" of *his* feigning. In the river marriage the reader is drawn into a vision that is more emphatically the poet's own and depends less upon an explicit contrast to history. Poet and reader become closer collaborators in such visionary moments. The insistence on the poet's golden world is no longer a generalized claim; the unobtrusive references to the poet's own life delicately suggest that the celebration of Britain's natural world is the task of a quite specific "gentle muse." The canto demonstrates the mythopoeic powers that claim a place for the poet's own nation in the ranks of the civilized world—and a place for his own poem among the epic formulations of myth.

Chapter 4

Mirrors
More Than One

In the proem to book 3, Spenser invited his queen to observe her reflection "in mirrours more then one" and specified Gloriana as the mirror of her rule and Belphoebe of "her rare chastitee." I have contended that we should not limit Spenser's "more then one" to just these two reflections. To Elizabeth *The Faerie Queene* is rather a hall of mirrors than a pair of looking glasses. Through Una, Belphoebe, Britomart, and later, in book 5, Mercilla, Spenser provides means for his queen to relate the virtue in question to her role as moral focus of the nation. And as in the Lucifera reflection in book 1, the poem is also capable of surprising her with cautionary images of female rule, distorted reflections from contorted fun-house mirrors. In specifically mentioning Gloriana and Belphoebe, Spenser was pointing to the place in that hall of mirrors where two of his most important *specula* were to be, a place where the illumination was most steady and ideal and where the flickering light of sublunary history would least interfere. As it happened, the mirror of ideal rule in Gloriana would never be placed; Guyon's chronicle allows us to understand the sort of position it would have occupied, but little more. We do, however, have the shimmering, silvery reflection that is Belphoebe, and this image of the queen, especially in the subtle coloration it receives in book 4, provides us with a valuable index of the direction taken by the historical dimension of *The Faerie Queene*. In a sense, Belphoebe herself becomes more than a single mirror.

Critics sometimes speak of the poem as if it had a static design, as if Spenser foresaw with some precision how books 4, 5, and 6 would progress as he composed the first three. But without denying the poet a general conception, one can see in the unfolding of the historical dimension a poem that was developing in ways quite unforeseen by the poet in the 1580s. Belphoebe in particular enables us to gauge something of the way the poem shifts and adjusts in response to what Spenser learned about political power and its possessors in the 1590s. The passages in which she appears in books 2 and 3 were composed several years earlier than the passage in which she appears in book 4, and in fact Spenser in 1590 could not have even foreseen the event that is shadowed in the episode in book 4. And yet the Belphoebe episodes have a kind of thematic consistency: each deals with the questions of honor and service of the queen. The combination of thematic consistency and response to an unforeseen historical situation allows us to discern what was happening to the historical dimension of the poem.

The characterization of Belphoebe also exhibits a degree of consistency not usually evident in characters who make isolated appearances in different books. She always possesses a certain elevated detachment from common human affairs, a concern for absolutes and ideals that allows her little understanding of less-than-ideal human traits. Belphoebe's vocational chastity in fact holds her above knowledge of the darker side of human nature; she is in all her appearances surprised at the passions of lesser mortals, innocent of the suspicion that she herself could move them. Spenser no more intended actual characterization of the queen than the various portrait painters intended realistic representation in the many idealized paintings of her. He uses the language of literary compliment as the painters continued to use the unlined face their queen had shown the world some twenty-five years earlier, and his use of the virgin-huntress motif is in part analogous to the visual emblems of virginity employed by the painters. But claims for realism aside, it is also clear that Spenser knew something of the woman whom he invited to peer into the reflecting glass of his ideal Belphoebe. Harry Berger has suggested that there is "a shade of the sinister" about the ambiguity of Belphoebe's self-conscious awareness (best shown perhaps in her elaborate costume) combined with her sublime innocence—"girlish vanity and a majesty that passively accepts homage, art and abandon, purpose and instinct."[1] One may hedge at the word sinister and still agree. Spenser has expressed something in Belphoebe about the complex woman who nobly chose virginity for reasons of state and yet sometimes took personal offense at marriages in her court. Spenser insists in the letter to Raleigh that Belphoebe shadows the queen's private person separately from her rule. But such a separation cannot finally be made; Elizabeth the woman was a queen and a superb politician. We never forget in reading that Belphoebe bears a relationship to Elizabeth, and over the course of three books, the realization grows that this relationship cannot be fully explained by the words idealization or flattery.

i / "In woods, in waues, in warres"

Belphoebe's first appearance, in canto 3 of book 2, clearly delineates her mythic, ideal nature as well as her reference to the queen. A blast from a horn announces her and strikes fear into the craven hearts of Bragadocchio and Trompart. Bragadocchio dives off Guyon's horse into some bushes, while Trompart, more curious, stays to see what will happen:

> *Eftsoone there stepped forth*
> *A goodly Ladie clad in hunters weed,*
> *That seemd to be a woman of great worth,*
> *And by her stately portance, borne of heauenly birth.*
>
> [2. 3. 21]

There follows a ten-stanza description of Belphoebe, a kind of chaste *blason*. Spenser uses the language of the sonneteers to express her physical beauty. But he appears to structure the *blason* on the line of Vergil that describes Venus's appearance to Aeneas as a virgin huntress: "Virginis os habitumque gerens et virginis arma" (1. 315); the description proceeds from Belphoebe's face to her costume to her boar spear and "bow and quiuer gay." Belphoebe becomes a paradoxical blending, an "infolding" of Venus and Diana.[2] The poetry of the description similarly expresses this paradoxical doubleness of Belphoebe in its tendency to ascend from physical to moral qualities. The beauty of her eyes, for example, is spoken of in conventional terms of fire and stars, and Cupid tries to kindle his "lustfull fire" in her eyes—but vainly: "For with dredd Maiestie, and awfull ire, / She broke his wanton darts, and quenched base desire." Her ivory forehead seems fit for Love to engrave his triumphs, but "All good and honour might therein be red." The most curious example of this simultaneous kindling and quenching of passion occurs in the celebration of her legs. Belphoebe appears no less concerned about her costume than her royal prototype, and the description dwells on her tucked up skirt and "gilden buskins of costly Cordwaine," carefully fastened with a rich jewel just below the knees. But just where a more amorous *blason* would venture on to a celebration of thighs and adjacent demesnes, Spenser presents a simile for such finely set off legs:

> *Like two faire marble pillours they were seene,*
> *Which doe the temple of the Gods support,*
> *Whom all the people decke with girlands greene,*
> *And honour in their festiuall resort.*

[2. 3. 28]

The marble pillars can be counted on to cool the expectations the *blason* may arouse, but the civic festival of the conclusion rather startles the reader. The poet is suggesting the appeal of physical beauty which comes to stand for something much more important. The beauty of Belphoebe is made abstract and sacred and becomes the focus not of desire but of veneration. The poetry makes that beauty analogous to the temple honored as the embodiment of social cohesion. The Venus-Diana paradox thus symbolizes a love that is not individual or sexual but broadly inclusive, indeed social. Spenser's *blason*, curiously, works in a political direction.

It is with such an understanding of Belphoebe that we must see Bragadocchio's amorous lunge. Upton suggested that Bragadocchio and Trompart referred to the Duc d'Alençon, Elizabeth's ardent suitor of 1579–80, and his agent Simier.[3] Nothing specific in the episode makes us think of Alençon and Simier in particular, and one suspects that the poet could easily have given them some French association to make the connection if he had so intended. And yet I feel there is something suggestive about Upton's notion. In 1590 the controversy over the Alençon marriage was ten years dead, and the threat the marriage once represented to Elizabeth's Protestant subjects must by then have appeared quite remote. The queen herself was now several years past the age for marriage, and therefore praise of her virginity had become more tactful and nec-

essary than ever. In retrospect loyal subjects must have thought—
or discreetly appeared to think—that their queen had never intended to marry, that her virginity was as vocational as Belphoebe's.
If Bragadocchio and Trompart in some way recall Alençon and Simier, they appear not as representatives of the political crisis of
1579–80 (for Belphoebe is scarcely threatened by them) but as comic
figures out of the past who do not understand what all Englishmen,
in 1590 at least, understand. Since the pair does not allude with any
specificity to Alençon and Simier, I would prefer to see them as
fictional representatives of all those earlier "threats" to the queen's
unmarried state, threats that appear in the 1590s as comically un-
substantial Bragadocchio's knightly prowess. Like him, all those
suitors of the queen had tried to possess for themselves a love that
had to remain virginal to provide a common blessing for the nation.[4]
Belphoebe bends her javelin against Bragadocchio's advance and,
like Oberon's fair vestal thronèd by the West, runs off in maiden
meditation, fancy free.

But the political comedy of the scene, appealing though it is,
represents only one side of the episode. Trompart salutes Belphoebe
in imitation, or in parody rather, of Aeneas's response to Venus
when she appears to him as a virgin huntress. Trompart and Bragadocchio are as sorry versions of Aeneas and Achates as Paridell is
in book 3. Guyon, the true Aeneas of book 2, never sees Belphoebe
or hears her words on honor and service. He would have best understood her response to Bragadocchio's question why she is not at
court enjoying love instead of running around in the wilderness:

> Who so in pompe of proud estate (quoth she)
>> Does swim, and bathes himselfe in courtly blis,
>> Does waste his dayes in darke obscuritee,
>> And in obliuion euer buried is:
>> Where ease abounds, yt's eath to doe amis;
>> But who his limbs with labours, and his mind
>> Behaues with cares, cannot so easie mis.
>> Abroad in armes, at home in studious kind
> Who seekes with painfull toile, shall honor soonest find.
>
> In woods, in waues, in warres she wonts to dwell,
>> And will be found with perill and with paine;
>> Ne can the man, that moulds in idle cell,

> *Vnto her happie mansion attaine:*
> *Before her gate high God did Sweat ordaine,*
> *And wakefull watches euer to abide:*
> *But easie is the way, and passage plaine*
> *To pleasures pallace; it may soone be spide,*
> *And day and night her dores to all stand open wide.*

[2. 3. 40–41]

What is so fitting in the sylvan fiction but curious when we consider the context of royal allusion is Belphoebe's blame of court life. Spenser provides Belphoebe with something of the same view of court life as that of the satirist of *Mother Hubberds Tale*. If she were more aware of human frailty, she would notice that the court, as she conceives of it, is a fitting aspiration for the likes of Bragadocchio. She finds honor "in woods, in waues, in warres," and the terms evoke an Elizabethan ideal of service that we associate with contemporaries like Hawkins, Drake, and Norris, as well as with such familiars of Spenser as Raleigh and Sidney. In the fiction her phrases "painfull toile" and "wakefull watches" and the sweat demanded at honor's gate (the Hesiodic phrase calls up all the sternness of the *Works and Days*) are the best descriptions of Guyon's plodding, literally pedestrian, and seemingly unheroic quest. Though Guyon never sees her, Belphoebe appears to the reader as the ideal fulfillment of the virtue he achieves with so much effort; it is in the nature of Guyon's virtue that he must do without such a vision of fulfillment. Belphoebe's comic encounter with Bragadocchio and Trompart becomes not simply a retrospect upon the queen's determination not to marry; it also celebrates her as the ideal exemplar of heroic temperance.

Not only must Guyon do without a vision of the fulfillment of his virtue, he must also confront the negative side of honor and honorable service in the Cave of Mammon. As Belphoebe faces the false knight in Bragadocchio, Guyon sees a false image of royalty and honor in Philotime ("Love of honor"). It is precisely the kind of court that arouses Belphoebe's disdain:

> *A route of people there assembled were,*
> *Of euery sort and nation vnder skye,*
> *Which with great vprore preaced to draw nere*
> *To th' upper part, where was aduaunced hye*

> *A stately siege of soueraigne maiestye;*
> *And thereon sat a woman gorgeous gay,*
> *And richly clad in robes of royaltye,*
> *That neuer earthly Prince in such aray*
> *His glory did enhaunce, and pompous pride display.*
>
> [2. 7. 44]

But more importantly, Philotime pretends to the kind of radiance that distinguishes Belphoebe, a pretense all the more pathetic because she had once possessed such "heauenly" beauty:

> *Her face right wondrous faire did seeme to bee,*
> *That her broad beauties beam great brightnes threw*
> *Through the dim shade, that all men might it see:*
> *Yet was not that same her owne natiue hew,*
> *But wrought by art and counterfetted shew,*
> *Thereby more louers vnto her to call;*
> *Nath'lesse most heauenly faire in deed and vew*
> *She by creation was, till she did fall;*
> *Thenceforth she sought for helps, to cloke her crime withall.*
>
> [2. 7. 45]

Philotime holds an emblematic golden chain of ambition that stretches from heaven to "lowest Hell." In response to Guyon's question, Mammon tells him that she is his daughter, that "honour and dignitee" are from her alone, that she is worthy of heaven but has been thrust down by envious gods. Because Guyon does not make the expected Bragadocchian lunge, Mammon offers her in marriage to him. Unfailingly courteous, Guyon turns down the proposal and protests his mortal unworthiness and a previously plighted troth.

In the episode both the thematic concern for honor and the now-realized image of the kind of court she shunned cause us to recall Belphoebe's high-minded appeal, and we see the irony in the reversed confrontations of Guyon and Bragadocchio by the kind of honor they each desire. As with Lucifera in book 1, we have in Philotime one of those negative, distorted images that are to be found in Spenser's hall of royal mirrors. Philotime not only casts a reversed image of idealized Belphoeban honor. What is disquieting is that her court is a quite recognizable version of the more sinister side of the actual court Spenser knew:

> *Some thought to raise themselues to high degree,*
> *By riches and vnrighteous reward,*
> *Some by close shouldring, some by flatteree;*
> *Others through friends, others for base regard;*
> *And all by wrong wayes for themselues prepard.*
> *Those that were vp themselues, kept others low,*
> *Those that were low themselues, held others hard,*
> *Ne suffred them to rise or greater grow,*
> *But euery one did striue his fellow downe to throw.*

[2. 7. 47]

I do not mean that Spenser is satirizing the Elizabethan court while using Belphoebe to pacify the queen. The common concern for honor in the two episodes suggests that each may be seen as a possibility. Neither is necessarily more "realistic," and both allude to elements of the Elizabethan government we recognize as actual. If Drake and Raleigh responded to the honor to be gained in waves and wars, mere courtiers like the Earl of Oxford found a version of Philotime's court more to their liking. Spenser creates in Belphoebe an idealized fictional image of what seemed to him finest in his queen's career. By her own temperate self-denial Elizabeth saved England from the dangers, still fresh in memory, of a foreign royal marriage; moreover, the firm political center of gravity she provided had spurred the explorations of the New World and martial endeavors of the 1580s. Spenser suggests something like this, I believe, in projecting the radiant image of Belphoebe as the fulfillment of Guyon's virtue. But one must keep in mind Belphoebe's idealized, mythic nature; like Guyon she is a Faery and belongs therefore to the kind of golden world we see in Guyon's Faery chronicle. As the Faery chronicle is able to omit silently the less happy aspects of Tudor rule, so the characterization of Belphoebe can submerge those elements of the court and policy of Elizabeth that we know from satires like *Mother Hubberds Tale* disturbed Spenser. Some of these darker elements appear in the court of Philotime and in other details of the Cave of Mammon. Philotime does not, to be sure, represent the queen in any explicit sense; indeed, insofar as she has any specific political reference, she would recall, especially in the lovers lured by her seeming beauty, Mary Queen of Scots. But Spenser pointedly insists that Philotime images the moral corruption of which all monarchs are capable: every pillar of her presence chamber is decked "With crownes and Diademes, and titles vaine, / Which mortal Princes wore, whiles they on earth did rayne" (2. 7. 43). Though not specifically allusive, Philotime is a clear, unhesitating image of the corruption of honor and service possible when the Belphoeban ideal is compromised. Similarly, Mammon himself represents the central temptation of the men who were rising from the ranks of the gentry to positions of power and importance in the government. In the next reign Mammon's cave would become a specific reality, and titles of honor would be bought and sold.

ii / "Dying her serue, and liuing her adore"

In their base-mindedness Bragadocchio and Trompart respond with foolish inadequacy to the paradoxical nature of Belphoebe. In Belphoebe's appearance in book 3, we see the full and proper response by Prince Arthur's squire, Timias. His pursuit of the lustful Foster into the forest and his battle with the Foster and his two brothers delineate Timias as a devotee of the honor that dwells in woods and wars. It is, in fact, only when Timias achieves his victory over the three brothers that the reader even learns his name, which means "honored." When Timias is mortally wounded in the battle, the narrator reflects that the honor he has achieved will avail him nothing unless he is found and healed (3. 5. 26). Belphoebe, who does find and care for him, thus becomes the one who confers life and honor on the squire, and Timias responds by devoting that life to her service.

Spenser intensifies the Venus-Diana paradox of Belphoebe's nature by modeling the episode on Ariosto's story of Angelica's discovery and healing of the wounded squire Medoro and her sudden falling in love with him (*Orlando Furioso* 19).[5] In Ariosto the relationship of Angelica and Medoro develops into a frankly sexual love idyll. Spenser's story cannot, of course, because Belphoebe is an unassailable virgin huntress who shadows an unassailable virgin queen, and Timias correspondingly feels himself to be a mortal serving a goddess. But the source of Spenser's imitation indicates initially why the episode creates such ambivalence in the love of Timias for Belphoebe. He is a mortal and feels all the pangs of usual mortal love. The first impulse he feels is not dissimilar therefore from the impulse felt by Medoro or indeed by Bragadocchio before his lunge. Timias, however, responds simultaneously to the side of Belphoebe that commands worship and respect. Like Trompart, he first speaks to her in imitation of Aeneas's response to Venus disguised as a hunting nymph; but Timias, like Aeneas and unlike Trompart, recognizes a heavenly reality beneath the appearance:

> *Mercy deare Lord (said he) what grace is this,*
> *That thou hast shewed to me sinfull wight,*
> *To send thine Angell from her bowre of blis,*
> *To comfort me in my distressed plight?*
> *Angell, or Goddesse do I call thee right?*
> *What seruice may I do vnto thee meete,*
> *That hast from darkenesse me returnd to light,*
> *And with thy heauenly salues and med'cines sweete,*
> *Has drest my sinfull wounds? I kisse thy blessed feete.*
>
> [3. 5. 35]

Aeneas's doubt—"An Phoebi soror? an Nympharum sanguinis una?"—becomes Timias's doubt whether Belphoebe is angel or goddess. The Vergilian imitation may recall Trompart's response, but the difference here underscores the specifically religious nature of Timias's reaction: he venerates Belphoebe and, though quite helpless, immediately offers his service to her. She protests her mortality; the "commun bond of frailtee" requires mortals to aid each other. But we recognize his reaction as fitting nonetheless.

This mortal-heavenly ambivalence is paralleled by more Venus-Diana associations. Around Belphoebe's secluded pavillion are both myrtle trees, sacred to Venus, and laurels, sacred to Diana and Apollo. The birds there sing "gods high praise" and "their loues sweet teene."[6] Timias, responding to both sides of the paradox, sees her as a heavenly maid as she goes about the quite earthbound task of changing the plasters on his wound. He loves her because she is fair and because she restores his life. He is drawn to her as a lover and yet is instinctively aware of her vocational chastity.

As with the episode of Belphoebe's escape from Bragadocchio, the apparent love story here actually works in a political direction, and we need to ask what exactly the doubleness of Belphoebe means as it relates to the queen and how one is to understand the apparently tormented love of Timias. The ambivalent figure of Belphoebe, radiantly attractive and perfectly chaste, idealizes of course an important cult image of Queen Elizabeth created by her courtiers. She was adored all her reign as a queen of love, a mistress who subdued men's hearts, and after it became clear she would not marry, she was also revered as a chaste Diana. One cannot suppose that this image was fostered simply by the personal vanity of the queen; pleased though she surely was by the flattering attention, such an intelligent woman undoubtedly recognized its usefulness in winning and maintaining political loyalty. A central difficulty for a sixteenth-century queen was that she could not evoke the kind of political expression traditionally used by kings, expression based on martial habits of mind, to control men. J. E. Neale notes that "the royal household still remained a great masculine community of about fifteen hundred persons"; to control and win the loyalty of such a community was a task of no mean difficulty for an unmarried woman.[7] If she invoked the usual feudal role, she ran the risk of amazonian associations that would be considered unseemly, especially in view of the role the religion assigned to women. But as a chaste mistress, the queen could summon many similar chivalric associations to spark loyalty. The admixture of Neoplatonic ideas and sonnet conventions deriving from Petrarch resulted in the familiar queenly image that cannot but strike the twentieth century as remote and slightly bizarre. We do not have difficulty in accepting the kind of political expression that surrounded sixteenth-century kings, for abundant contemporary analogies exist. But we cannot fail to be a little surprised at men in their twenties and thirties confessing their undying love for an aging spinster. Such confessions by men like Raleigh and Essex were, of course, expressions of political loyalty, and we can be sure that Elizabeth understood the game she was playing—and its value. The ambivalence in the figure of Belphoebe derives from the necessary ambivalence in the queenly image itself. In order to see the full import of the Timias and Belphoebe episode, we must take seriously this cult image of Elizabeth as a vehicle for the expression of personal political loyalty to her.

It is perhaps discomfort at these Elizabethan modes of political expression that has caused most critics to shy away from the question why Spenser should have shadowed Sir Walter Raleigh in Timias. Only the narrator's uncertainty about what kind of herbs Belphoebe uses to heal Timias's wound directly indicates that Timias is to be connected with Raleigh, but the fame that Raleigh gained by his introduction into England and frequent use of a particular herbal restorative makes the allusion virtually certain:

> *There, whether it diuine* Tobacco *were,*
> *Or* Panachaea, *or* Polygony,
> *She found, and brought it to her patient deare*
> *Who al this while lay bleeding out his hart-bloud neare.* [8]
>
> [3. 5. 32]

The specific identification of Timias with Raleigh will become more important in the continuation of the story in book 4. What is significant here is the role of lover that Raleigh played before the queen. Raleigh, of course, had no special claim on the role, for it had been and would be played by others of the queen's favorites. Apart from their friendship, Spenser probably chose to shadow Raleigh because of the extraordinary verve and conviction with which he played the part; though others donned the same mask, few did so with such consistency and flair. In his recent study of the histrionic in Raleigh's life and art, Stephen J. Greenblatt has suggested that Raleigh "must have been deeply sensitive and responsive, in a way surpassing mere calculation, to the personality of the queen."[9] Raleigh left many records of his role as devoted lover of the queen, and for us, as for Spenser, the most significant record exists in his poetry. At several points Spenser's characterization of Timias reminds us of specific moments in which Raleigh plays out the role in his verse.

In the continuation in book 4, Raleigh's specific performance becomes important to the poem, but in book 3 Spenser focuses on the role itself as a response to the public image of the queen's "private person." Basically the role attempts to respond fully to the queen's nature—to her womanhood *and* to her sovereignty. As a mistress she must be loved passionately and exclusively, but as a chaste goddess she must be revered. In more mundane (or modern) political terms, one supposes, courtiers were expressing both their high respect and their intense personal loyalty to the sovereign. But in the pretense there may have also been a kind of half-conscious psychological delicacy that went beyond political considerations. As ruler, Elizabeth had to forego consciously most of the satisfactions of a private life; even with Leicester she could never with impunity forget for long that she was a queen. Anthropologists tell us of the compensations that a tribe offers to its chief for the burden of rule. In Elizabeth's court the considerable attention afforded her femininity may well have been such a compensation for the fact that she had indeed sacrificed much of her life as a woman to the exigencies of rule.

Spenser asserts that this relationship of queen and courtier becomes a variety of love; as he expresses it in the first stanza of the canto, it is one of the "pageants" love plays in "diuerse minds." Because Belphoebe is a paradoxical "infolding" of Venus and Diana, a full response to each side of her reality becomes the lover's dilemma. Timias's lyric complaint (stanzas 45–47) focuses on this dilemma and the resolution of it. Love at first seems "To blot her honour, and her heauenly light" in its usual earthly fulfillment. But love's opposite, hate, is equally impossible, and death is to be preferred:

> *Dye rather, dye, and dying do her serue,*
> *Dying her serue, and liuing her adore;*
> *Thy life she gaue, thy life she doth deserue:*
> *Dye rather, dye, then euer from her seruice swerue.*

[3. 5. 46]

The idea of service seems inadequate because of the lover's unworthiness, but the analogous service of God by men resolves the dilemma: since God receives the service of the humblest men, Belphoebe too may receive his love and service. Rather like the analogy Redcross learned of between Cleopolis and the transcendent New Jerusalem, love and service of Belphoebe becomes an analogue to love and service of God.

Though this may settle things rationally, the role demanded that the lover maintain a pose of hopeless, unfulfilled love. Therefore, Timias, though suffering within, retains unspoken his passion for Belphoebe:

> *Yet neuer he his hart to her reuealed,*
> *But rather chose to dye for sorrow great,*
> *Then with dishonorable termes her to entreat.*

[3. 5. 49]

Behind this refusal to confess his love lie some of Raleigh's verses to the queen in which he protests that his silence (which the poem breaks!) argues the depth of his love:

> *For knowing that I sue to serue*
> *A Saint of such Perfection,*
> *As all desire, but none deserue,*
> *A place in her Affection:*
> *I rather chuse to want Reliefe*
> *Then venture the Reuealing;*
> *When Glory recommends the Griefe,*
> *Despaire distrusts the Healing.*

> *Thus those desires that aime too high,*
> *For any mortall Louer,*
> *When Reason cannot make them dye,*
> *Discretion will them Couer,*
> *Yet when discretion dothe bereaue*
> *The Plaints that they should vtter,*
> *Then your discretion may perceiue,*
> *That Silence is a Suitor.* [10]

In response to Timias's suffering, Belphoebe, as a "gracious Lady," spares no pains "to do him ease, or do him remedy." She applies "Many Restoratiues of vertues rare, / And costly Cordialles." If we wonder why the cordials of a wood nymph should be "costly," we may suspect that Spenser is suggesting with delicate wit that real-life adherents of the gracious royal lady received certain restoratives for their "suffering" in her service. It was a common Elizabethan conceit that the best "cordial" was gold; in his Elegy 11 Donne concludes that "Gold is Restorative . . . Because 'tis cordiall." [11] Outside of Faeryland "restoratives" could be more negotiable; certainly Raleigh received his share of such royal ministrations. Though the role required a lingering malady of hopeless love, Spenser appears to hint, such wounded hearts received their cordial.

If Spenser wittily intimates something of this sort, he does not do more than glance at it, for his main purpose is to suggest how the relationship of Timias and Belphoebe forms a part of the complex of analogies that love creates. Consequently he turns from Timias to trace the origin of Belphoebe's chastity. He uses the image of the rose with its rich symbolic implications to express the mystery of bountiful chastity. But in the metaphor he also subsumes the viewpoint of the natural man in Timias. To ordinary human vision there is something negative, evasive, overly delicate about virginity as a state of life, and the image of the natural flower discreetly suggests this:

> That dainty Rose, the daughter of her Morne,
>   More deare than life she tendered, whose flowre
>   The girlond of her honour did adorne:
>   Ne suffred she the Middayes scorching powre,
>   Ne the sharp Northerne wind thereon to showre,
>   But lapped vp her silken leaues most chaire,
>   When so the froward skye began to lowre:
>   But soone as calmed was the Christall aire,
> She did it faire dispred, and let to florish faire.
>
> [3. 5. 51]

But such a merely natural view is as limited as the simply earthly derivation of the queen's lineage. Spenser insists that chastity, like royal ancestry, has a heavenly origin as well. In the next stanza the poet asserts this origin: God planted it in paradise "to make example of his heauenly grace" and then engrafted it to the "stock of earthly flesh" so that men would "admire"—in the Latin sense of "wonder at"—its glory. Chastity, utterly unexpected by such as Bragadocchio, evokes an almost religious awe in Timias. (Indeed, Spenser's language here reminds us how important was the residual fervor of the cult of the Virgin to the success of this image of the queen.) This flower yields the fruit of honor and "chaste desire."

Although the poet insists that such chastity is not the abnegation of love but an expression of "perfect loue," there is still a sense of paradox in the poetry:

> In so great prayse of stedfast chastity,
>   Nathlesse she was so curteous and kind,
>   Tempred with grace, and goodly modesty,
>   That seemed those two vertues stroue to find
>   The higher place in her Heroick mind:
>   So striuing each did other more augment,
>   And both encreast the prayse of woman kind,
>   And both encreast her beautie excellent;
> So all did make in her a perfect complement.
>
> [3. 5. 55; emphasis added]

Though steadfast in chastity, she is *nonetheless* courteous and kind to her lovers; the paradox comes from the specifically erotic meaning of "courteous" and "kind" in Renaissance love poetry. Spenser intends to transvalue the words and with them the meaning of the relationship of Timias and Belphoebe. She is not simply the cruel fair of amatory poetic conventions; in the more-than-natural vision of the analogy between Belphoebe's chastity and divine love, "perfect loue" and "spotlesse fame of chastity" are reconciled and united. Hence Timias's resolution of the dilemma of desire and unworthiness in terms of God's acceptance of man's unworthy service is consonant with the narrator's derivation of regal chastity from divine love. In such a relationship, by implication, a feminine sovereign can love her subjects perfectly and receive in return their devoted service. What appears ambivalence—in Belphoebe or in the queenly image—becomes participation in the mystery of perfect love and chastity. As in book 2 Belphoebe advances Elizabeth as the ideal fulfillment of Guyon's virtue, so here Belphoebe projects the queen as the fulfillment not only of chastity (the announced subject of book 3) but also of love (the book's real subject). The allegorical core of book 3 is the vision of fertility in the Garden of Adonis (canto 6), but Spenser places this reconciliation of announced and real subjects in close proximity to that core to emphasize the derivation of that reconciliation from the queen. And no doubt significant to the idealization of Elizabeth's chastity in 1590 is the suggestion that Belphoebe's grace and modesty "both encreast her beautie excellent." The mortal spinster continues to age, but her Faery counterpart teaches her to grow more beautiful by continuing to play the part she played all her life.

iii / *"High displesure, through misdeeming bred"*

Between the publication of the first three books of *The Faerie Queene* and the appearance of the second three in 1596, the brazen world of history impinged enough upon the poet's golden world to force Spenser to consider anew the roles played by queen and courtier. The continuation of the story of Timias and Belphoebe in book 4 (cantos 7 and 8) quite obviously allegorizes Raleigh's five-year loss of royal favor occasioned by his marriage to Elizabeth Throckmorton in late 1591. The term "historical allegory" does indeed fit the

episode in the two cantos, for in them Spenser abandons the allusive technique that characterized the introduction of contemporary
elements in the first three books. The episode in book 3 just considered, for example, refers to no specific event. It alludes generally, initially by the suggestion of tobacco, to Raleigh's reception
into royal favor, and it relates more broadly, as we have seen, to
the evolving roles played by the queen and her courtiers. Even in
Bragadocchio's vain assault on Belphoebe, we do not feel the weight
of a specific event in the fiction; the Alençon controversy or other
royal marriage schemes bear an important, but general and retro-
spective, relation to the episode. In cantos 7 and 8 of book 4, however, the fiction is specifically constructed—for the first time in the
poem—to shadow a contemporary situation.

The distinction between historical allusions and historical allegory is quite crucial to our assessment of the relation of the poem
to history, for the continuation of Timias's story represents something of a qualification of the poet's differentiation, considered in
chapter 3, between his ideal fictional world and history's morally
ambiguous world. History has in fact exerted pressure on the gold-
en world and forced the poet to take up again the question of
honor and service in a way he could not have foreseen in 1590. The
ideal world is finally reasserted, to be sure, but in a curious way.
The resolution of the book 4 episode puts the fictional world not
simply in juxtaposition to historical patterns but in actual contra-
vention of the historical situation at that moment.

The story behind Raleigh's loss of favor has been considerably
elucidated by A. L. Rowse's use of the diary of Sir Arthur Throckmorton, Lady Raleigh's brother.[12] In the spring of 1592 Raleigh had
just departed on an expedition to prey on Spanish treasure ships
when he was suddenly called back and, after several weeks, thrown
into the Tower. As captain of the Yeomen of the Guards, Raleigh
had been much in the company of the queen's maids of honor, and
one of them, Elizabeth Throckmorton, proved to be with child by
him in late 1591. Raleigh had secretly married her in November of
1591, and she gave birth to a son the following March. Rather than
reveal the affair to the queen and ask for her forgiveness, Lady
Raleigh returned to the court in late April to continue to pass
herself off as a maid of honor. By the end of May, however, the
queen learned of the situation. The offense of their marrying with-

out royal permission was serious enough, for the queen stood *in loco parentis* to her maids of honor; in addition, the circumstances of the marriage could have been counted upon to irritate a queen who genuinely attempted to maintain a moral tone in her court that would set it off from the more notorious courts of Europe.[13] But the offense was aggravated not only by the deceit of the attempted return to court and Raleigh's denial of the marriage in a letter to Cecil but also by the couple's continued failure to express regret over the circumstances or beg the queen's pardon when the whole matter became known. Rather than acknowledge the offense, Raleigh displayed extravagant grief at his loss of the queen's favor during the five weeks he spent in the Tower. Meanwhile, the expedition that Raleigh had been about to command had seized an exceedingly wealthy prize, the Spanish carrack *Madre de Dios*. Since his help was required in sorting out the shares of the rich booty, he was released from the Tower, but his wife remained there until the end of the year. She was never allowed to return to court, and Raleigh himself was not admitted back into royal favor until 1597, the year after the publication of the second part of *The Faerie Queene*.

There can be no doubt that the episode in book 4 allegorizes Raleigh's disgrace. The allusion to Raleigh in the reference to the salubrious qualities of tobacco in book 3 creates a presumption that Timias will continue to refer to Raleigh in the continuation of the story. Raleigh himself used the name Belphoebe, apparently while writing in the Tower, to contrast his earlier relationship with Elizabeth to his loss of favor:

> *A Queen shee was to mee, no more Belphebe,*
> *A Lion then, no more a milke white Dove;*
> *A prissoner in her brest I could not bee,*
> *Shee did vntye the gentell chaynes of love.* 14

In addition, Spenser's version of the familiar tag "Indignatio principis mors est" at the beginning of canto 8 certainly looks beyond Belphoebe the hunting nymph in its reference:

> *Well said the wiseman, now prou'd true by this,*
> *Which to this gentle Squire did happen late,*
> *That the displeasure of the mighty is*
> *Then death it selfe more dread and desperate.*

But the most suggestive evidence that Spenser continues to shadow Raleigh comes in the actual characterization of Timias. A reading of Raleigh's *The Ocean to Cynthia* allows one to understand what Spenser is doing with Timias. For the forlorn squire is an evident representation of the kind of role Raleigh created for himself while in disgrace, especially while he had ample time for such creation during his stay in the Tower. Spenser may have based his characterization on the fragmentary poem, if he knew it, or he may have written from what he knew of his friend's extravagant, melancholy turn of mind. *The Ocean to Cynthia* itself extends into verse the elaborate display of bitterness and despondency that Raleigh put on while in disgrace.[15]

Spenser also took a cue from another poem of Raleigh's published in *The Phoenix Nest* in 1593 (anonymously, but in a "Raleigh group"):

> *Like to a Hermite poore in place obscure,*
> *I meane to spend my daies of endles doubt,*
> *To waile such woes as time cannot recure,*
> *Where none but Loue shall euer finde me out.*
>
> *My foode shall be of care and sorow made,*
> *My drink nought else but teares falne from mine eies,*
> *And for my light in such obscured shade,*
> *The flames shall serue, which from my hart arise.*
>
> *A gowne of graie, my bodie shall attire,*
> *My staffe of broken hope whereon Ile staie,*
> *Of late repentance linckt with long desire,*
> *The couch is fram'de whereon my limbs Ile lay,*
>
> *And at my gate dispaire shall linger still,*
> *To let in death when Loue and Fortune will.*[16]

After he falls into Belphoebe's disgrace, Timias chooses "a gloomy glade" in which to make his cabin, breaks his weapons, "wilfully" cuts his garments, and lets his hair and beard overgrow his face.

> *There he continued in this carefull plight,*
> *Wretchedly wearing out his youthly yeares,*
> *Through wilfull penury consumed quight,*
> *That like a pined ghost he soone appeares.*
> *For other food then that wilde forrest beares,*

> *Ne other drinke there did he euer tast,*
> *Then running water, tempred with his teares,*
> *The more his weakened body so to wast:*
> *That out of all mens knowledge he was worne at last.*

[4. 7. 41]

When Arthur chances to come upon Timias's retreat, he supposes at first it is the abode of "some holy Hermit." The suggestion that Timias's suffering is willful indicates the extravagance of it all, but it is not really made to seem quite comic. Spenser appears to be drawing upon his reader's association of Timias's sorrow with the actual loss of favor by Raleigh.

What is most fascinating about this association is that the pressure of the actual upon the fiction causes a strange blurring of the moral focus that is uncharacteristic of Spenser's poem. The narrative attitude toward Timias's guilt is curiously ambivalent. The head verse to canto 7 suggests that Belphoebe has reason to question his faith:

> *Amoret rapt by greedie lust*
> *Belphebe saues from dread,*
> *The Squire her loues, and being blam'd*
> *his dayes in dole doth lead.*

But what actually occurs places less blame on Timias. His fight with the Carl of Lust is in a sense a return engagement, for the Foster and his two brothers were examples of similar passion in book 3. But if Roche is right about the reference to male genitalia in the Carl—and I suspect he is—then Timias is up against lust in a more explicit and savage form.[17] His earlier wound in the thigh can perhaps be seen as a kind of projection of his own first reaction to Belphoebe, but the Carl of Lust appears too gross and disgusting to have anything to do with the courtly Timias. On the other hand, Timias is not able to slay Lust; the Carl's ungallant use of Amoret as a shield renders Timias comparatively ineffective against him. His powerlessness appears analogous to Scudamour's at the House of Busirane, and as the chaste Britomart had power there, so Belphoebe rather effortlessly slays this decidedly explicit representative of male lust.

The ambiguity of Timias's relation to all this is emphasized by the fact that we view the scene of his ministrations to Amoret through Belphoebe's eyes. Belphoebe releases the prisoners in the Carl's cave and returns with them to find Timias:

> *Thence she them brought toward the place, where late*
> *She left the gentle Squire with* Amoret:
> *There she him found by that new louely mate,*
> *Who lay the whiles in swoune, full sadly set,*
> *From her faire eyes wiping the deawy wet,*
> *Which softly stild, and kissing them atweene,*
> *And handling soft the hurts, which she did get.*
> *For of that Carle she sorely bruz'd had beene,*
> *Als of his owne rash hand one wound was to be seene.*

[4. 7. 35]

Belphoebe is tempted to slay them both with the same arrow she has just used on Lust:

> *But drawing nigh, ere he her well beheld;*
> *Is this the faith, she said, and said no more,*
> *But turnd her face, and fled away for euermore.*

[4. 7. 36]

Spenser has kept the moral focus just soft enough to avoid the question of the guilt or innocence of Timias's prototype. Is the wound from his "rash hand" merely to Amoret's reputation? Or should we take up the hint in the poet's reference to her as "that new louely mate" and indulge in some old-fashioned allegorizing by substituting the abstraction Married Love for Amoret's fictional identity at this point? This second alternative, whatever its other demerits, would at least conform to the actuality of Raleigh's marriage. But the poem itself does not insist that we ask such questions, for by focusing on Belphoebe, it suggests the hastiness of her judgment and Timias's inability to explain or beg mercy. (He might, for example, have explained that he was just giving Amoret the same first aid that Belphoebe had once given him.) Timias's guilt or innocence therefore becomes almost irrelevant, and we are instead left slightly uncomfortable about Belphoebe's haste.

Spenser's treatment of Belphoebe must of necessity be delicate, for he is suggesting that the fault in her (and therefore in her prototype) is the ill-considered judgment to which she has subjected the unfortunate Timias. As Belphoebe pursues the Carl of Lust, the

poet uses a simile to bring out a certain aspect of the Diana archetype that lies behind her:

> As when Latonaes *daughter cruell kynde,*
> *In vengement of her mothers great disgrace,*
> *With fell despight her cruell arrowes tynde*
> *Gainst wofull* Niobes *vnhappy race,*
> *That all the gods did mone her miserable case.*

[4. 7. 30]

The simile has an unexpected double edge. The story of Niobe
compliments Belphoebe's swiftness and toxophilitic accuracy, but
by linking her to the Diana who is *"Latonaes* daughter," it suggests
as well the imperious vengefulness of Latona toward Niobe. The
"cruell kynde" formula points to the cruelty that resulted from
Diana's filial kindness. The simile hints at the imperious, rather
acerbic quality of Diana on occasion—the Diana we see in canto 6
of book 3 who speaks with the scornful hauteur of absolute chastity. Belphoebe, of course, is not allowed to become so sharp, but
in her wrath toward Timias and Amoret, she considers them worthy
of the same arrow that has just slain lust in its most savage and
disgusting form. The virginal mind is evidently not used to making
distinctions in such matters. Whatever Timias's ministrations to
Amoret may mean, it is clear that they are not to be so simply
equated with the Carl of Lust. Belphoebe, however, tempers her
wrath and merely flees from Timias. The poetry of stanza 37 delicately hints at the language of court: Timias attempts to sue for
grace, but "For dread of her displeasures vtmost proofe," he cannot approach her. She threatens "mortal arrowes" that force him
to retreat "with foule dishonor."

The analysis, the *"un*folding" (to use Wind's term) of Belphoebe begun in the *"Latonaes* daughter" simile continues in the
resolution of the story by the dove that leads Belphoebe back to
Timias. This is an evident imitation of the incident in the sixth
Aeneid in which twin doves guide Aeneas to the golden bough.
There Aeneas recognizes the doves as sacred to Venus: "Tum maxi-
mus heros / maternas agnoscit avis . . . " (192–93). The feminine
dove that comes to Timias had, like him, "lost her dearest loue."
As sacred to Venus, the dove appears to represent an aspect of Belphoebe that she does not fully recognize in herself. In *The Ocean to*

Cynthia, we should recall, Raleigh himself characterizes that side of the queen that formerly favored him as "a milke white Dove." Belphoebe is regally aloof throughout the episode, remote from any emotion except anger at the moment she sees Timias and Amoret. But the dove qualifies this aspect of Belphoebe's character. It is the dove that comes first and sings to Timias "a lamentable lay, / So sensibly compyld, that in the same / Him seemed oft he heard his owne right name" (4. 8. 4). Belphoebe's reaction to the dove is important.

> *She her beholding with attentiue eye,*
> *At length did marke about her purple brest*
> *That precious iuell, which she formerly*
> *Had knowne right well with colourd ribbands drest:*
> *Therewith she rose in hast, and her addrest*
> *With ready hand it to haue reft away.*
> *But the swift bird obayd not her behest,*
> *But swaru'd aside, and there againe did stay;*
> *She follow'd her, and thought againe it to assay.*
>
> [4. 8. 10]

The dove does not obey because it is the unacknowledged part of Belphoebe's self; it is what leads her out to find Timias in spite of herself. In stanza 12 the pronouns become ambiguous so that the distinction between the dove and Belphoebe vanishes. The dove has brought Belphoebe back to the point at which she first found the wounded Timias; it has restored her womanly pity and desire "to do him any grace."

Unknowingly, Belphoebe accuses herself in her questions about his plight:

> *Ah wofull man, what heauens hard disgrace,*
> *Or wrath of cruell wight on thee ywrake?*
> *Or selfe disliked life doth thee thus wretched make?*
>
> [4. 8. 14]

Timias tactfully acknowledges the role of fate and his own willful loathing of life in his plight, but in the language of court he places the largest share of blame on her "misdeeming":

> *Ne any but your selfe, O dearest dred,*
> *Hath done this wrong, to wreake on worthlesse wight*

> *Your high displesure, through misdeeming bred:*
> *That when your pleasure is to deeme aright,*
> *Ye may redresse, and me restore to light.*

[4. 8. 17]

The terms are political, of course, as well as courtly ("dearest dred" echoes the poet's own address to the queen in the proem of book 1), and when we learn that Timias is "receiu'd againe to former fauours state," the hortative import of the episode becomes clear. What is surprising about this hortative conclusion is that Spenser interjects the poem into a specific political situation. In 1596 Raleigh was still in disgrace. The ideal that the fiction asserts is thus placed not simply in juxtaposition to the actual, as Faery chronicle had been juxtaposed to British chronicle in book 2, but thrusts itself upon the actual and seeks to alter it. Raleigh was received back to court the following year, and though Raleigh's participation in the raid on Cadiz probably had more to do with that reception, Spenser might have credited his poetry with a scarcely characteristic success in the realm of *praxis*.

In taking account of a real crisis in a subject-sovereign relationship, the Timias and Belphoebe story of book 4 suggests certain things about the development of Spenser's vision in the second half of *The Faerie Queene*. In being constructed to reflect an actual situation, the fiction as ideal is challenged by the actual. The distinction between the poet's golden world and the brazen world of history becomes less sharp because of the acceptance by the fiction of such a challenge. There are two ways one can view this altered relationship. On the one hand, Spenser appears more willing to take the risk of submitting his poetic vision to the vicissitudes of history, and the poem exhibits a fundamental honesty by, in effect, partially revising its earlier optimism about the roles played by queen and courtier. But on the other, the continued importance of the ideal to the poem may mean that the poet is courting danger when he abandons his technique of deriving moral meaning from the juxtaposition of golden and historical worlds. For the poet may begin to make ideal of actual—to gild over, as it were, the brazen world. We can see elements in these cantos of book 4 that would validate both ways of viewing what is happening to the poem. But book 5 will require of us a choice.

A positive consequence of the altered relationship of poetry to history visible in the episode in book 4 is an unusual degree of psychological subtlety that appears to come from the moral ambivalence in the fiction. Spenser's narrative rhetoric generally leaves no mistake about the moral issues involved in a situation; he is always concerned with motivation and psychological consequences, but the narrative voice is ever a judge of moral realities. We see this less in evidence in the completion of the Belphoebe story. We cannot, as we have seen, be certain of the degree of Timias's culpability in the episode or of his exact relation to the Carl of Lust. For obvious reasons the poet cannot introduce overt narrative disapproval of Belphoebe, but it also becomes evident that Timias's melodramatic suffering is not wholly undeserved or wholly Belphoebe's doing. Spenser manages to catch in Timias something of Raleigh's willful, theatrical nature. And similarly with Belphoebe. In the earlier episodes the poem presented her as the radiant resolution of Venus and Diana, an "infolding" of apparent opposites. But the cantos of book 4 represent analysis instead of resolution, an "unfolding" of Belphoebe for the sake of psychological understanding. Instead of a poetic image of *discordia concors*, the dove that leads Belphoebe out of herself suggests latent conflict in her mind. In terms of its reference to the queen, the episode urges the reassertion of the mild and the womanly, the aspect of the Venerean dove, which the poet implies has been suppressed by a Diana-like severity in her treatment of Raleigh. In effect, Spenser hints that there is ambivalence after all in the role Elizabeth played, that there was perhaps inevitable conflict between womanly understanding and the Cynthian aloofness of queenship. Though without fully intending to, Spenser has broached the central question about the personality of a ruler: is it possible to rule effectively and yet retain unscathed such personal values as friendship, loyalty, and love? The conclusion expresses rather his hope than the conviction he earlier held.

Spenser pays a price, though not exorbitant, in the way the political dimension sits slightly askew from the moral design of book 4. In the first three books of the poem, the "mirror" for the queen, Una in book 1 and Belphoebe, predominantly, in books 2 and 3, returned a reflection that related the virtue in question to Elizabeth's role as moral focus of her kingdom. In each case this reflection mythopoeically projected some moral accomplishment of the queen and gave the reader a sense of the immanent reality of the values of Faeryland in his own world. But in book 4 this does not happen. Belphoebe, far from being the achieved image of friendship, actually becomes a negative image. Her "high displesure, through misdeeming bred" exemplifies a pitfall of friendship. And the positive conclusion reflects not what the queen has done but what she is being urged to do.

This minor inconsistency in the political dimension of the poem, interesting in itself, is not as consequential as the moral ambiguity that I have suggested is released by the allegorizing of an actual situation. There exists the danger that the amoral quality of history may color or subvert the moral values that remain so important to Spenser's poetic world. If the poet is gilding the brazen world of history, he runs the risk that where the gilding was inadequate, some of the brass may in time show through. Because Raleigh was a poet and presented himself, moreover, to both contemporaries and posterity with consummate histrionic skill, time has dealt gently with him. But one may nevertheless wonder what Spenser thought of his friend's deceit in hiding his marriage and his stubborn refusal to acknowledge the affront he had offered his benefactress. Here, perhaps, we catch sight of just a spot of brass. We cannot be too concerned about it, for the moral issue is not consequential and the fictional representation of the situation is delicate and well conceived. But in the broad historical sweep of book 5, psychological considerations were of necessity to prove less absorbing. The demands made upon poetry by the actual political world were greater, and most importantly, the moral issues were of far more consequence.

Chapter 5

Myth and History
in the Legend of Justice

In book 5 the historical dimension of *The Faerie Queene* reaches a climax. As the book progresses, history exerts an influence on the narrative that becomes virtual control by the final four cantos. By canto 9 even filial piety could not prevent James VI from seeing the reference to Mary Queen of Scots in the trial of Duessa. At the same time the artistry of the poem undergoes a crisis. No other book exhibits so much distance between high and low points. Spenser's mythopoeic powers are severely tested by the subject of the Legend of Justice, and both the successes and the failures of that testing are remarkable. Inevitably, and not without reason, some readers have blamed the insistence of historical reference for the failings of the book. From our distance of nearly four centuries, we know that some of the events and policies the poet asks us to consider were not unassailable examples of justice. But it is not simply Spenser's insistence on an historical context for justice that causes the crisis in the poem, for the historical immediacy of other books of the poem, especially book 1, has a fascination even for readers far removed in time. On the other hand, critical commentary by readers who believe the book a success has minimized or neglected history and attempted to show the workings of myth.[1] These readers have treated history as an unimportant—and perhaps embarrassing—appendage of Spenser's moral allegory; at most the historical allusions simply illustrate the moral allegory. But Spenser never uses contemporary history as mere illustration, and book 5 in particular is seriously engaged with the contemporary world. To avoid noticing that the Legend of Justice consistently directs readers toward history is to rob it of a substantial part of its moral pretension. The book demands to be read as in part a commentary on the operations of justice in the contemporary world, and we must finally judge its use of myth in portraying these operations.

Among recent critical discussions, only Angus Fletcher's coordinates of labyrinth and temple have proved able to retain history and myth both in the consideration of book 5. Fletcher speaks of the "prophetic moment" at which "the prophetic order of history is revealed."[2] Prophecy in this sense is not the prediction of the future but "a visionary interpretation of the life of the spirit" (p. 37). I would suggest further that prophecy is the imposition of moral judgment upon public experience. The prophet is moral interpreter of the past *and* judge of the present. In applying the term to Spenser, we should realize that Vergil's example is at least as important as that of the visionaries of the Old Testament. Fletcher sees the "prophetic moments" in *The Faerie Queene* as the points at which the labyrinth of history is made to cross the threshold of the temple of timeless spiritual and moral truth. Suggestive though Fletcher's discussions of Spenser's mythmaking are, however, I do not feel that they finally allow us to see the crisis of historical vision that the Legend of Justice represents. Fletcher describes what may be seen as the Platonic idea of book 5 rather than its often problematic reality; there are more questions about the success of what Spenser achieved, I feel, than Fletcher has allowed. But Fletcher's use of the term prophecy may suggest an origin of the difficulties many readers have seen in book 5. The poem fails when Spenser is unable, for a variety of reasons, to make his poem an authentic vehicle of prophecy, to judge history in sufficiently moral terms. At certain points he exhibits a compulsion to justify the claims of history beyond his desire to advance our moral understanding.

But I do not believe that the failure is complete or that it derives from the poet's desire to direct the poem toward history. The central three cantos contain some of Spenser's most effective mythmaking, mythmaking that brilliantly suggests the relation of history to concepts of justice. Because book 5 contains such extremes as the evocative vision of the Temple of Isis and the flat-footed allegorizing of Henri of Navarre's change of alliance, it requires more sorting out and questioning of its successes and failures. My objective is a better understanding of the nature of the crisis that Spenser's poetic vision undergoes.

i / *"Thy great justice":*
The Question of Subject Matter

In the proem Spenser portrays his awareness of the discrepancy between the ideal of justice and what men usually make of it. He affects a pose of nostalgia for the golden age, "the image of the antique world," when true justice reigned. Commonplace though the notion of a golden age was, Spenser's pose may startle us slightly, for his usual ploy in these proems is to find the virtue so dazzlingly expressed in his queen and her realm that he must throw a fictional veil over it so men may look upon it. Now he takes a position seemingly quite contrary to this:

> *Let none then blame me, if in discipline*
> *Of vertue and of ciuill vses lore,*
> *I doe not forme them to the common line*
> *Of present dayes, which are corrupted sore,*
> *But to the antique vse, which was of yore,*
> *When good was onely for it selfe desyred,*
> *And all men sought their owne, and none no more;*
> *When Iustice was not for most meed outhyred,*
> *But simple Truth did rayne, and was of all admyred.*
>
> [5. Proem. 3]

As Donald Cheney notes, antiquity here is a state of mind, "a symbol of the Ideal as it exists before passing through the distorting lens of the Actual."[3] We are prevented from supposing that the poet is actually comparing the here-and-now to some more just age by the comic tone he adopts in describing the signs of the zodiac knocking each other about: the ram has forgotten where he belongs and has "shouldred" the bull, who in turn has butted Castor and Pollux, who land on and crush the crab, who drops into the lion's grove. It strikes a modern as rather a scenario for an animated cartoon than a serious lamentation about injustice. The poet pretends to knit his brows and worry that the declension of the sun will cause it to forsake us altogether in time. The comedy actually projects extreme positions toward the ideal and actual to prepare for the balancing synthesis. The pose of nostalgia for an antique (and impossible) ideal and comic pessimism for the woeful present lead to a truer— and Christian rather than classical—derivation of justice: the goddess of Justice resembles, and indeed *is*, God in his ruling capacity. God allows princes to share in his rule and gives them a participation of his justice. The final stanza brings us to the expected figure who resolves ideal and actual, a goddess we at first are made to think is the Justitia or Astrea of the preceding stanza:

> *Dread Souerayne Goddesse, that doest highest sit*
> *In seate of iudgement, in th'Almighties stead,*
> *And with magnificke might and wondrous wit*
> *Doest to thy people righteous doome aread,*
> *That furthest Nations filles with awfull dread,*
> *Pardon the boldnesse of thy basest thrall,*
> *That dare discourse of so diuine a read,*
> *As thy great iustice praysed ouer all:*
> *The instrument whereof loe here thy* Artegall.
>
> [5. Proem. 11]

"Iam redit et virgo," and as the poet returns her to our consciousness, the stylized pessimism and gloom of the preceding stanzas are dispelled. The return of the ideal and antique Astrea has been accomplished in the rule of another royal virgin. The golden age is an ideal and the actual can appear all too grim, but a princess of such wit and might can assert the ideals of peace and plenty against an iron age. The proem ends by making essentially the point made in the *April* hymn to Eliza.

But there are some puzzling things about this celebration of the return of Astrea in the person of Elizabeth. Though the poet says in the third stanza that he will not form justice and its processes ("ciuill vses lore") from the mold of the present, he is, nevertheless, treating of the queen's justice. Does the distinction represent an unwillingness to delve into the mechanics of contemporary law but a recognition that justice always exists in time and in a social context? If so, why has the return of Astrea not been more efficacious in restoring justice to the "common line / Of present days"? Is the queen's justice not the system of justice over which she presides but merely her own personal ability to deal justly? In what sense is Artegall an "instrument" of the queen's justice; is he simply executive power, analogous to a police force, or will he represent law as forensic process? Readers of Spenser know that they cannot demand precision from the proems, which are designed to be playful and tantalizing, but the puzzles here do not go away as we read the book. We can sense from his prose dialogue, *A View of the Present State of Ireland*, that Spenser may himself have wondered how the queen he esteemed for magnific might and wondrous wit could have pursued such inconsistent and irresolute policies in Ireland. And the nature of Artegall's instrumentality will remain disturbingly ambiguous in the poem; in early cantos, as we shall see, he does portray the forensic aspect of the law, but in later cantos he bears more resemblance to a squadron of Elizabeth's warships or a detachment of marines. We might take the proem to mean that the poem is to be more jurisprudential than concerned with the specific application of law, but a genuinely prophetic intention must face and judge specific events and specific laws. The poem, moreover, is manifestly concerned with facing the specifics of the contemporary world.

The puzzling features of the proem mirror, I think, some of Spenser's own ambivalence about his task as celebrant of his queen's justice and foreshadow some of the ambiguities of the book as a whole. There is, first of all, a question to be asked about its subject matter. Many fictions, of course, celebrate justice; in fact, any fiction that treats seriously of human evil will in large measure be concerned with justice. But concern with *legal* justice is another matter. Does Spenser mean to consider justice as a moral absolute or the justice which is effected by law? The question is crucial, and not simply because legal justice may sometimes result in what we may recognize as moral injustice. Rather, fictions that concern moral justice may actually not be about law at all; indeed, they may imply the absence or debility of law. The distinction between fictions dealing simply with justice and those preoccupied with legal justice may perhaps be appreciated by brief reference to two twentieth-century popular genres, the western and the detective novel. In the former, though justice is always at issue, the law is typically powerless. There is rarely a question about whether a crime has been committed or who is responsible; in the near absence of law, the problem facing the oppressed victims of injustice is to find someone strong and resourceful enough to punish the oppressor. The hero is most often not an agent of the law, and even when he is, the problem remains to find aid and support in apprehending the malefactor. Typically the conclusion is a scene of violent confrontation, the gunfight, between the forces of good and bad. The very existence of law is problematic in the western, and even when law has tenuous foothold, it must be upheld by right-thinking men of strong fists and sure aim. The detective fiction, on the other hand, presupposes and indeed celebrates the rule of law. Its plot is analogous to a forensic process; it must be proved that a crime has taken place (that the death was a murder is not always initially evident), and facts must be established that point unmistakably to the guilty. Even when the detective is not an official agent of the law, he is generally in a sort of fraternal relationship—or rivalry—with the police. In their pure form such fictions conclude with the arrest or the confession of the guilty, and the reader knows that the detective's case, if not his adventure, will become a process in a court of law. Law in fact is an implicit hero in such fictions, for all the astuteness of the detective would be to no end if the law were not sophisticated enough to accept his case and powerful enough to punish the guilty.[4]

There was, of course, no classical or Renaissance equivalent of the detective fiction; moreover there appears no myth or fiction that similarly presupposed and celebrated the rule of law. If Spenser wanted to celebrate his queen's justice as a rule of law, he had to fashion such a fiction for himself with very little help from the body of classical myth that is his constant source. But in fact he appears to be pulled both ways. He begins, as we shall see, by constructing episodes that concern legal justice, but they are in uneasy tension with mythic patterns more closely resembling the western. One such pattern is the career of Hercules, the primitivism of which militates against an attempt to celebrate something so complex as Tudor law. This tension is evident through much of the book, and at the conclusion the primitivistic mythic pattern, which implies the absence of law, prevails.

For the ultimate source of this tension in book 5, we have to look to Spenser's own ambivalence about the law's effectiveness, which grew in him from his experience of Ireland. Law is an important topic of his *View of the Present State of Ireland*, and there we see grave doubts about the power of law to bring civility and justice to the land that became the poet's adopted home. As a colonial official whose work often involved him in legal processes, Spenser had a detailed, if not always precise, knowledge of the law. By the time he wrote the *View*, shortly after completing the second three books of *The Faerie Queene*, he had obviously come to believe that English law, far from pacifying Ireland, was actually working against the attempts to bring order and stability. Irenaeus, who is Spenser's spokesman in the dialogue, asserts that English laws, though "good still in themselues," in Ireland "worke not that good, which they shoulde and sometyme allsoe perhaps that evill which they woulde not."[5] Irenaeus includes in his indictment both common law and statutory laws of Parliament. He advances several reasons for the failure of law in Ireland: in many parts English law was never established or acknowledged by the inhabitants, and even now law and its penalties are irrelevant in a land continually in rebellion. But through Irenaeus Spenser advances a doubt that English law could ever be a fully effective force, for it does not agree with the disposition of the Irish, and "lawes oughte to be fashioned vnto the manners and Condicion of the people to whom they are mente and not to be imposed vnto them accordinge to the simple rule of righte" (p. 54). From this we might expect that Spenser would be sympathetic to Irish customary law, and he does admit that there is often "a greate shew of equitye in determyninge the right between partie and partie" in what he terms "Brehon law" (p. 47). But he concentrates instead on what he considers the negative elements of that law, elements that he calls repugnant to the law of God and man. He objects in particular to the penalty for murder, which is simply to pay a recompense, like wergild, to the slain man's kin. The theme that emerges most prominently from the discussion of law in the *View* is that English law has proved not only powerless but of negative value in Ireland. Irenaeus mentions one provision of the common law after another that the Irish have managed to subvert. Whenever Eudoxus, the other interlocutor of the dialogue, suggests some remedy for the application of a law, Irenaeus typically mentions another detail that would turn the proposed remedy itself into a problem. From this a reader is led to despair that law, any law, could possibly reform and civilize the country. Irenaeus states this explicitly when he comes to suggest cures for Ireland, "for it is vaine to prescribe lawes wheare no man careth for kepinge them nor feareth the daunger for breakinge them" (p. 147). His melancholy conclusion is that only the imposition of quite massive military power will bring order to the country, and only when it is thus reduced will the imposition of law be of any effect.

Such experience and opinions do not, of course, necessarily disable Spenser as an apologist for his queen's legal justice, but we may well wonder whether they would allow him the necessary conviction to delineate the moral justice within it. And this he must do if he is to establish a genuinely prophetic dimension in the Legend of Justice. The potential difficulty lies not only in his low estimation of the utility of law in Ireland but in his faith in Elizabeth and her role in England's history. Has the faith, so evident in book 1, that history has made his queen an instrument of God's justice survived the further experience of Ireland? The question is not to be answered by reference to the *View*, which was written with purely practical and political ends in mind, but by the quality of Spenser's mythopoeia in the Legend of Justice. Because history is so prominent in the book, his treatment of it must carry the conviction of prophecy to win over readers who may themselves disagree with the poet's historical judgments. Since prophecy, as I am using the term here, is essentially the imposition of moral categories upon public experience, Spenser must achieve an allegory that will convince readers, even skeptical readers, that he understands the relationship between justice as moral virtue and justice as it is practiced in his political world. It is not that we must agree with his judgments of history—surely few readers in the latter half of the twentieth century, after the Reformation and Counter-Reformation have finally ended, would endorse the estimate of history in book 1—but that we must find in his allegory a deep pondering of the relation of justice and history. It is such a pondering that one feels is immanent in Vergil's poetry, especially in the second half of the *Aeneid*. Anything less may breed suspicion in a skeptical reader that the poet himself doubts, perhaps only unconsciously, that history can bear moral scrutiny. Simple assertion by a poet is hardly enough, and it may in fact be a defense against unrecognized doubt.

ii / Artegall and Positive Law

The problems begin early in book 5. In the first four cantos the poet makes Artegall fill two roles. He is a knight on a quest to release a damsel from the tyrant Grantorto, whose name suggests the very root of injustice. Spenser links Artegall with Bacchus and Hercules as primordial righters of wrong. Fletcher suggests that this is the myth of the "social bandit," the Robin Hood figure who first brings justice to a society suffering from the oppression of a tyrant.[6] The myth of social banditry is very close to the western in its presupposition of the near absence or corruption of the law; it delineates right and wrong as basic and easily discernable categories—in this sense it is about justice—but it cannot really treat the rule of law or cope with issues with which law must deal in a society as complex as Elizabethan England. Spenser's announced subject, his queen's justice, appears far beyond the jurisprudential capabilities of the myth of social banditry, and for this reason he makes Artegall a more up-to-date "instrument" of the queen's justice: Artegall appears to be a justice of the assizes who rides in circuit with an iron sheriff to hear difficult cases.[7] The tension between the roles is evident in the first few stanzas of canto 1. After suggesting Artegall's mythic ancestry, Spenser also decides to give him an education of sorts. Few readers, I expect, read stanzas 6 and 7 without wincing to learn that Astrea, goddess of justice, in effect kidnapped Artegall as a child by alluring him "with gifts and speaches milde" and took him to a solitary sylvan law school where he learned principles of justice and equity:

> *Of all the which, for want there of mankind,*
> *She caused him to make experience*
> *Vpon wyld beasts, which she in woods did find,*
> *With wrongfull powre oppressing others of their kind.*

This academic dispensing of justice upon wild animals looks like an uneasy blend of Hercules in infancy with the sort of education a proper judge might be expected to have. Young Hercules tames the beasts and the law student has his moot court.

In these first four cantos Artegall seems more evidently a judge than a social bandit. The fiction is a bit mechanical and more than usually episodic, and the machinery of the cantos reveals itself in the fact that we can follow Artegall's judicial circuit quite closely with a map contained in a paragraph of Tudor jurisprudence. Without defending the artistry of the cantos, it is possible to see the episodes in them as structured by an idea that Elizabethans called "positive law." In his very popular dialogue on law and justice, *The Doctor and the Student*, Christopher St. German calls this positive law simply the "law of England," that is, common law.[8] The primary ground of English law, St. German says, is the "law of reason," or the theologians' natural law. There is a remarkable correspondence between Artegall's exploits in these first four cantos and St. German's exposition of this primary ground of England's law. The Student of Law in the dialogue explains that the "law of reason" is divided into "two degrees":

that is to saie the lawe of reason primarie, and the law of reason secondarie, by the law of reason primarie be prohibite in the lawes of England, murther, that is the death of him that is innocent, periurie, deceit, breaking of the peace, and many other like. And by the same lawe also it is lawful for a man to defend him self against an vniust power so he kepe due circumstance.[9]

These crimes against the "lawe of reason primarie" appear to furnish a basis for Artegall's administration of justice in the first four of the six episodes in these cantos. In the first episode Artegall convicts Sanglier of murder and perjury. In the second he defends himself against a giant who represents unjust power of formidable proportions and notable deceit:

> His name is hight Pollente, *rightly so*
> *For that he is so puissant and strong,*
> *That with his powre he all doth ouergo,*
> *And makes them subiect to his mighty wrong;*
> *And some by sleight he eke doth vnderfong.*

[5. 2. 7]

It is clear that the primary danger of the egalitarian giant is the threat he represents to peace and order: Artegall first sees "full many people gathered in a crew," then the giant stirring them up with his novel doctrine of redistribution of wealth. After Talus shoulders the giant over the cliff, the people, gathered "in tumultuous rout," still seem about "to stir vp ciuill faction," but a cop like Talus can be counted on to deal with that sort of breaking of the peace. At the marriage tournament of Florimell and Marinell, Artegall uncovers the notable deceit (and perjury) of Bragadocchio's claim to have rescued Marinell and exposes the fraud that the false Florimell represents. All of Artegall's dealings of justice in these episodes exemplify quite accurately (though not, of course, in exact order) St. German's list of what is prohibited and allowed by the "lawe of reason primarie."

After Bragadocchio's deception has been uncovered, Guyon steps forward to claim his horse, on which Bragadocchio has been bouncing along ever since the second canto of book 2. This incident and the case of Amidas versus Bracidas in the following canto appear to illustrate what St. German calls the "lawe of secondarie reason general." This second part of the law of reason "is grounded and deriued of that generall lawe or general custome of propertie, wherby goodes mouable & vnmouable be brought into a certaine propertie so that euery man may know his owne thinge."[10] The case of Guyon's horse proves fairly simple to decide, and after the animal gives a rather tardy display of ferocity at being handled by another than Guyon, restitution is easily made. The case of Amidas and Bracidas is more complex, but Artegall gives a decision based on a maxim (fictional, it seems[11]) of property law repeated to each brother: "That what the sea vnto you sent, your own should seeme" (5. 4. 17–18). He then formally expresses his opinion for the legal record as a proper judge must:

> For *equall right in equall things doth stand,*
>   *For what the mighty Sea hath once possest,*
>   *And plucked quite from all possessors hand,*
>   *Whether by rage of waues, that neuer rest,*
>   *Or else by wracke, that wretches hath distrest,*
>   *He may dispose by his imperiall might,*
>   *As thing at randon left, to whom he list.*
> *So* Amidas, *the land was yours first hight,*
> *And so the threasure yours is* Bracidas *by right.*

[5. 4. 19]

It is immediately after this decision that Artegall happens upon the adventure that proves his undoing. I think that in Artegall's ensuing combat with Radigund, Spenser is in part displaying the limit of positive law and suggesting the necessity of another principle when "respect of person" enters the realm of justice. Radigund entangles the ordinary workings of law, and only the principle of princely equity, embodied in Britomart, can cope with the injustice of subverted common law.

One need not suppose that Spenser wrote these first six episodes of book 5 with a finger marking the page in St. German's dialogue. In the *View* Spenser displays a keen layman's interest in the workings of the law, and the general sort of jurisprudence of the dialogue would likely have been a common possession of men whose work brought them close to the law. What I am suggesting is that some such pattern seems more to structure the narrative than the myth of social banditry; beneath Artegall's armor we are more likely to discover the black of a judge's robe than the Kendal green of a Robin Hood.

But there are elements of the myth of social banditry in the narrative, and the combination of those elements with the fiction embodying the jurisprudential idea becomes the problem. Fletcher, who believes that the myth is predominant, comes close to admitting the problem; he suggests that much of the interest of the book derives from the fact that "with curious ambivalence, Spenser combines in Artegall certain features of the social bandit and certain features of a more refined, postlegal justiciar."[12] Such ambivalence there is indeed, but it appears unconscious on the poet's part and it creates a basic confusion. You cannot, after all, insist that Robin Hood be both a just outlaw and a circuit-riding justice; the first role assumes the absence or corruption of law, and the second the healthy administration of established law.

In the most haunting episode in these four cantos, Spenser has his judge and sheriff suddenly and unexpectedly employ not the justice but the summary tactics of a social bandit; the result illustrates what happens to this vacillation between myth and jurisprudence when it confronts history. Artegall's encounter with the egalitarian giant produces some of the most rhetorically impressive poetry in the book; contrary ideas of justice and social order are juxtaposed in a grave debate. In its strength it may remind us of the debate between Redcross and Despair in book 1. What engrosses us initially are the good intentions and the hubris of the giant who intends to refashion all things "as they were formed aunciently" and yet does not really know how divine justice disposed creation.

His analogies to the world of nature indicate his unawareness of nature's workings. Whether as judge or orator, Artegall counters with an argument that eloquently expresses a basis in faith for the hierarchy of Elizabethan society. The biblical cadences of the poetry have an authentic ring of conviction. The earth and sea, Artegall tells the giant, are not augmented or diminished by their constant change, and the disposition of all things works in accordance with the will of God:

> *They liue, they die, like as he doth ordaine,*
> *Ne euer any asketh reason why.*
> *The hils doe not the lowly dales disdaine;*
> *The dales doe not the lofty hils enuy.*
> *He maketh Kings to sit in souerainty;*
> *He maketh subiects to their powre obay;*
> *He pulleth downe, he setteth vp on hy;*
> *He giues to this, from that he takes away.*
> *For all we haue is his: what he list doe, he may.*
>
> [5. 2. 41]

Here if anywhere Spenser presents the alternative to the pose of pessimism in the proem. The view of nature's continually wearing down and human society's growing worse and worse is echoed in the giant's inadequate reasoning. The giant not only looks back to an ancient age of innocence, he wants to model postlapsarian society on the lost ideal of absolute equality. And balance in hand, he intends to start right now. Artegall, as legal spokesman for hierarchical society, argues that such a plan of geological and social reform is not only foolish but impious in its refusal to accept God's will. The giant is a bit obtusely literal-minded, and most readers, with the benefit of the next two centuries of political thought, could easily supply him with enough ammunition to level Artegall's demonstration. But the interesting thing is that the debate continues, and there appears the prospect that the giant, if not Artegall, will learn something from it. Suddenly Talus grows impatient with the giant's way of thinking:

> *Whom when so lewdly minded Talus found,*
> *Approching nigh vnto him cheeke by cheeke,*
> *He shouldered him from off the higher ground,*
> *And down the rock him throwing, in the sea him dround.*
>
> [5. 2. 49]

As far as we can see, Artegall has not given any order for this, but he does not rebuke Talus either. The orderly forensic process has been rudely interrupted by the violence of the executor of law turned outlaw. It is not that Talus employs the *justice* of a Robin Hood (who, in any event, would have at least sympathized with the argument of the egalitarian giant) but that he, a guardian of legal process, nevertheless resorts to the methods of the social bandit. The fact that a riot breaks out in response to this appears designed to justify Talus's fears and what he did. The giant's violation of law in conducting an illegal assembly scarcely necessitated his summary execution (even Sanglier, the convicted murderer, got off with a lighter sentence), especially since Artegall had the situation so well in hand. As anyone who has taught the poem will testify, few readers are impressed by the justice of the conclusion.[13]

A reader who seeks to know why the episode ends this way, why the debate is suddenly terminated by the shoot-from-the-hip violence of Talus, will find a part of the answer in the historical reference of the giant. His arguments are not simply hypothetical constructs to enable Artegall to get in a few licks for Elizabethan order and degree; they are the views, suitably parodied, held by the Anabaptists, who believed that the hierarchical structure of society was responsible for the inequities of wealth and poverty. The Anabaptists were felt as a threat far out of proportion to their actual numbers in Elizabethan England, and John of Leyden and the excesses of Munster remained fresh memories in the 1590s.[14] But the fear came not simply from memories of Munster. If Spain represented the main military challenge to Elizabethan England, the radical Christian socialism of the Anabaptists was the most salient philosophic threat. Within a decade the social teaching of the Anabaptists would be metamorphosed on the London stage into the terrible lesson Lear learns on the heath; leveling would be enacted when a king stripped himself to the condition of a poor naked wretch and asserted that a barking watchdog was the great image of authority. But in the 1590s not even Shakespeare was yet prepared to consider the challenge represented by the social vision of the Anabaptists. Spenser knew that his readers would recognize the radical threat of this vision in the egalitarian giant and would generally acquiesce in the necessity of its destruction. The threat to society was felt to be too real and pressing to require full consideration of all the philosophic or juridical questions. Hence Talus's solution to the problem. The legal primitivism of the social bandit's methods provides an easier way out than further development of Artegall's judicial role. The effect is doubly disheartening because myth is not used, as it had been in book 1, to project an understanding of history but merely to accept one of history's all-too-common fears: titans and giants, as everyone knows, must always be toppled. But no image could be more ludicrous for the tiny groups of visionaries who renounced violence and authority. Artegall's black robes and the jurisprudential patterning of these four cantos may not create high poetic appeal, but they at least would have provided a more honest basis for treating a threat to the peace and order of society.

But there is more to Talus's sudden brutality than contemporary fear of the Anabaptists. Elizabethans, with good reason, felt themselves to live under an almost constant threat of rebellion, and Spenser's experience in Ireland made him even more than usually sensitive to this threat. Like his contemporaries he viewed Ireland not as a foreign land England was attempting to conquer and subdue but as a part of Britain since Henry II's conquest. The warfare that Irish clans waged more or less continually against English rule was therefore not opposition to colonial encroachment but rebellion of disloyal subjects. A life lived at this frontier of English rule made Spenser even more ready than the average Londoner, it seems clear from the *View*, to answer threats of rebellion with powerful force. The giant, in the ideas he embodies, refers clearly to the Anabaptists, but in psychological terms the threat he represents focuses Spenser's own preoccupations and fears. How real the threat was can be judged from the fact that Spenser and his family were driven from their home by Irish "rebels" two years later. In Talus's action it is almost as if we see the fears of a colonial official suddenly expressing themselves in a disputation that has hitherto been academic and civilized.

iii / "That part of Iustice, which is Equity"

But in the second half of canto 4 and for the next three cantos, Spenser creates a fiction whose mythic power enables him to respond to the pressure of history without endangering his moral allegory. Alluding to Hercules' submission to Omphale but also drawing on Tasso and Ariosto, the poet strengthens the romance element of the book. Although Artegall's capture by Radigund suggests a limit to the efficacy of positive law, there is not the same insistence on jurisprudence and literal judging of cases. Artegall and Talus begin to look more like knight and squire than judge and sheriff. And when equity is advanced as a principle grounding and supplementing positive law, the point is made symbolically by Britomart's strange, polysemous vision in the Temple of Isis. The vision, in fact, is one of the most memorable moments in *The Faerie Queene* and daringly advances the relationship of male and female psychology as a metaphor for the balance of law and equity.

The story of Radigund's capture of Artegall and his rescue by Britomart's victory over her has a Vergilian breadth and generosity in its historical suggestiveness. In the proud and beautiful Radigund, Spenser makes his first allusion to Mary Queen of Scots in book 5. The rescued Sir Terpine tells Artegall that his plight came of trying to avenge the wrong wrought by "a proud Amazon" who had defied all the knights of Maidenhead. In naming Radigund, Terpine calls her "a Princesse of great powre, and greater pride." Artegall is an "instrument" of law, but Radigund rules through a separate system of law; she proposes for their combat the condition that if he is vanquished, "he shall obay / My law and euer to my lore be bound" (5. 4. 49). Artegall's helplessness when he sees Radigund's radiant face suggests in retrospect the inadequacies of the usual processes of law in dealing with Mary, but the medium of that reference, the insistence on the awesome beauty of the Amazon Queen, acknowledges and compliments as well the legendary beauty of the Queen of Scots. (When Spenser comments on the political power of woman's beauty at the beginning of canto 8, he even gives Radigund the famous golden tresses of Mary.) The generosity of the portrayal lies not only in its concession of great beauty to Radigund but also in its setting of Britomart and Radigund upon equal footing in their violent combat. Typologically the combat suggests the twenty-year struggle of the two queens. Spenser has Britomart end the struggle as Elizabeth ended hers: she strikes off the head of her still proud and defiant rival. There is little in Radigund to which Mary's supporters—or James—could, or did, object. Spenser's generous construction of myth here resembles in its minor way Vergil's great stroke of generous sympathy in creating the tragedy of Dido to encompass the historical tragedy of Rome's destruction of Carthage. In her beauty, power, and proud defiance, Radigund remains a fitting tribute to Elizabeth's most dangerous rival.

The full import of Radigund, an import that is moral and psychological as well as historical, lies in the difference between her and the figures in the poem she most closely resembles. When she paces forth to do battle with Artegall, the poet describes her apparel in terms oddly reminiscent of those used of Belphoebe in book 2. Radigund wears "a Camus light of purple silke" (5. 5. 2) and elaborately described buskins. She appears poetically an "infolding" of Belphoebe and Britomart. Like Belphoebe she is beautiful and free (especially of male dominance); like Britomart she is an armed knight who must function as a man in a man's world. An historical context for the resemblance, I would suggest, is the relativity of the propaganda battle waged by supporters of Elizabeth and of Mary. A part of the rhetoric of this propaganda consisted in linking one's own queen with quite evidently positive exemplars of female leadership, usually such biblical figures as Deborah or Judith, and in styling the opposing queen a Circe, a Medea, a Jezebel, or a Delilah.[15] The lists of rhetorical exempla, of course, could be used equally by either side. Spenser appears to counter the relativity of such argumentation by starting in an opposite direction; Radigund at first resembles rather than obviously opposes the "mirrors" of Elizabeth. A reader is required to distinguish the significance of the characters, as he must distinguish the moral quality of queenship, not by appearance but by deeds. Spenser even allows Radigund an association with a symbol used to praise the virginity of Elizabeth: her shield appears "As the faire Moone in her most full aspect" (5. 5. 3). When Artegall, having momentarily overcome Radigund, unlaces her "sunshinie helmet," he discovers the beauty of her face even amid the blood and sweat, "Like as the Moone in foggie winter's night, / Doth seeme to be her selfe, though darkned be her light" (5. 5. 12). The image is vaguely sinister, and we recall that the moon is also a symbol of impermanence and change. But even more importantly, the moon dimmed by winter fog seems a parody of Elizabeth's own icon, to be used again in canto 9 of Mercilla, of a sun bursting through a veil of clouds. What distinguishes

Radigund from Belphoebe and Britomart is that she psychologically emasculates the men she encounters. Men cannot serve her and remain men; she will not accept their masculinity but dresses them in women's attire and sets them, as Omphale set Hercules, to do her housework. This alludes, one supposes, to Mary's notorious power over men, even over seemingly loyal Englishmen, and we should recall that even Spenser's own earlier patron, Lord Grey, had come under the suspicion of influence by the Queen of Scots.[16] But there is a basic inconsistency in Radigund: the femininity of her costume contradicts her impulse to unman the knights she captures, and after putting the disgraced Artegall to work at a distaff, she conceives a secret passion for him. Radigund fulfills not the chastity potentially implied by the moon imagery but the inconstancy. Psychologically she veers back and forth between femininity and a desire to dominate men utterly. Femininity has not been reconciled with the virtues necessary for leadership, as it so eminently is in Belphoebe's virginity and as it will be in Britomart's understanding of queenship. If this likewise represents Spenser's judgment of Mary Stuart's leadership, it is shrewd indeed, for femininity and queenship were ever at odds in her career.

At the center of book 5, and between Artegall's submission to Radigund and Britomart's rescue of him, stands Britomart's sojourn at the Temple of Isis. What the reader learns there provides a kind of intellectual key by which Artegall can be released from his thralldom. Literally, of course, the release comes through Britomart's strength of purpose, confirmed in the temple by the vision of her future rule and marriage to Artegall. But the poet also asserts in the opening stanzas of canto 7 that justice will be anatomized in the canto, and this anatomy, the reader understands, will be the key. The primary symbols of the temple are the Egyptian gods Isis, the silvery moon-linked goddess worshipped there, and Osiris, the crocodile god of justice who is capable of "forged guile" and "open force" unless controlled by Isis.[17] But Spenser starts further back by suggesting a euhemeristic origin of the Isis and Osiris myth. Justice, he insists, is the most sacred thing on earth because it is derived from "highest Ioue" and its skill is thence revealed "to Princes hearts":

Well therefore did the antique world inuent,
   That Iustice was a God of soueraine grace,
   And altars vnto him, and temples lent,
   And heauenly honours in the highest place;
   Calling him great Osyris, *of the race*
   Of th'old Ægyptian Kings, that whylome were;
   With fayned colours shading a true case:
   For that Osyris, *whilest he liued here,*
The iustest man aliue, and truest did appeare.

His wife was Isis, *whom they likewise made*
   A Goddesse of great powre and souerainty,
   And in her person cunningly did shade
   That part of Iustice, which is Equity,
   Whereof I haue to treat here presently.
   Vnto whose temple when as Britomart
   Arriued, shee with great humility
   Did enter in, ne would that night depart;
But Talus *mote not be admitted to her part.*

[5. 7. 2–3]

Talus might not be admitted because he is the strong right arm of Artegall, who in Britomart's dream is linked to Osiris. Talus is the embodiment of masculine open force, and the Temple of Isis is a distinctly feminine sort of sanctuary. Even the priests seem effeminate with their long, carefully combed locks and silver-hemmed linen robes. One might almost say that it is a temple of the female imagination—Isis sets a conquering foot upon the crocodile who represents her husband—and that it answers, like the Wife of Bath's wish-fulfilling heroine, the question of what all women desire: maistry.

   To say this would be to express the definite relationship of the temple to Radigund's emasculating establishment. But we must avoid missing the equally important difference. Britomart's dream, though not the most obstinate allegory on the banks of the Nile, is a complex bit of mythmaking and subtly suggests the difference between her and Radigund. And because Spenser is intensely interested in the question of female rule, the difference must of necessity extend to that between his queen and Mary. While doing sacrifice to Isis, Britomart sees herself suddenly transformed into a queen. But in the midst of her royal felicity a "hideous tempest" blows the sacred fire into "outragious flames" that threaten her and the temple itself. The crocodile of Isis awakens and swallows both flames and tempest but then (just like a man) "swolne with pride of his owne peerelesse powre" threatens to devour Britomart as well. Isis, Radigund-like, beats back the crocodile and brings him under control:

> Tho turning all his pride to humblesse meeke:
> Him selfe before her feete he lowly threw,
> And gan for grace and loue of her to seeke:
> Which she accepting, he so neare her drew,
> That of his game she soone enwombed grew,
> And forth did bring a Lion of great might;
> That shortly did all other beasts subdew.
> With that she waked, full of fearefull fright,
> And doubtfully dismayd through that so vncouth sight.

[5. 7. 16]

The ambiguity of "her" in the second line suggests that Isis and Britomart become identified. The image of fertile sexual union definitively distinguishes the Temple of Isis from Radigund's achievement of seemingly liberated dominance. When the priest interprets the dream for the troubled Britomart, he tells her that the fire storm is rebellion and that the crocodile represents Artegall, who is "Like to *Osyris* in all iust endeuer." The lion stands prophetically for the son and heir she will bear to Artegall. The reader knows that the lion also symbolizes the British crown. As a whole the dream suggests how essentially complementary are male and female strengths in the stability of rule.

Similarly, the stability of justice depends on two complementary principles: the "male" strength of positive law—objective and bound to precedent, rigorous, precise in its demands—and the "female" strength of equity—subjective in application, not bound to precedent, and therefore able to change its mind from case to case. To see how Spenser arrived at this anatomy of justice and what he meant by it, we need to look briefly at the special meaning of equity in sixteenth-century English law. The vitality of Spenser's symbols in the Temple of Isis derives in fact from the way he exploits the *donnée* of a female sovereign in his analysis of British justice. Aristotle saw equity as the root of justice and a correction of the possible injustice of law: "the equitable is just, but not the legally just but a correction of legal justice."[18] The law speaks universally, but equity corrects the universal by covering exceptions. Some English theorists in the sixteenth century felt that equity was a feature of the common law itself and operated whenever some law was corrected or modified by a competing legal principle, maxim, or statute; equity in this sense is the built-in competition that keeps the reach of any law from becoming absolute.[19] But the more usual application of the term referred to the particular way equity was institutionalized in courts and procedures connected with the royal prerogative. Prime among such institutions was the Court of Chancery, over which the lord chancellor presided. The court actually derived from the king's council and was always considered an extension of the monarch's conscience (thus the chancellor was sometimes called the "keeper of the king's conscience"). The Chancery Court was designed to offer relief in the absence of common law or the absence of common law jurisdiction. In theory, though not always in practice, the court was not in competition with the common law but supplemented it for the more complete operation of justice. Quite in accord with contemporary jurisprudence, Spenser derives equity from the sovereign by associating Isis with the royal Britomart. Because his own sovereign is a woman (and typologically "prophesied" by Britomart), Spenser is able to suggest this essentially feminine quality of equity. Moreover, here as nearly everywhere in *The Faerie Queene* feminine strength proves more reliable and finally more durable. But mindful of the imbalance of Radigund's "law" and of the dangers of unchecked subjectivity, Spenser insists upon a harmony, in law as in psychology, that resolves the conflicts of opposites. As Kermode notes, the poet favors the claims of imperial equity.[20] But the dream image of sexual *discordia concors* makes equity and the common law a fused whole of British justice.

Meanwhile Artegall is still enthralled by Radigund, and one must ask how the anatomy of justice in Britomart's dream can free him. Because decisions of equity (as, for example, in the Chancery Court) were given *ad personam* rather than *ad rem*, equity could consider "respect of person" in settling cases. Readers sometimes assume that Spenser's equity is synonymous with mercy and is mainly illustrated, though perhaps rather oddly, in Mercilla's tearful vacillation about Duessa. But though equity that derived from the sovereign's prerogative could give relief where positive law did not, it was not to be identified with mercy. Equity could also close gaps in the working of positive law. Equitable procedure was invoked in the unusual (and not notably merciful) trial of the Queen of Scots. A special commission established by an act of Parliament was impaneled to try Mary, and Elizabeth required that Parliament ratify the commission's judgment of Mary. Elizabeth herself was concerned to point out that Mary had not been tried according to the "strictness and exact following of common form," that Mary's royal estate forbade such proceeding by the course of common law.[21] Mary's trial had to contend with "respect of person" to an extraordinary degree. These facts explain, I believe, why Britomart's dream provides a kind of intellectual key that is necessary for the release of Artegall and her defeat of Radigund. In contemporary fact, positive law, the queen's usual "instrument" for maintaining the peace and security of her realm, proved unable to accomplish justice because its application to a foreign queen was subject to some doubt. Even Parliament's Act of Association could have no force until Elizabeth's decision to act. Justice could only be done when Elizabeth agreed to use the juridical power of equity that emanated from her throne. One might also say that the dream vision of Britomart portrays in a surrealistic way what Elizabeth had to understand to deal at last with Mary: that positive law and princely equity are interdependent.

Although these cantos allude effectively to these legal and historical matters, their success obviously does not lie in their precision of contemporary reference. It stems, I believe, from their suggestive correspondence with the poet's mythmaking in other books of the poem. One feels that certain things are being drawn together in these cantos. Radigund's capture of Artegall by her overwhelming beauty and her feminizing of previously manly knights appear a more explicit version of Acrasia's effect upon men. Perhaps even more significantly, Artegall's self-betrayal to Radigund, his imprisonment, and Britomart's faithful search for him recall the basic myth of the Legend of Holiness. Dolon, indeed, appears analogous to Archimago—and bears a similar historical reference.[22] Most importantly, the typological dimensions arising from the envisioned union of Britomart and Artegall closely resemble those projected by the betrothal of Una and Redcross: Spenser now meditates the role of his queen in the stability of British justice as he had there meditated her accomplishment in achieving a purified Christian church. (Paradoxically, the virginity of the queen effects much of the insistence on sexuality and marriage in *The Faerie Queene*, for the poet is able to envision her in various roles of mystic betrothal, marriage, and perfect love.) The combat of Britomart and Radigund climactically summarizes the many contests or polarities of female rule in the poem; through that combat we come to suspect that all those polarities related in some sense, sometimes even unconsciously on the part of the poet, to the great twenty-year war of nerves between the two queens. Some of those polarities—and their reference to Elizabeth and Mary—have been evident all along: Una and Duessa, for example, or Belphoebe and Acrasia. But other, less obvious duels of queenship show up in the fierce glare provided by the violently female battle of book 5: the opposition between Britomart and Malacasta, between the true and false Florimells, between Cambina and Ate. Because these cantos spring from Spenser's deepest mythopoeic sources, they remain faithful to the poem's basic impulses and structures. They acquire a sense of historical immediacy in their allusion to what was probably the greatest political and legal challenge of Elizabeth's career, but myth remains in control and shapes, with a certain generosity rather than fear, the response to history. Spenser's poetic genius expresses itself most fully in images and fictions of psychological understanding. He is not primarily a philosopher but a psychologist, and his mythmaking functions best when it demonstrates for us, as it does here, a relationship we did not suspect between ideas and human impulses and motivations.

iv / *Justice, Mercy, and Historical Allegory*

The quality of Spenser's mythmaking falls drastically in the final five cantos, however, as the urge to justify contemporary history, not understand it in psychological terms, masters the poem. The result is historical allegory on a large scale. From the beginning of canto 8 to the end of the book, Artegall administers justice in a broader sphere, as if the concept of justice is being expanded to include what we would call international law.[23] When in canto 8 Artegall is joined by Arthur, as a symbol of British power, the two of them set out to conquer various forms of foreign injustice. Such a development was perhaps inevitable at a time when Englishmen felt their sceptered isle surrounded by the forces of foreign injustice. Several of the episodes vigorously portray contemporary political or military crises; Arthur's defeat of the Souldan, in particular, cleverly allegorizes the victory over the Spanish Armada. But the episodic structure of the first four cantos returns, and at the same time there is a curious similarity to several of the episodes. The battles with the Souldan, with Geryoneo, and with Grantorto all follow the same basic pattern: Artegall and Arthur rescue symbolic maidens from symbolic oppressors. The poet's powers of invention appear concentrated on the satiric fashioning of the tyrannical oppressors. With the Souldan, for instance, he wittily subverts Philip II's Apollo *impresa* by turning Apollo into a Phaethon.[24] And in the Malengin episode he exploits the Proteus myth to portray the almost preternatural shiftiness of the Irish guerillas. But the poem appears far less inventive in using myth to project psychological and moral understanding.

The feature of these cantos most perilous to the moral dimension of the poem is the fact that Artegall and Arthur, once they venture into an international sphere of operation, become more an executive force than arbiters of right and wrong. As in the liquidation of the egalitarian giant, Spenser resorts to the legal primitivism of the social-bandit myth instead of developing Artegall's role as justiciar. Characteristically there is little to judge, for the issues are already decided. Samient simply tells Artegall and Arthur how the Souldan oppresses Mercilla. When Belge's ambassadors come to Mercilla's court, the poet narrates how Geryoneo has wronged her, and Arthur is left with only a police action to accomplish. Nor do we ever learn why Grantorto is detaining Irena, what her cause is, or why Grantorto wants to execute her; his name notwithstanding, Grantorto's case against her could be as good as Mercilla's against Duessa for all the reader learns of it. Only in the trial of Duessa is a real judgment rendered, and then we hear of it in an offhand way—almost as an afterthought—in the next canto. Because the duties of Artegall and Arthur are simply executive, to punish wrongdoers, their difficulties are tactical rather than moral—how do you deal with man-eating horses and a spike-wheeled chariot? how do you contain a shape shifter like Malengin? how do you handle a giant with three sets of arms? Artegall, clearly, has doffed his judicial wig and accepted a military commission when he joins Arthur. At times we may even suspect they hold, like Drake or Raleigh, a privateer's license.

The relationship of history to the narrative fiction of these cantos determines their character and explains why Spenser is unable to maintain the earlier distinction between executive force and the legal sources of justice (we recall, for example, Talus's exclusion from the Temple of Isis). In five of the six basic episodes, historical events and persons are not suggested allusively (as Mary was suggested by Radigund's queenship and great beauty) but actually structure the narrative. The result is historical allegory of the type we first see in the conclusion of the Timias and Belphoebe story in book 4. Spenser retains his Vergilian motives toward history, but he abandons Vergil's allusive way of suggesting an historical dimension in favor of creating an entire fictional episode to allegorize a specific event. Fiction now waits upon history. Since the history that finds its way into the cantos concerns Britain's great contest with Spain in the 1580s and '90s—in the Low Countries, on the English Channel, in Ireland—it is scarcely surprising that executive force, i.e., power, proves much more engrossing than development of ideas of international justice. In the realm of *praxis*, such ideas were just as subservient to force in the sixteenth as in the twentieth century.

If indeed we ask how the concluding five cantos develop the idea of justice, we notice that the narrative fiction, perhaps because of the basic sameness of the episodes, elaborates the *idea* of justice very little. We have simply a piling up of just conquests of unjust tyrants. It is, for example, difficult to say what the Belge adventure adds to what the Souldan episode has already indicated about tyranny and injustice in international politics. Only when we refer the Belge episode to England's role in the Low Countries and consider it *vis-à-vis* the defeat of the Spanish Armada do we see any legal difference—in the one England sent a fire brigade to her neighbor's house and in the other the fire was on her own doorstep. But even this difference does not emerge in the fiction; the episodes vary only in so far as they delineate different historical situations.

In the case of Philip II's oppression of the Low Countries or the attempt to invade England from the channel, one does not feel the poem greatly mistaken in its view of injustice; Spanish policy was cruel, violent, and immoral. (Thematically, however, the poem also gains little, for one must attribute the victory over the Armada more to seamanship and lucky weather than to Elizabeth's justice.) But when the poet insists that we consider the British role in Ireland, as he does in the Irena-Grantorto story, the tables are turned on him. Even if we grant England's strategic danger from a possible Spanish base of operations in Ireland, it is no use pretending that England, through Lord Grey de Wilton, John Norris, or any of her commanders, brought justice and peace to the land that became the poet's troubled home. If "Great-wrong" oppressed Ireland, Artegall—and Spenser—were its servants, not antagonists. If the fiction waits upon history, its morality also waits upon history.

Although the court of Mercilla provides the only haven from all the military operations, it illustrates most poignantly what happens to the moral design of Spenser's poem when myth does not mediate history, when the poet's desire to give history its due outstrips his desire to generalize it through myth. And because the court of Mercilla also treats, now in far more explicit detail, the trial of the Queen of Scots, it offers the most significant comparison to the Radigund story. It may appear strange that Spenser should refer again to Mary, but a characteristic of book 5 is the way it keeps returning, almost obsessively, to the political threats to Elizabeth; Philip II and Spanish power appear in a series of metamorphoses: Dolon, the Souldan, Geryoneo, Grantorto. Ireland, it seems clear, did not offer much reassurance to a poet meditating political stability.

On the one hand the court of Mercilla is designed to resolve various thematic concerns of the book. As Aptekar points out, the image of Mercilla controlling "an huge great Lyon" beneath her feet recapitulates the icon of Isis controlling the Osiris-crocodile.[25] As an heraldic emblem the lion certainly represents the power of the crown of England, but his murmuring "with rebellious sound" also suggests the British people, proverbially changeable and rebellious unless firmly controlled by a gracious sovereign. The recapitulation of the Isis-Osiris image indicates that Mercilla too embodies equity in accord with law. Indeed, the fact that Mercilla's conscience must decide Duessa's fate suggests the extraordinary, equitable nature of this justice. And yet Mercilla's name and the symbolism of her attendants mean that we are to see more than law and equity resolved in her court. It is the place where, in the words of Psalm 85, "mercy and truth are met together, righteousness and peace have kissed each other." The Litae, a "beuie of faire Virgins" who attend Mercilla's throne, are the primary symbols of the reconciliation of virtues. They wait upon the judgment seat of Jove to calm his anger and stay his vengeance:

> They also doe by his diuine permission
> Vpon the thrones of mortall Princes tend,
> And often treat for pardon and remission
> To suppliants, through frayltie which offend.

[5. 9. 32]

Their names indicate something of the resolution Mercilla represents: Dice (δίκη, Justice), Eunomie (Good Law), Eirene (Peace), "goodly *Temperance*," and "sacred *Reuerence*." What is obviously to be expected in the court of Mercilla is an action that will portray a reconciliation of Justice and Mercy. The Legend of Justice has hitherto shown strict justice performed; now we expect to see it supplemented with a mercy that brings peace and harmony.

What we see instead is an increasingly close allegorization of the trial of the Queen of Scots. Mercilla is the most sharply etched figure of Queen Elizabeth as ruler in the poem, and the details of Mercilla's portrayal add up to an iconographic portrait of the queen in her imperial role. The throne embossed with the lion and the fleur-de-lis, the "cloth of state" that is a cloud with the familiar sunburst effect, and the prostrated "kings and kesars" at her feet reproduce the iconography of actual portraits. The rusty sword of peace at her feet, in fact, was a literal as well as an emblematic possession of Elizabeth.[26] Although Spenser is not interested in reproducing the legal details of Mary's trial (the special commission of jurors is reduced to Artegall and Arthur), he represents quite exactly the case against Mary in the trial of Duessa, "now vntitled Queene." Gone is the generosity that marked the treatment of Radigund: Duessa is brought in "as prisoner to the bar," and the poet insists that her "rare beautie" is "blotted with condition vile and base." Zeal, a prosecutor as skilled in rhetoric as law, does not hesitate to bring up old charges that Duessa has beguiled and ruined many a knight, but he admits that she is not being tried for this but for treasonous conspiracy against Mercilla. Caught up though he is by Zeal's persuasiveness, Spenser is nevertheless as honest as exact about the reasons for convicting Duessa; the prosecutor's first witness is Kingdom's Care, a "sage old Syre" whose pleasant English name rings more agreeably in a judicial proceeding than its continental equivalent, *raison d'etat*. The "law of Nations" and "Religion" also testify against her. In the "Peoples cry and Commons sute" Spenser suggests Parliament's appeal for Mary's execution. Duessa's defense is very close to the actual reasons for which Elizabeth hesitated to execute Mary; it is the same mixture of political and personal considerations:

> *But then for her, on the contrarie part,*
> *Rose many aduocates for her to plead:*
> *First there came* Pittie, *with full tender hart,*
> *And with her ioyn'd* Regard *of womanhead;*
> *And then came* Daunger *threatning hidden dread,*
> *And high alliance vnto forren powre;*
> *Then came* Nobilitie *of birth, that bread*
> *Great ruth through her misfortunes tragicke stowre;*
> *And lastly* Griefe *did plead, and many teares forth powre.*

> [5. 9. 45]

And like the vacillating Elizabeth, Mercilla cannot bring herself to render a final judgment, even though she knows Duessa to be guilty. The canto ends with Mercilla unable to let "iust vengeance" fall upon Duessa:

> *But rather let in stead thereof to fall*
> *Few perling drops from her faire lampes of light;*
> *The which she couering with her purple pall*
> *Would have the passion hid, and vp arose withall.*

> [5. 9. 50]

Although there is still doubt about the extent of Mary Stuart's guilt in the plots against the life of Elizabeth, there can be no doubt about the political expedience of her execution; as long as Mary remained alive, she was a focus for plots against the life of Elizabeth. But for a variety of reasons, some political, Elizabeth would have preferred to spare Mary. In fact, though with vacillation and tears, she did not. The trial and execution of the Queen of Scots is a fascinating amalgam of Tudor law, politics, and *raison d'etat*. A glowing exemplum of mercy tempering justice it assuredly is not. In spite of his design, Spenser seems, at least implicitly, to have recognized this. Canto 9 ends with Mercilla's indecisive tears; canto 10 begins with two stanzas on the relation of mercy to justice:

> *Some Clarkes doe doubt in their deuicefull art,*
>> *Whether this heauenly thing, whereof I treat,*
>> *To weeten* Mercie, *be of Iustice part,*
>> *Or drawne forth from her by diuine extreate.*
>> *This well I wote, that sure she is as great,*
>> *And meriteth to haue as high a place,*
>> *Sith in th'Almighties euerlasting seat*
>> *She first was bred, and borne of heauenly race;*
> *From thence pour'd down on men, by influence of grace.*

> *For if that Vertue be of so great might,*
>> *Which from iust verdict will for nothing start,*
>> *But to preserue inuiolated right,*
>> *Oft spilles the principall, to saue the part;*
>> *So much more then is that of powre and art,*
>> *That seekes to saue the subiect of her skill,*
>> *Yet neuer doth from doome of right depart:*
>> *As it is greater prayse to saue, then spill,*
> *And better to reforme, then to cut off the ill.*

The first stanza describes the virtue that so far appears to have been shown in Mercilla's court, and the second relates that mercy to the strict justice that may be in conflict with it. The fourth line of the second stanza has sometimes been felt to be in need of a gloss; William Nelson suggests that it means that strict justice may at times demand the death of the human "principal" to save the written "part" of the law.[27] But the greatest virtue, that which reconciles justice and mercy, satisfies strict justice while it mercifully seeks to save the human principal, to reform rather than exact punishment. The next stanza extols Mercilla's possession of this supreme virtue. Spenser has been accused of throwing up a "rhetorical smoke-screen" in these stanzas, and it is difficult to see how he is to be defended from the charge.[28] For the stanza that follows the praise of Mercilla's mercy suggests with an almost embarrassed obliquity the curious outcome of that mercy:

> *Much more it praysed was of those two knights;*
> *The noble Prince, and righteous* Artegall,
> *When they had seene and heard her doome a rights*
> *Against* Duessa, *damned by them all;*
> *But by her tempred without griefe or gall,*
> *Till strong constraint did her thereto enforce,*
> *And yet euen then ruing her wilfill fall,*
> *With more then needfull naturall remorse,*
> *And yeelding the last honour to her wretched corse.*

[5. 10. 4]

What has happened, we wonder, to Duessa? To what does "thereto" refer? The fact that there is a "wretched corse" to which last honor is yielded means that Duessa has been executed, but certainly the reader can be pardoned if he does not realize this until after another reading of the stanza. Such mercy as can be turned aside by "strong constraint" and contents itself with "more then needfull naturall remorse" may not be worth making such a fuss about. Spenser seems so circumspect about Duessa's execution that one suspects he realizes in some way what he has done.

What has gone wrong seems evident, even painfully so. Instead of fashioning a mythic fiction to convey at this climactic point in the book the crucial idea of a mercy that tempers justice, Spenser chose to make his fiction allegorize closely the trial of Mary Stuart. His own vision of mercy thus becomes no better than the mercy finally afforded Mary. Mary may not have deserved mercy, but this does not help Spenser's allegory. His devotion to his queen and her cause is evident, even touching, but as with Talus's summary execution of the egalitarian giant, the Legend of Justice falters.[29]

As we fault Spenser for becoming, like Sidney's historian, "captiued to the truth of a foolish world," we must also note that he exhibits a strange and melancholy honesty about that world even as he is taken captive. Once he commits himself to following contemporary history, he follows it faithfully, even if it leads, as in the case of Mary's trial, away from where he intended to go. In the allegorization of Henri of Navarre's change of alliance, the reader can see the almost comic doggedness of the poet's fidelity in pursuing the actual. In canto 11 Artegall and Talus rescue a shieldless knight who is beset by a "rude rout." Artegall asks him his name and why he has abandoned his shield. The knight replies that he is Sir Bourbon and that he has laid aside his shield because people dislike it so much that it has won him more enemies than friends. The shield, of course, is Henri IV's Protestantism, and Bourbon's "relicta non bene parmula" allegorizes Henri's famous judgment that "Paris is worth a Mass." Artegall scolds Bourbon sharply for giving up the shield, but when Bourbon simply changes the subject and asks for aid in rescuing his fickle lady Flourdelis, Artegall complies. Bourbon remains shieldless, Artegall says nothing more about it, and the lady is recovered. Bourbon appears to have been right: the shield was not so very important, and even someone so rigid as Artegail will drop the matter and join in the rescue. The allegory loses its moral point, but it follows history: Elizabeth rebuked Henri for his recantation, but she did not break the alliance that was aiding him. Artegall sternly lectures Flourdelis about her faithlessness, but Bourbon does not appear any less eager to have her and, still shieldless, snatches her up onto his horse and rides off. If there is any moral to this, it is that you listen politely to people like Artegall, then do the *politique* thing—Henri IV's lesson exactly and not, presumably, Spenser's.

The book ends in a melancholy gloom that testifies more to Spenser's fidelity to the world he knew than to his prophetic hope that he could transform or transcend it. By means of Artegall's rescue of Irena, Spenser attempts to assert fictionally the ideal in a cause very close to him, the pacification of Ireland. But it is a measure of the fragility of that ideal in the face of reality as well as of Spenser's honesty that the brazen world of historical fact overcomes the ideal even as it is asserted. Instead of ending on a note of victory and fulfillment, as all previous books of *The Faerie Queene* have ended, the Legend of Justice follows Spenser's political experience in Ireland. Eight stanzas chronicle an anticlimactic military victory over Grantorto, and sixteen stanzas recount the victory of Envy, Detraction, and the Blatant Beast over Artegall. The scope of the poet's vision contracts, and Artegall refers not so much to Elizabeth's justice or system of law as to her commanders in Ireland, particularly, it would seem, to Lord Grey, who came home to England in disgrace in 1582, and to Sir John Norris, who Spenser fears will follow Grey.[30] The reader's attention is directed not to the importance and magnificence of law in its maintenance of justice and mercy or even to an understanding of those virtues, but to the specific injustice that the poet feels has been done to one man and may be done to another. Artegall overcomes Grantorto, but the allegorization of Lord Grey (and perhaps his conflation with Norris) in the maligned Artegall belie both a fictional sense of victory and the asserted ideal of an Ireland saved from "great wrong." As the fiction becomes more closely tied to the truth of specific situations, it becomes increasingly unable to reach the mythic level of moral and psychological generalization at which the greatest sections of *The Faerie Queene* move.

The Legend of Justice fails finally to be prophetic poetry. Spenser appears to lack the conviction of the prophet who knows what is just and fashions the vehicle of his prophecy to express his conviction. When the poem falters, it is not because of the poet's inclination to consider political and historical issues, for prophetic poetry must move in just such a direction. Nor must we suppose that his support of established power and a successful monarch necessarily leads him astray; Spenser is ever his queen's champion, but his poetic interpretation of her career had previously achieved a delicate and complex, if partisan, intelligence. Rather he fails when he makes history as it is, not a vision of history as it should be, the vehicle of his prophetic morality. In doing so he paradoxically betrays a want of faith in history, for he implies that history needs his defense and that the contemporary world is not secure enough in its self-understanding to bear a moral vision of what it could be. We can see this, I believe, in the obsessive way the poem keeps returning to the historical figures who threatened Elizabeth's rule. Structurally the poem is overly insistent that we understand that Mary Queen of Scots and Philip II represented injustice. When the poet doubles and makes more explicit the reference to Mary in the trial of Duessa, he appears to mistrust the generosity and artistry of his portrayal of Radigund.

To explain why book 5 fails as prophetic poetry, it may be well to view it momentarily in the context of the intense 1590s. The last decade of Elizabeth's reign saw enormous change in the historical and political sensibilities of sophisticated Englishmen. The early

1590s, following hard upon the victory over the Armada and the resolution of the twenty-year threat of Mary and encompassing the wars in the Low Countries, were a time of patriotic fervor and loyalty in which England saw itself as an island threatened by swirling currents of Spanish power. These are the years of Shakespeare's early history plays, in which he accepts as a given the political terms of "Tudor myth." He shared with Spenser a faith in the nation's history that was born of the dangers and successes of the late eighties and early nineties. The recent foreign threats to England's safety and the concomitant plots against Elizabeth's life stimulated an art that placed a high value on patriotic celebration of nation and ruler. But in the second half of the decade the patriotic optimism would quickly fade. The war with Spain dragged on and on, consuming crown revenues and keeping taxes very high. Economic depression was deepened by continued crop failures; severe grain shortages caused prices to soar. The monopolies on the staples of daily life became so burdensome on average Englishmen that in 1597 Parliament was moved to act against this royal prerogative. A fin-de-siècle disillusionment and political skepticism replaced the patriotism of the early years of the decade. A literary locus of this new national mood is the dark weariness that infects the world of *Henry IV, Part 2*. In *Henry V* doubts about national history and the politics of kingship become even more prominent, and it is possible to see in that play what amounts to a counterargument that sharply qualifies the victory of England's hero-king. Perhaps *Troilus and Cressida* is the definitive manifestation of this skepticism. Ulysses's speech on degree, so often plucked from its context as an exhibit of the Elizabethan idea of hierarchy, surely functions in the play as a rhetorical ploy that ironically summons up an earlier world very different from the darkly antiheroic one that the characters are creating for themselves. At the turn of the century, military heroism of the sort that had stirred English blood in the 1580s began to look distinctly anachronistic. Essex, that odd amalgam of the old chivalric gallantry and the new cynicism, must have done much to stimulate Shakespeare's imagination as he wrote *Troilus*.

Spenser's Legend of Justice, published as it was in 1596, is caught uneasily between these national moods. In its explicit argument it is a patriotic defense of Elizabeth and her policies. But we catch sight of Spenser's discomfort from time to time, and the gloom at the end of the book seems indeed suggestive of the mood to come. There appears no open expression of political skepticism, but the tone of the conclusion implies dissatisfaction and a basic doubt of the processes of political reward. Spenser, in fact, writes himself into a decidedly awkward position: while praising Elizabeth's justice, he portrays a final lack of justice for the human instruments of her policy. Even the returned Astrea, we must conclude, cannot recognize slander for what it is and reward her unjustly maligned servants.

But even as we see book 5 caught between the shifting moods of the 1590s, we must also recognize that Spenser was hardly a passive spectator of political events. He had invested some fifteen years of his life in England's colonial policy in Ireland, and his estate of Kilcolman gave him a personal stake in the pacification of that land. It is worth noting that a part of Spenser's own experience of the law came in a series of bitter lawsuits over possession of parts of his estate with Lord Roche, one of the old Irish landowners near Kilcolman.[31] Spenser was clearly not inclined to admit the defeat of English policy in Ireland, and yet, in spite of the conclusion of book 5, he did not see it as one of Elizabeth's major successes. When he came to write the *View* a year or so later, he expressed his disillusionment and recommended that stern military measures be taken against the rebellious Irish. The sections of book 5 that concern Spenser's experience in Ireland are hardly too close to actual history, but when we reflect upon that experience, we must see in the poem more wish fulfillment than moral prophecy. Artegall's anticlimactic rescue of Irena from Grantorto is little more than whistling in the dark, and Spenser must have realized this when he came to quite different conclusions in the *View*. It is even less pleasant to consider the conclusion as exhortation to Elizabeth, for as such it sinks into the moral bog that the *View* is.

Even more disturbing is the wish fulfillment evident in Talus. There is something at once childlike and grotesque about the conception of an "immoueable, resistlesse" iron man who enforces the decrees of justice. He reminds a modern of Superman, who is likewise impervious to weapons and easily surmounts all physical barriers in apprehending criminals. Imaginatively, Talus appears to answer the need that Spenser felt, and expressed in the *View*, for massive military support of English policy in Ireland. This aspect of Talus is nowhere more evident than in the Malengin episode, in which Spenser portrays the Protean shiftiness of the Irish guerrillas. Artegall cannot handle Malengin, so Talus is dispatched to finish him off. Spenser gives this to us in a stanza of scarcely concealed delight:

> But when as he would to a snake againe
> Haue turn'd himselfe, he with his yron flayle
> Gan driue at him, with so huge might and maine,
> That all his bones, as small as sandy grayle
> He broke, and did his bowels disentrayle;
> Crying in vaine for helpe, when helpe was past.
> So did deceipt the selfe deceiuer fayle,
> There they him left a carrion outcast;
> For beasts and foules to feede vpon for their repast.

[5. 9. 19]

The gratuitous brutality of Talus, evident almost whenever he is turned loose by Artegall, disturbs one all the more in that the narrative voice renders no judgment of it. One must assume that Spenser's experience of Ireland not only inured him to such brutality but made him prone to countenance it in the defense of what he took to be right. When one ponders the violence Spenser embodied in Talus, C. S. Lewis's judgment seems scarcely too harsh: "Spenser was the instrument of a detestable policy in Ireland, and in his fifth book the wickedness he had shared begins to corrupt his imagination."[32]

Talus is an odd creation of a poet to whom the epithet "gentle" has so often been applied. But those who know Spenser's poetry well may be less inclined to relinquish the adjective than to see Talus, and much else in book 5, as the untimely product of bitterness and frustration. If one does not want to justify or excuse the failings of book 5, he may nevertheless wonder how Spenser, had he lived another decade, might have revised or extended his poetic meditation on kingship and political power. It is not only the extraordinary turn of Shakespeare's imagination in the twilight of Elizabeth's reign that makes one suppose that Artegall, Talus, and Mercilla would not have been Spenser's final images of achieved justice. Much happened to Spenser himself before his premature death early in 1599. The *View*, of course, represents more melan-

choly second thoughts about Irish affairs. But he would also per-
sonally witness a collapse of English policies in Ireland in 1598, and
he and his family would be driven from their home by rebellion.
(Ben Jonson later told Drummond of Hawthornden that "a little
child new born"—Spenser's or a servant's?—died when the house
at Kilcolman was burned.[33]) During the week that Spenser died in
London, Essex was being dispatched to Ireland with the largest expedition undertaken in Elizabeth's reign. In the *Prothalamion* Spenser had looked toward Essex as "Great England's Glory," and such
an expedition must have appeared to answer his hopes of pacification. But a year later Essex's adventure would also have ended in
failure, and two years later he would be in active revolt against
Gloriana. One cannot speculate, of course, how Spenser would
have responded to such failures and perplexities of his hopes, but
we may suppose that his response to history would have been
complicated—and perhaps deepened—by such experiences. Book
5 is caught uneasily in the midst of uncompleted historical events
to which the poet was responding in a very partial and personal
way. In its failings we can see the fragility of his faith in history—
and sense some of the motives for his unexpected withdrawal from
history in the Legend of Courtesy.

Chapter 6

The Return
to Pastoral Vision

While amid the variety of book 6, the reader feels that a great deal has happened to *The Faerie Queene* since the opening lines of book 1. We do not really need to go back to the letter to Raleigh to realize that Spenser's plans, indeed something of his poetic vision, have changed since we set out with the Redcross Knight and Una. Things happen unexpectedly in book 6: the hero drops out of sight in the central six cantos; when he reappears, he promptly abandons the quest that the reader has been led to suppose is thematically central; the hero returns to the quest only after the innocent shepherds, including the wise Meliboe, have been brutally slaughtered; and finally, when the quest has been completed and the monster captured, the Blatant Beast escapes—not only from its Faeryland chain but from Faeryland itself. The Beast suddenly turns into a real-life threat to the poet. It is evident, moreover, that the Ariostan technique of books 3 and 4 does not really explain the variety and unexpectedness in the narrative of the Legend of Courtesy.

Perhaps the most striking discontinuity in the entire poem is the difference in tone between books 5 and 6. What many readers have felt to be a grim determination in the narrative of book 5 gives way to an amplitude and ease in book 6. The differences between justice and courtesy account in large part for the tonal and structural differences between the two books.[1] The patrons of either virtue differ from one another like brothers of radically divergent temperaments, the elder taking after his father and the younger resembling the mother. There is something absolute and unswerving about Artegall; he does not need to concern himself with envy and detraction because they are not relevant to the tasks he has to do. His role is a corrective one, and he is able to win decisive victories within the well-defined boundaries in which he operates. Calidore, however, moves across a larger terrain where decisive victory is impossible and somehow irrelevant. His courtesy is close to the very basis of human intercourse; as humble as the common words and customs that lubricate everyday social life, it is also the very ground of society. Though it blossoms "on a lowly stalke," it "spreds it selfe through all ciuilitie." We can see the distinction between Artegall and Calidore in the difference between legal battles to establish a basic human right and the reforming of a society's values to make such battles unnecessary. Both endeavors are always needed, but it is evident that the latter is bound to be forever incomplete. Calidore's victories have a more positive side to them, as we see in the reforming of Briana and Crudor, but they are likely in a world of "infected will" to prove as inconclusive as the temporary capture of the Blatant Beast. Because Calidore's quest can have no definitive conclusions, both hero and poet have leisure to search and explore.

But the most significant change of vision in the Legend of Courtesy concerns the historical dimension we have been tracing through the poem. This dimension, from its most complete (if not most satisfying) manifestation in book 5, virtually disappears in book 6. This should surprise us, for although justice is most tied to the specifics of history, Spenser also defines his courtesy as existing in a social context. In the proem he avers that courtesy springs from his queen and flows into her court. We may naturally suppose, then, that book 6 will somehow suggest the contemporary loci, in persons or institutions, of courtesy.[2] But when the poem looks momentarily beyond itself, it alludes not to anything historical or public but, in Colin's vision on Mount Acidale, to the poet himself. Most strikingly though, book 6 is the only book of *The Faerie Queene* that has no fictional character shadowing the queen. The metaphorical hall of mirrors that I proposed ends with book 5, and in book 6 we turn a corner and enter another chamber. The central figure, in fact, in Colin's vision of poetic inspiration is his own mistress, and he asks Gloriana's pardon for allowing his lady this focal position:

> *Pardon thy shepheard, mongst so many layes,*
> *As he hath sung of thee in all his dayes,*
> *To make one minime of thy poore handmayd,*
> *And vnderneath thy feete to place her prayse,*
> *That when thy glory shall be farre displayd*
> *To future age of her this mention may be made.*
>
> [6. 10. 28]

The apology is delicately made, but the fact remains that Gloriana's prototype would look in vain in book 6 for any images of her glory. Colin is clearly speaking retrospectively to Gloriana about the many lays "sung of thee in all his dayes."

Indeed, book 6 represents an implicit reaction to Spenser's initial desire to engage the questions of power and rule in his ethical vision. For this reason the book demands some consideration in a study where it may at first appear quite out of place. In the first three books of *The Faerie Queene*, Spenser considers the relation of the virtue in question to his queen by means of fictional typologies that he points up in brief and controlled allusions. The negative aspects of the contemporary and political world find their way into the poem through satiric characters like Lucifera, Philotime, Bragadocchio, or Paridell or through the moral antitypes of Elizabeth, Duessa, Acrasia, or Malacasta. But in the second half of the poem, and in book 5 in particular, historical allegory tends to remove the delicacy and caution that had maintained the fiction as a suggestive "type" of the actual; the ideal and mythic "golden world" of the fiction becomes increasingly involved in the actual world until the latter seems to overpower and control the fiction. As I suggested in the last chapter, the poet's curious evasiveness about Duessa's execution and perhaps the narrative sameness of the last three cantos seem an implicit recognition that something is amiss in the attempt to consider history in Faeryland terms. The disappearance of any sense of a positive historical dimension in book 6 appears to confirm the suspicion that the poet sensed the peril involved in making history not only the focus but also the vehicle of his prophetic morality. When he does refer to political power in the final stanzas of book 6, it is in a wholly negative way. Poetry, far from being heeded, has won "a mighty Peres displeasure"; a poet must not seek to influence but only to please. His Vergilian intentions toward history and power have failed.

The bow to the queen in the proem to book 6 suggests something of the changed status of the historical dimension. As in the proem to book 5, Spenser contrasts the present state of society with the ideal he embodies in his "Antiquitie." The present age *seems* well stocked with courtesy;

> Yet being matcht with plaine Antiquitie,
> Ye will them all but fayned showes esteeme,
> Which carry colours faire, that feeble eies misdeeme.

Contemporary courtesy, he asserts, is a glittering imposture, brass that is mistaken for gold, for true courtesy is rather a state of mind, "And not in outward shows, but inward thoughts defynd." But unlike the proem to book 5, there is no rhetorical posturing that suggests comic exaggeration in the strictures on the present. Rather we hear only earnest insistence on the secret, inward springs of poetry and courtesy. Then almost as if calling himself back from a reverie to the task at hand (and recollecting the title of his poem), the poet makes the expected bow in the direction of the one locus of contemporary courtesy that must be excepted from his general censure:

> But where shall I in all Antiquity
> So faire a patterne finde, where may be seene
> The goodly praise of Princely curtesie,
> As in your selfe, O soueraine Lady Queene,
> In whose pure minde, as in a mirrour sheene,
> It showes, and with her brightnesse doth inflame
> The eyes of all, which thereon fixed beene;
> Yet meriteth indeed an higher name:
> Yet so from low to high vplifted is your name.
>
> Then pardon me, most dreaded Soueraine,
> That from your selfe I doe this vertue bring,
> And to your selfe doe it returne againe:
> So from the Ocean all riuers spring,
> And tribute backe repay as to their King.
> Right so from you all goodly vertues well
> Into the rest, which round about you ring,
> Faire Lords and Ladies, which about you dwell,
> And doe adorne your Court, where courtesies excell.

The compliment is altogether graceful, and it would probably be wrong to characterize it as merely perfunctory. Nevertheless, we may suspect that Spenser is by now adept enough at turning such stanzas as these that only a part of his attention is needed. For the figurative language of the first of the stanzas fits oddly with the preceding stanzas. It is peculiar that the poet should insist that the brightness of the queen's courtesy dazzles the eyes of beholders just after he has deprecated the false courtesy that pleases the eye and blinds the judgment. Similarly, his likening of the queen's mind to a "mirrour sheene" is a little disconcerting in view of the disdain for the vision of superficial worldlings who see "but in a glas." Spenser does not, one would guess, imply any sly innuendo here, and the discords are merely the slips of fingers playing an old piece a little inattentively. In any case, the cycle of courtesy is begun from the queen and ended in her without any mention of its having passed through or informed the poem. In the proem to book 5, we recall, as well as in the proems to the first three books, the poet had insisted that the queen was the *subject* as well as the inspiration of his poem. Now, however, Elizabeth may well sense from the very beginning that she is to be confined to the role of a mere onlooker.

The first stanza of the narrative itself presents an etymology for courtesy that makes even more striking the lack of a fictional mirror for the sovereign: "Of Court it seemes, men Courtesie doe call, / For that it there most vseth to abound." Of all the virtues, then, we might most have expected courtesy to find its "allegorical core" in a representation of the English court, just as mercy and justice were united within such a representation in the court of Mercilla. But our further understanding of the Legend of Courtesy makes us realize that the book intends more to qualify than to substantiate this etymology. Indeed, the sources of courtesy become more and more remote from any court life. Calidore comes from the Faery Court, but he is the only practitioner of courtesy we see who does. The squire Tristram, though of noble blood, has been brought up entirely in the forests. Calepine, Calidore's surrogate in the middle cantos, is not Spenser's usual Faery knight; he is rather, as Cheney has suggested, "a more typical representative of mankind."[3] Calepine in turn is aided by a representative of courtesy at the furthest remove from the court, the Salvage Man, who utterly lacks the graces of speech and comely conduct and whose courtesy is rather an instinctive human sympathy. Even Calidore's courtesy is tested and completed during his sojourn among the shepherds, and the sanest advice he receives comes from the old shepherd Meliboe, whose experience of court has been entirely negative. Calidore finally accomplishes the rescue of Pastorella as an armed knight disguised as shepherd, and surely we are to see his effectiveness as a result of this acquired dual identity. If courtesy is correctly etymologized from *court*, it is nevertheless wrong to limit its practice to the court or indeed even to find its true source there.

i / *"Rare thoughts delight"*

The actual "allegorical core" of book 6 comes in Colin's vision on Mount Acidale in canto 10, and what replaces the concern for the political and historical is, paradoxically, concern for the inner processes of poetic vision and the challenges to that vision. As it did in the marriage of the Thames and the Medway in book 4, the poem again, but now more fully and decisively, turns in upon itself and considers its own fonts. Instead of searching in the political world for the means of realizing ethical ideals, the poet projects his own aesthetic experience as relevant to the ethical concerns of the poetic fiction. His own aesthetic experience becomes a more trustworthy guide to the problem of finding the relation of the ethically ideal to a reality often harshly at variance with the ideal.

The vision on Mount Acidale presents most clearly the poet's concern for his own aesthetic experience, but it is by no means the sole expression of this concern in book 6. Even before he draws a curtain and leads us into this symbolic representation of the processes of the imagination, Spenser calls our attention, both implicitly and explicitly, to these processes. The proem to the book begins with just such a suggestion that we notice that the poem is composed in time by a man who, like all engaged in immense intellectual projects, feels both exhilaration and tedium in his work:

> *The waies, through which my weary steps I guyde,*
> *In this delightfull land of Faery,*
> *Are so exceeding spacious and wyde,*

> *And sprinckled with such sweet variety,*
> *Of all that pleasant is to eare or eye,*
> *That I nigh rauisht with rare thoughts delight,*
> *My tedious trauell doe forget thereby;*
> *And when I gin to feele decay of might,*
> *It strength to me supplies, and chears my dulled spright.*

The poet resembles the knights in his poem, for he too is engaged in a quest. His quest is for "the sacred noursery / Of vertue," but he can reach it only if he responds to the promptings of a source he represents initially as external to himself, his muses:

> *Guyde ye my footing, and conduct me well*
> *In these strange waies, where neuer foote did vse,*
> *Ne none can find, but who was taught them by the Muse.*

The quest metaphor for the creative process, as well as the more conventional plea for inspiration, suggests the poet's uncertainty about the outcome of that process. The imagination is a "delightful land," and its paths are spacious and wide. But at the same time the ways that lead to the object of the quest are "strange" and require careful guidance. The tedium of the journey is relieved by "such sweet variety," and the weary traveler can be "nigh rauisht with rare thoughts delight." There could scarcely be a better compact description of the kind of pleasure *The Faerie Queene* affords the reader as well. Here if anywhere the poet draws himself very close to his reader's experience of the poem.

The opening stanzas of the final canto present another image of the process of composition. On the surface it reminds one of Ariosto's metaphor at the beginning of his last canto: the poet's ship is finally reaching port, and he spies all his friends and well-wishers on the shore. But Spenser looks not to the port but back over the voyage, and he is concerned to point out to his reader the pattern of the "strange waies":

> *Like as a ship, that through the Ocean wyde*
> *Directs her course vnto one certaine cost,*
> *Is met of many a counter winde and tyde,*
> *With which her winged speed is let and crost,*
> *And she her selfe in stormie surges tost;*
> *Yet making many a borde, and many a bay,*

> *Still winneth way, ne hath her compasse lost:*
> *Right so it fares with me in this long way,*
> *Whose course is often stayd, yet neuer is astray.*

Though the simile is nautical, it conveys the same sense of traveling a definite course through broad and open space. And like the "strange waies" of the quest, the course involves a devious pattern of tacking, riding out tides at anchor, seeking sheltered water in freshening weather, and so forth. Only the land-loving passenger, certain that the shortest distance between two points is a straight line, is confused by the mariners' tactics. The poet insists that what to the reader may seem an aimless narrative path has been as carefully plotted as the ship's strange course:

> *For all that hetherto hath long delayd*
> *This gentle knight, from sewing his first quest,*
> *Though out of course, yet hath not been mis-sayd,*
> *To shew the courtesie by him profest,*
> *Even vnto the lowest and the least.*
> *But now I come into my course againe,*
> *To his atchieuement of the* Blatant beast;
> *Who all this while at will did range and raine,*
> *Whilst none was him to stop, nor none him to restraine.*
>
> [6. 12. 2]

The simile is tantamount to an invitation to go back over the poet's navigation to see the coherence of it all.

The image of a ship tacking seems, in fact, a curiously exact analogy for the effect of the narrative in book 6. Many things appear to happen more than once—as we read, we think we have seen this spot in the narrative before, but when we check our bearings, we find we have moved forward in thematic development. Perhaps the best example of this narrative "tacking" comes in cantos 2 and 3. Calidore, having reformed Crudor and Briana, comes upon Tristram, who has just slain the knight who oppressed Aladine and Priscilla. When the dead knight's lady tells her story, we learn that he had come upon the two lovers sitting together "in ioyous iolliment / Of their frank loues." Calidore satisfies himself that justice has been done, knights Tristram, returns the wounded Aladine to his father, and solves Priscilla's problem of compromised reputation by a bit of equivocation to her father. Calidore no sooner returns to his quest than

> He chaunst to come whereas a iolly Knight,
> In couert shade him selfe did safely rest,
> To solace with his Lady in delight . . .
>
> [6. 3. 20]

Again? we ask, realizing that Calidore's interruption of the lovers is the same situation in which the slain knight found himself in the very last canto. We soon understand, of course, that this encounter not only illustrates Calidore's civility as a contrast to the other knight's incivility but that the episode develops the connection of the Blatant Beast to slander and infamy; this lady, Serena, is not as lucky in her escape as Priscilla.

This narrative doubling is analogous to, but not the same as, the thematic doubling that is so frequent in *The Faerie Queene*. Thematic doubling is evident when, for example, the Redcross Knight defeats the dragon of Error only to fall into error when he is deceived by Archimago; he escapes from the Palace of Pride only to be captured by Orgoglio. In each case the narrative expression of the sin is altered so that the reader will understand an altered—and more subtle—appearance of what is essentially the same reality. But in book 6 the narrative situations and motifs are themselves reduplicated. Thematically, either contrast or development may be implied by the parallels. The Salvage Man's rescue of Calepine and Serena, for example, parallels Tristram's rescue of the discourteous knight's lady in canto 2. The courteous Tristram is a prince whose only education has been the hunting and hawking afforded by the forests; the Salvage Man is unaccommodated man, "the thing itself." If Tristram's formation has been inadequate for a prince, the Salvage Man's is inadequate for a human being. The hermit, whose advice cures Timias and Serena from the bite of the Blatant Beast, has his authority from his retirement after an active life of knighthood. Meliboe, who affords hospitality and advice to Calidore, is a version of the hermit whose authority has a negative sting to it; he enjoys his pastoral *otium* after ten years of futile court service. The foundling motif introduced in Calepine's rescue of the baby from the bear is recapitulated in the story of Pastorella's infancy. Some of the parallel motifs involve evident contrast. The Salvage Man assumes an incongruous knightly role and identity when he puts on Calepine's armor to protect Serena (the poet leaves us with the impression that the armor doesn't quite fit); Calidore, however, integrates his identities as knight and shepherd when he puts shepherd's weeds on over his reassumed armor to rescue Pastorella. Crudor's being forced in battle to "stoup to ground with meeke humilitie" prefigures his actual reformation to true courtesy. When Turpine is enforced to a similar posture by Arthur, we learn by subsequent events that it signals nothing more than fear and cowardice.

It is perhaps this recurrence of motifs and narrative situations that led Berger to describe the tone of book 6 as "oddly reflexive."[4] Indeed, Spenser does implicitly call attention to his allegorical technique by such narrative doubling. We are also aware of a sense of freedom in the narrative; things happen unexpectedly, almost capriciously, in the Legend of Courtesy. The freedom is of course the projection of the poet; it comes to stand for the play of his own imagination. As Kathleen Williams has pointed out, the words *chance* and *fortune* occur very frequently in book 6.[5] Many things are expressly said to happen by good or bad fortune. This insistence on fortune, I think, gradually produces the realization that it is the poet himself who, like a Prospero, is structuring such "fortune." Things that seem to happen fortuitously are actually happening by grace of a poetic mind and imagination that have some hidden end in view.

This is nowhere more evident than in the short, self-contained episode of Calepine's rescue of the baby from the bear in canto 4. The thematic relation of the episode to courtesy is hardly self-evident, but one may suspect that Berger's principle of "conspicuous irrelevance" applies well here.[6] Under the Salvage Man's care, Calepine is recuperating from the wounds suffered at Turpine's hand. He decides one day "To take the ayre, and heare the thrushes song." It is then that "An hard aduenture with vnhappie end" befalls him. The unhappy end is Calepine's separation from Serena, but the baby-and-bear episode ends in quite another key. Potential unhappiness there is indeed: a bear is carrying off a baby "betwixt his bloodie iawes." As it "chaunst," Calepine lacks his armor and is able to give chase to the kidnapping bear. When he overtakes the bear, the animal is forced to drop the baby and defend itself. Calepine has no weapon but catches up a stone lying at hand—"so fortune him did ayde"—and thrusts it down the bear's throat. Without much difficulty Calepine is able to strangle the bear, then turns his attention to the wailing baby. Because of his pursuit Calepine has become lost in the forest and can only wander about with the baby "as fortune fell." The scene becomes almost comic when the infant's feeding time arrives and the crying of "his louely little spoile" perplexes and annoys the inexperienced Calepine. But just at sunset, "by good fortune," they arrive in an open meadow where a woman is complaining of *her* fate and fortune. As it happens (and as the reader surely expects it will happen), the lady is lamenting her childlessness. She explains to Calepine that she is "th'vnfortunate *Matilde*," whose husband has had the "happie fortunes" of conquering a giant and thereby seizing a large estate. But "cruel fate" has decreed them childless; at their deaths their lands will revert to the giant. If you need a baby, Calepine says in effect, I just happen to have one here:

> *If that the cause of this your languishment*
> > *Be lacke of children, to supply your place,*
> > *Lo how good fortune doth to you present*
> > *This litle babe, of sweete and louely face,*
> > *And spotlesse spirit, in which ye may enchace*
> > *What euer formes ye list thereto apply,*
> > *Being now soft and fit them to embrace;*
> > *Whether ye list him traine in cheualry,*
> *Or noursle vp in lore of learn'd Philosophy.*

[6. 4. 35]

"Fortune" arranges things for all concerned: Calidore is glad to be rid of his young charge "whereof he skilled nought," Matilde has a baby, and the child has been snatched from the jaws of a bear to be the heir of Sir Bruin. With this last detail, which we did not expect, the poet adds a whimsical grace note to the symmetry of the piece; we are amused not only at the precision of the poet's "fortune" but also at its caprice. Calepine will continue wandering until the end of canto 8, when "by chance" he is brought to the rescue of Serena just in the nick of time. As in the old movie serials, Calepine rushes onto the scene just as the cannibal priest raises the knife to slay her.

Such insistence on fortune and the symmetrical working out

of the little subplot cannot help but make us aware of the poet who is pulling the strings. The conclusion of the baby-and-bear story (as well as Calepine's cliff-hanging rescue of Serena) affects us like the end of a classic comedy: all the lovers are suddenly reunited and properly paired off, and we are amused at the symmetrical artificiality of it all. Life is never quite so neat, and yet the story has in some sense been an imitation of life. The pleasure we feel derives from our recognition that mind and imagination have, however temporarily, imposed themselves decisively upon an obstinate reality.

ii / "But vertues seat is deepe within the mynd"

Canto 9 begins with yet another metaphor for the process of composition: the narrator is "iolly swayne" who has left several furrows of rich soil unplowed; lest Calidore's name be dishonored, it is necessary to return to those furrows and finish the work. The homely metaphor (based, it would seem, on the narrative metaphor of Chaucer's knight[7]) makes Calidore's reputation, indeed his quest, one with the process of composition. The reader who has felt the reflexive quality of the narrative of book 6 will not, then, be entirely unaware of what to expect when that quest quickly leads Calidore away from castles and courts, cities and towns and into the "open fields." Immediately the narrative grows more leisured, and the poet describes what Calidore sees in the fields. Shepherds are singing to their flocks "Layes of sweete loue and youthes delightful heat." The image of quiet contentment taps a current of poetic associations reaching back to springs in the hills of Sicily; we know that we have left the heroic world and arrived in the pastoral. We cannot yet be sure why the mode of the poem has changed, but because poetry has ever been, since Theocritus, a natural subject of pastoral, we sense that the poem may become explicitly reflexive, that it will attempt a return to its own fonts. We expect in pastoral to learn about basic things.

Calidore is led into the pastoral experience by Pastorella's beauty, but once he has entered the world of the shepherds, he is held both by her beauty and by the eloquence of Meliboe, her foster father. As Meliboe tells of his youthful attempt at court life, his disillusionment with it, and his final return to pastoral *otium*, Calidore is "rapt with double rauishment,"

> *Both of his speach that wrought him great content,*
> *And also of the obiect of his vew,*
> *On which his hungry eye was alwayes bent;*
> *That twixt his pleasing tongue, and her faire hew,*
> *He lost himself, and like one halfe entraunced grew.*
>
> [6. 9. 26]

To determine the nature of Calidore's pastoral experience, we must take a closer look at Pastorella and Meliboe. Despite her large role in the last four cantos of book 6, Pastorella remains a somewhat vague heroine. She never acquires the more distinct characterization that is afforded Britomart, Belphoebe, or Una. This is surely because Pastorella is never allowed to speak for herself; the poet tells us the effect of her speech but never allows us to hear it. Pastorella, indeed, seems rather abstract. Like Florimell, she wins male hearts at first glance. Coridon, Calidore, and the brigand chief are all captivated by her beauty; shepherds and their antitypes, the merchants, recognize her rare quality. We, like Calidore, first see her among the shepherds and assume she is a part of the pastoral world. But like Shakespeare's Perdita she has come from a courtly world and finally returns to it. Like other characters in book 6, she has what Cheney has called a "mixed identity."[8] She is both shepherdess and gentle born, and she therefore transcends court and pastoral worlds. Perhaps the diminutive of her name is the point: she is pastoral, but only a little pastoral. At the beginning of canto 10, Calidore's service to Pastorella is contrasted with his duty to Gloriana. Only by turning from that duty and abandoning the quest can he come to know Pastorella. Although Spenser gives us various symbolic representations of courtship, Calidore is the only character in all *The Faerie Queene* whom we see fall in love in anything like the way ordinary mortals do. He finds himself forced to stop what he was doing and to cultivate a private garden of entirely new experiences and emotions. We might say that Calidore, stopped in mid-career, suddenly discovers in Pastorella not only love but the private life he had not hitherto known.

Meliboe, her foster father, is more clearly identified with the pastoral landscape. He is an actual shepherd, and the contentment he enjoys derives from his acceptance of the simple life. But elements of his portrayal indicate that the true pastoral is not to be confused with rural life, sheep, or even poverty. Spenser has modeled Melibœ on the shepherd in the *Gerusalemme Liberata* with whom Erminia stays after she has tried to come to Tancredi disguised in Clorinda's armor but is frightened off by Christian warriors. Melibœ's contentment with his rustic life and his youthful ambition as a royal gardener echo Tasso's shepherd. But an important difference in Spenser's shepherd proves crucial to Calidore's pastoral experience. In the *Gerusalemme Liberata* Erminia asks the old shepherd how they are able to survive in the middle of war. He replies:

> *d'ogni oltraggio e scorno*
> *la mia famiglia e la mia greggia illese*
> *sempre qui fur; né strepito di Marte*
> *ancor turbò questa remota parte.*

> *O sia grazia del Ciel, che l'umilitade*
> *d'innocente pastor salvi e sublime;*
> *o che, sí come il folgore non cade*
> *in basso pian ma su l'eccelse cime,*
> *cosí il furor di peregrine spade*
> *sol de gran re l'altere teste opprime;*
> *né gli avidi soldati a preda alletta*
> *la nostra povertà vile e negletta.*

[7. 8–9]

Here my family and flocks have always been untouched by any ravage or abuse; the din of war still does not disturb this remote region. It is either the grace of Heaven which exalts and guards the humility of the harmless shepherd, or as the lightning does not strike the plain but upon the highest peaks, so the fury of foreign swords falls upon the heads of great kings, and our humble and neglected poverty does not allure the soldiers greedy for prey.

Spenser's Melibœ says nothing about such literal benefits of poverty, and his praise of pastoral life emphasizes the inward sources of contentment:

> *Surely my sonne (then answer'd he againe)*
> *If happie, then it is in this intent,*
> *That hauing small, yet doe I not complaine*

Of want, ne wish for more it to augment,
But doe my self, with that I haue, content.

[6. 9. 20]

He is content not because he feels safe but because he does not long for more than he has. In the next canto pillaging brigands destroy the literal pastoral world; Meliboe's having been modeled on Tasso's shepherd becomes, finally, ironic. But from the very beginning the same irony is expressed by his name. Meliboeus in Vergil's first eclogue is the shepherd whose lands have been seized for returning veterans and who must leave the pastoral landscape and its ease. The implications in Meliboe's name are fulfilled when the brigands break into the pastoral world. They steal his sheep, ransack his house, and take him and his family captive. When Meliboe himself is killed, the impermanence of the literal pastoral is shockingly underscored; of the characters who meet untimely ends in *The Faerie Queene*, none seems so blameless and representative of such positive values as Meliboe.

What is true and enduring in the pastoral world is represented by the frank advice Meliboe gives Calidore. The knight, partly out of a courteous desire to praise the situation of his host and partly, one feels, out of a sincere appreciation of the simplicity he is experiencing after the rigorous difficulties of his quest, wishes that he too had been granted the "fortune" to be a shepherd:

That euen I which daily doe behold
The glorie of the great, mongst whom I won,
And now haue prou'd, what happinesse ye hold
In this small plot of your dominion,
Now loath great Lordship and ambition;
And wish th'heauens so much had graced mee,
As graunt me liue in like condition;
Or that my fortunes might transposed bee
From pitch of higher place, vnto this low degree.

[6. 9. 28]

Meliboe mildly rebukes him for this wish:

In vaine (said then old Meliboe) doe men
The heauens of their fortunes fault accuse,
Sith they know best, what is the best for them:

For they to each such fortune doe diffuse,
As they doe know each can most aptly vse.
For not that, which men couet most, is best,
Nor that thing worst, which men do most refuse;
But fittest is, that all contented rest
With that they hold: each hath his fortune in his brest.

[6. 9. 29]

Meliboe, unlike Tasso's shepherd, holds for a pastoral of the mind: "It is the mynd, that maketh good or ill, / That maketh wretch or happie, rich or poore." After the insistent vacillation between "good" and "bad" fortune earlier in the narrative, the question is now settled decisively. Men do wrong to accuse "fortune," for the contentment or discontent of their own minds creates that "fortune." A man who is satisfied with his lot is "fortunate"; one who is not is "unfortunate." It is not, finally, one's state in life but his state of mind that creates whatever contentment exists. Calidore seems not to understand fully, for he interprets Meliboe's words to mean that a man must take his life in hand; he will rest on the pastoral shore his bark, "which hath bene beaten late / With storms of fortune and tempestuous fate." Meliboe has insisted on a divinity that shapes their ends, but Calidore begs leave to rough-hew his for a time.

Some critics have been quite stern with Calidore for taking leave of his quest.[9] And indeed, the poet himself seems to chide the knight at the beginning of canto 10. But he softens his criticism of Calidore's truancy by admitting the attraction of the "happie peace" of pastoral *otium* in opposition to the "painted show" and "false bliss" of pursuing courtly favor. Spenser is dealing here with a basic sort of human problem, the seemingly inevitable opposition between external duties or responsibilities and satisfactions that are private and personal. We are left caught between the poet's blame and his mitigation of the blame, and not surprisingly readers, according to their own predilections, line up on one side or the other of the question. Those who are inclined to blame Calidore for abandoning his quest point to the stanza that compares the newly transformed knight to Paris as a shepherd:

who had seene him then, would have bethought
On Phrygian Paris *by* Plexippus *brooke,*

> *When he the loue of fayre* Oenone *sought,*
> *What time the golden apple was vnto him brought.*
>
> [6. 9. 36]

But Cheney is surely right in seeing the simile not as an unflattering comparison of Calidore to the effeminate Paris but as indicative of the choice that seems to lie before Calidore.[10] Calidore is compared not to the Paris of the Trojan War (on whom Paridell is modeled) but to the shepherd Paris "What time the golden apple was vnto him brought."

The myth of Paris's choice was universally interpreted as representing the choice among the active life (symbolized by Juno), the contemplative life (Minerva), and the life of pleasure and love (Venus). Natalis Comes, like most mythographers, insisted that Paris's choice of pleasure over political power or philosophical contemplation was reprehensible but thoroughly human.[11] But Ficino allowed the possibility that the exclusive choice of any one of the three goddesses would involve suffering.[12] In choosing pleasure, Paris scorned wisdom and power and fell into misery. Hercules had to choose between Juno and Venus, and although Juno rewarded him, he was vexed with constant struggles, Ficino notes, and was never happy on earth. And in the *Philebus* Socrates properly chose Minerva, but the scorned Venus and Juno revenged themselves upon him in his death. Ficino commends Lorenzo de Medici for honoring all three goddesses in his way of life.

Calidore has come from the active pursuit of the Blatant Beast and will eventually return to the active life. While "resting his bark" on the shore of the pastoral world, he pursues Pastorella and discovers the pleasures of courtship and love. And it is in the pastoral world that he is afforded a glimpse of the contemplative life in Colin's vision of the graces. After that vision Calidore "had no will away to fare" but desires to stay with Colin; only the "enuenimd sting" of the dart of love forces him to return to Pastorella. Spenser does not, however, intend primarily to distinguish between love and contemplation in the pastoral episode. Venus, "when she did dispose / Her selfe to pleasaunce," resorts to Colin's Mount Acidale, and Pastorella's foster father appears, with his philosophical cast of mind, a devotee of Minerva. Rather, love and contemplation are united in the pastoral world, and together they form the two halves of the private life Calidore is discovering. It is that private life which Spenser sets off against the active.

Surely the poet wants us to see moral ambiguities in Calidore's abandonment of the pursuit of the monster that runs from book 5 into book 6. Calidore has responsibilities not entirely dissimilar to those of Artegall, and when he turns wearily from the quest of the beast, he is giving up his responsibilities toward society and history. He is trying to find some personal quietude and in a sense is making a separate peace with those threats to society expressed in the beast. We are made to feel uneasy about his decision to abandon the quest that has been laid upon him. But at the same time we recognize that something positive happens to Calidore in the pastoral world, that the retreat from duty is not wholly blameworthy and may indeed be necessary for the knight of courtesy.

Although "gentlenesse of spright / And manners mylde were planted naturall" in Calidore (6. 1. 2), he does in fact learn a few things about courtesy in the pastoral world. In the matter of conduct, he learns from Melibœ that he should not tempt hospitable poor people with large offers of gold; Melibœ rebukes his attempt to pay for hospitality and counsels instead a learning of country ways:

> But if ye algates couet to assay
> This simple sort of life, that shepheards lead,
> Be it your owne: our rudenesse to your selfe aread.
>
> [6. 9. 33]

Calidore finds that he must bring himself to his new friends' level rather than make them rise to his. But essentially he learns to step out of himself. In doffing his knightly armor, Calidore puts off a part of his identity and assumes a new. Pastorella leads him to this, for she will have none of his "queint vsage," and "did litle whit regard his courteous guize" (6. 9. 35). Instead of teaching her his courtly ways, he himself becomes versed in country things—keeping sheep, driving wolves away, and doing the evening milking. In Sidney's *Arcadia*, Musidorus also learns to perform rustic duties while dressed as a shepherd, but Sidney makes it clear that this sort of thing is quite beneath the dignity of a knight. Calidore, however, obviously enjoys the simple tasks and learns, like another courtly young man in another pastoral, "some kinds of baseness /

Are nobly undergone and most poor matters / Point to rich ends."[13] Spenser's understanding of the fonts of the pastoral impulse in human experience is altogether closer to Shakespeare's. Calidore acquires new forms of courtesy, forms that please the rustic people more than courtliness; his natural gentility must find new expression. "Loue so much could," comments the poet on the unexpected transformation of knight into swain.

From Colin Clout, Calidore learns more theoretical things about courtesy. As he approaches Mount Acidale, Calidore does not know that the vision of the "hundred naked maidens" dancing in a ring has anything to do with him in particular, and finally curiosity gets the better of his courtesy. He steps into the open, and to Colin's displeasure the vision disappears. Colin nevertheless agrees to explicate the vision and explains that the maidens are the Graces who attend Venus. The three in the center are those who "doe chiefe on her attend" and represent an unfolding of the Heavenly Venus. They are the daughters of "sky-ruling Ioue" and Eurynome. If the reader seeks further explication, he may learn from Comes that Eurynome means "wide law" and the Graces represent the "fertility of the fields and abundance of crops," which do not come "except by the benefits of peace."[14] Spenser chooses mythological figures with both cosmological and ethical implications. The Graces, as an unfolding of the Heavenly Venus, suggest the harmony of nature becoming harmony among men:

> These three on men all gracious gifts bestow,
> Which decke the body or adorne the mynde,
> To make them louely or well fauoured show,
> As comely carriage, entertainement kynde,
> Sweete semblaunt, friendly offices that bynde,
> And all the complements of curtesie:
> They teache vs, how to each degree and kynde
> We should our selues demeane, to low, to hie;
> To friends, to foes, which skill men call Ciuility.
>
> [6. 10. 23]

Calidore learns that courtesy comes to him from outside of himself, that his courtesy is a participation in larger processes that begin in a divinely ordered nature and end in civility among men, the "friendly offices that bynde." But "end" is not the exact word: the

Graces dance in a circle, and the process is conceived of as cyclic. Man's civility fulfills the promise of harmony in nature and becomes, as social response to the law of love, itself a form of worship. Calidore's learning about the exterior context of his courtesy is analogous to his learning to step outside of himself among the shepherds. In both instances courtesy is transformed from conduct to an inward awareness of the reasons for such conduct.

With the capture of Pastorella by the brigands and the death of Meliboe and the other shepherds, Calidore finds that the pastoral world he has taken for secure is as fragile as his vision of the Graces. The woods that had echoed the dancing of the Graces "did nought but ecchoes vaine rebound." Calidore puts his armor back on and resumes his own identity and role, but he conceals the armor with shepherd's weeds; the art of our necessities is strange, and the rustic dress and shepherding skills prove useful to him in rescuing Pastorella. Calidore becomes both knight and shepherd. With the resumption of his knightly role, he finally takes the advice Meliboe had given him: "But fittest is, that all contented rest / With what they hold: each hath his fortune in his brest." The truth of Meliboe's advice is confirmed ironically by his death; the true pastoral is not to be confused with shepherding, ease, or the operations of fortune. The literal pastoral world does not afford protection to Meliboe or to the other shepherds. Rather, "it *is* the mynd that maketh good or ill." Calidore's choice as "Phrygian Paris" proves not really a choice at all: he will not stay with Colin and cannot keep Pastorella without returning to the active life. But what is true in the pastoral of Calidore's experience transcends the literal pastoral world, and can be taken back into his active life: the knowledge that true contentment is an interior thing and has nothing to do with "fortune." Calidore also takes with him Colin's lesson that human courtesy is only a part of a whole, that courtesy is cooperation with a larger order of things. Thus the poet tells us at the opening of the final canto that all that has delayed Calidore from his quest "yet hath not been mis-sayd." The moral ambiguities of the delay remain, but all has served "To show the courtesie by him profest."

iii / *"The Crowne which* Ariadne *wore"*

In Colin's vision and explication we are led to the realization that there exists a relation between courtesy and poetry. Courtesy is the most aesthetic of the virtues ("the poetry of conduct," in C. S. Lewis's happy phrase[15]), and thus we feel that a vision of the imagination and of aesthetic processes lies with strange propriety at the allegorical core of the Legend of Courtesy. Two things primarily impress us in Colin's vision: first, the harmonious perfection—indeed, the *artificial* perfection, in the Renaissance sense of the word —of the setting and the dance; and second, the way things keep reminding us of other passages in Spenser's poetry. We know we have seen Colin piping to dancing maidens before; we have listened to another waterfall to which songs are attuned, and we have heard other echoes rebounding through other woods. We have seen another maiden dancing with the Graces and "there aduanst to be another Grace." And when Calidore interrupts, we sense that we have seen Colin break his bagpipe before, that the gesture, like everything else on Mount Acidale, points to something beyond itself. We are not wrong, of course, about this sense of the *déjà vu*, for the echoes of the *Shepheardes Calender*, the *Epithalamion*, and the *Amoretti* are real. It is evident that Spenser is recalling the opening of his poetic career as well as his more personal lyric poetry. Colin is not identical to Edmund Spenser, but the persona appears to be an objectification of one aspect of the poet Spenser. One might tentatively define this aspect as that part of the poet that delights in the elements of poetry—words, song, myth, and the human emotions to be celebrated. It is an element of the poet in the Colin who tells Hobbinol in the *June* eclogue, "I play to please my selfe, all be it ill." It is the poet who delights in rivers and etymologies, who celebrates natural processes and a queen who brings peace. It is the poet who composes his most joyful poem for his own bride. For this part of poetry, Spenser claims a place among the "friendly offices that bynde." This poetry, like courtesy, can teach us how "We should our selves demean" because it teaches what it is to be human.

The center of Colin's inspiration is the "country lasse" whom we recognize as the lady celebrated in the *Amoretti*. What perhaps surprises us most is that this country lass has replaced the "mayden

Queene" who danced with the Graces in the *April* eclogue. The center of inspiration has shifted in Colin's maturity from national concerns to personal, from the realm of politics and history to the private garden. As we notice this significant alteration within the recapitulation of the vision of *April*, we should also note the elements of Spenser's poetic career that are *not* evoked by Colin's vision on Mount Acidale. The vision does not make us recall the satiric eclogues of the *Shepheardes Calender* or *Mother Hubberds Tale;* we do not think of the allusive adumbration of the English Reformation in book 1 of *The Faerie Queene*, of the historical chronicles of books 2 and 3, of Artegall and Talus, or of the trial of Duessa. Only the dancing of the "fourth grace" evokes an association with that historically committed poetry, and the poet has negated the association by altering (with apologies, to be sure) the identity of that grace. In the vision on Mount Acidale, we see the climax of the reflexive movement of book 6; the narrative, after turning in upon itself, now momentarily stops while the persona of the poet appears and affords us a glimpse of poetic inspiration and ideals. That these ideals include balance, harmony, and a suggestion of the unity of divine, natural, and human realms does not surprise the reader. But that the principal source of inspiration would turn from the national and public, the image of a gloriously successful monarch, to the poet's own private world could not have been foreseen by the reader of the first five books of the poem.

Paradoxically, this reflexive book of *The Faerie Queene* comes also from Spenser's experience of Ireland. For Ireland appears for him to have been a strangely two-sided world. On the one hand it was the enormous political problem that he presents in the *View*: an uncivilized land of rebellion and guerrilla warfare. It was a place where one must go to law to retain the land granted him by the crown, a land fatal to political and military reputations. But Spenser also found Ireland a land of extraordinary beauty and fruitfulness, and in the *View* he describes it warmly:

And sure it is, it is a moste bewtifull and swete Countrie as anye is vnder heaven, seamed thoroughe out with manye goodlye rivers replenished with all sortes of fishe moste aboundantlye sprinkled with manye swete Ilandes and goodlye lakes like little Inlande seas, that will carye even shipps vppon theire waters, adorned with goodly woodes fitt for buildinge of howsses and shipps so comodiously as that if some princes in the worlde had them they woulde sone hope to be Lordes of all the seas and ere longe of all the worlde. Allsoe full of verye good portes and havens openinge vppon Englande and Skotlande as invitinge us to Come vnto them to see what excellente Comodities that Countrye Cane afforde; besides the soile it self moste fertile fitt to yealde all kinde of fruite that shalbe committed thearevnto. And Lastlye the heavens moste milde and temperate thoughe somwhat more moyste then the partes towardes the weste.

[*View*, p. 62]

This is the Ireland that became Spenser's home; it is the backdrop for his personal lyric poetry, the *Amoretti* and the *Epithalamion*. This is the land that Colin Clout gratefully returns to in the poem that portrays Spenser's visit to England in 1589–90. Delight in this Ireland is quite obviously the impulse behind the etiological fables of rivers in that poem and in the *Mutability Cantos*. By putting Colin and his vision of the Graces at the center of Calidore's experience of the pastoral world, Spenser reveals a contentment he found in his own experience of a pastoral Ireland, a contentment we would not have expected on the evidence of book 5.

But there is one final aspect of Colin's vision that bears notice: it is exceedingly fragile. At Calidore's approach the dancing maidens vanish and cannot be recalled at will even by Colin. It is curious that the knight of courtesy, the one who can best benefit from a vision of the fonts of his virtue, should be responsible for the destruction of that very vision. But in fact it is Calidore, the knight entrusted with the quest by Gloriana, who is closer to that side of the poet *not* represented by Colin and his vision. Calidore is engaged—or should be—on a mission to benefit society. Because the beast has rushed from the Legend of Justice into the Legend of Courtesy, Calidore's mission is, whatever its more gentlemanly course, an extension of Artegall's. Like the committed poet, Calidore has obligations to society and a task to fulfill. The heroic poet cannot change his title or take back his dedication (much less pay back his royal pension). Though Calidore may benefit from a sojourn among the shepherds, it is clear that he cannot be released from the role he must play. And that role, which he carries with him even in rejection of it, appears to be what threatens Colin's fragile vision.

The most striking thing about the second half of canto 10 and the final two cantos is the contrast they bear to the vision on Mount

Acidale. The destruction of the pastoral world and the death of Meliboe shock the reader grown accustomed to the conventions of allegorical romance, who has come to suppose that what is good and beautiful will endure. But clearly we are on the very edge of Faeryland—an edge that borders on the poet's experience of the other, the dangerous and brutal, Ireland. Not only brigands exist at this edge of Faeryland, but also merchants eager to buy slaves. The battle among the brigands themselves is confused and terrifying, and when the candlelight goes out, the utter darkness "leaues no skill nor difference of wight." Even Calidore's victory is a more recognizable part of the real world than of the chivalric; he very practically stands in the entry so that he car. kill the brigands one by one as they come upon him, until the whole place is filled with bodies.

With Pastorella's return to the light and her discovery of her real parents, we return momentarily to the romance mode. Calidore achieves his quest and captures the Blatant Beast. We assume that the final tone will be one of conclusive joy and triumph. But the final four stanzas undo all of Calidore's quest and leave the Blatant Beast at large. The beast ranges through time as well as space and threatens even the present moment:

> So now he raungeth through the world againe,
> And rageth sore in each degree and state;
> Ne any is, that may him now restraine,
> He growen is so great and strong of late,
> Barking and biting all that him doe bate,
> Albe they worthy blame, or cleare of crime:
> Ne spareth he most learned wits to rate,
> Ne spareth he the gentle Poets rime,
> But rends without regard of person or of time.

[6. 12. 40]

The beast's attack is like the pitch-black battle of the brigands: it knows no distinction of person, skill, or time. The final stanza leaves us with the poet himself, not with the persona who expresses only a part of him but with the man who feels the terrible irony of his position:

> Ne may this homely verse, of many meanest,
> Hope to escape his venemous despite,

> *More then my former writs, all were they cleanest*
> *From blamefull blot, and free from all that wite,*
> *With which some wicked tongues did it backebite,*
> *And bring into a mighty Peres displeasure,*
> *That neuer so deserued to endite.*
> *Therfore do you my rimes keep better measure,*
> *And seeke to please, that now is counted wisemens threasure.*
>
> [6. 12. 41]

The reference to Burghley and the bitter irony of the last two lines bring us curiously close to the satiric tone of *Mother Hubberds Tale* or the moral eclogues of the *Shepheardes Calender*. If we wonder which of the poet's "former writs" could have given offense, it is in fact these works that come to mind. Like the allusions to Spenser's other poems in Colin's vision, the final stanza casts a glance back over the poet's career. Since some of those "former writs" have produced not reform but the mighty peer's displeasure, doubt is cast on their effectiveness and the utility of moral satire. Far from any positive effect, the poet's satire has served mainly to bring even his heroic poem into suspicion. Like the outcome of Calidore's quest, the career of the committed poet seems inconclusive; it has failed to affect those in power decisively—or perhaps even at all. Before Calidore brought the Blatant Beast into temporary custody, it had broken into the "sacred Church," robbed and spoiled the chancel and the altar, "and blasphemy spoke." All was "confounded and disordered there." Spenser is thinking not of the Puritans, who were more symptom than cause of the problems in the English church, but of the attitudes and policies he had countered in the satiric thrusts of *May, July,* and *September*. The poet's quest of the beast goes back to the beginning of his poetic career. But now the final undoing of Calidore's accomplishment, whether by "wicked fate" or "fault of men," implicitly recognizes the failure of those moral eclogues. The forces that the poet had combatted in his satiric thrusts are not only still active but are now attacking the poet himself.

The irony of the poet's position is too basic to admit resolution, and it is with the recognition of this irony, rather than resolution of it, that book 6 concludes. But the central image of Colin's vision suggests something of the way poetry relates to the forces that threaten harmony and order and make forever inconclusive its moral effect. The poet's simile for the rings of Graces, the three Graces within the larger circle of a hundred Graces and Colin's lady "as a precious gem" within the inmost circle, obviously looks beyond the literal, descriptive similarities:

> *Looke how the Crowne, which* Ariadne *wore*
> *Vpon her yuory forehead that same day,*
> *That* Theseus *her vnto his bridale bore,*
> *When the bold* Centaures *made that bloudy fray,*
> *With the fierce* Lapithes, *which did them dismay;*
> *Being now placed in the firmament,*
> *Through the bright heauen doth her beams display,*
> *And is vnto the starres an ornament,*
> *Which round about her moue in order excellent.*

[6. 10. 13]

Critics have noted the confusion in the mythology of the stanza; the battle of the Centaurs and the Lapiths occurred at the wedding of Pirithous and Hippodamia, not of Theseus and Ariadne.[16] But the real question is why Spenser brings the battle of the Centaurs and Lapiths into his simile for the harmonious dance of the Graces. Cheney suggests that the image is one of *discordia concors*, of harmony arising from strife.[17] He properly links the strife involved in the brigands' destruction of the pastoral world and its inhabitants to the "bloudy fray" of the simile. But I think one may perhaps go further and suggest that the battle of the Centaurs and Lapiths represents also the kind of violent, uncivilized challenge to poetic vision that concerns the poet at the conclusion of book 6. The Blatant Beast, like the Centaurs in Comes's interpretation of them, personifies the elements in human nature that keep men from harmony and community.[18] The mention of the "bloudy fray" at the heart of the simile for Colin's vision anticipates the irony of the poet's position at the end. The beauty of "the Crowne which *Ariadne* wore" cannot prevent the dark side of human nature from being expressed; it cannot even save Ariadne from the pain of her abandonment by Theseus. But the crown becomes immortal and outlasts the strife of the Centaurs and Lapiths. "Such was the beauty of this goodly band" of Graces in Colin's vision, the poet comments, and such is the beauty of a poet's accomplishment, the reader is left to infer. The ambiguities and ironies of the poet's position in a social and political world remain, but the beauty of his vision and a hope for its moral permanence are asserted. Ariadne's crown is not what the committed poet had foreseen as his accomplishment, but it is compensation for the Vergilian laurel that his ruler would never bestow.

With book 5 Spenser finds increasing difficulty in relating the contemporary world he wishes to celebrate to the moral values of Faeryland. I suggested that a part of this difficulty lay in the national disillusionment that was gathering at the conclusion of Elizabeth's long reign, and I proposed Shakespeare's histories of the late 1590s as more conscious and explicit loci of this political skepticism. *Henry IV, Part 2* and *Henry V* evince doubts of increasing specificity about the relation of kingship and political power to moral, humane values. At this point Shakespeare abandons English history as the vehicle for exploring the relation. Spenser's death in 1599 and his very different kind of genius keep any comparison imprecise. But the fact that readers of the Legend of Courtesy have found comparison with Shakespeare's late romances almost unavoidable may invest it with interest. The turn in Spenser's poem toward the freer, ampler world of romance prefigures the similar turn in Shakespeare's career. *Cymbeline, Winter's Tale,* and *The Tempest* involve similar "returns" to the pastoral world, where characters discover, or perhaps rediscover, things vitally important to human civility. In these plays considerations of history and probability are left far behind, for the romance world treats human nature with a kind of higher mythic generalization; human passions and hatred are represented as more sudden and intense than would appear probable, but so too are the loyalties, reconciliations, and healings of love. And in both the late romances of Shakespeare and the Legend of Courtesy, one feels that the poet's art is turning in upon itself to consider its relation to "nature," the nature of man and the nature of his world. "What Shakespeare does through Prospero," Kathleen Williams has written, "Spenser does in this last peaceful legend; he gives a new perspective upon the ordered world of his poem and the world of experience, and upon the relation between them."[19] Both poets, of course, represent as well the violence in men that ever challenges the attempts at a moral ordering of experience, but it is the perspective of Colin or Prospero that seems most salient in our recollection of these romances.

By placing the country lass at the center of Colin's vision, Spenser stresses the personal, indeed inward, nature of his vision. In book 6 he moves quietly but unmistakably away from the historical ideal which had earlier been a part of his inspiration. It would be wrong to argue that he turns upon and emphatically rejects these sources; Spenser's loyalties were too deep for such an explicit and abrupt volte-face. But the reading of the Legend of Courtesy I have proposed indicates a growing lack of confidence in such sources exterior to the poet, sources that invariably involve the violent, malevolent, or merely clumsy in human society. Colin Clout, taught by the muse, creates a vision that springs ultimately from within, and Calidore too learns in the pastoral world to look inward to the fortune that is in his breast. Both confirm the poet's assertion in the proem that "vertues seat is deepe within the mynd, / And not in outward shows, but inward thoughts defynd."

Some critics have wondered whether the lesson Calidore learns from Meliboe represents moral escapism, a suspicion kindled by Spenser's recognition of the problems of any retreat from an imposed duty. But it is only in the move away from history in book 6 that Spenser begins to develop this idea of interiority, the necessity of discovering moral value "deepe within the mynd." This is the germ of something new in *The Faerie Queene*, and as much as book 6 seems to reflect back over the poet's career, it also looks forward to new poetic possibilities. The Legend of Courtesy has seemed a completion to some readers, but this book, more than the Letter to Raleigh, convinces me of the unfinished state not only of the poem but of Spenser's vision. Like Shakespeare, Spenser was experiencing the disillusionment with history affecting Englishmen in the mid and late 1590s, and from this came the new valuation of inward sources of inspiration and moral worth. It is not usual to think of Spenser among those artists who died in the middle of their life's work. But Spenser's work was no more complete than Chaucer's, and in some ways perhaps, given the tantalizing accomplishment of the *Mutability Cantos* and the possibilities of a "Legend of Constancy" in an inconstant age, even more unfinished. Disciples complete the work of their masters, and the disciple to whom Spenser was "a better teacher than Scotus or Aquinas" would nourish the germ of pastoral inwardness. As man and poet, Milton writes large this turn from this historical to the inward as the source of moral value. Milton was never to write the historically committed epic on an Arthurian subject, the poem that was to be "doctrinal and exemplary to a nation." Instead, after his faith in history has been eroded by history, he comes to write an epic that throws power and action into the ironic gloom of Satan's domain, a domain that the final two books extend deep into human polity. All of *Paradise Lost* moves toward the quiet assertion of "a paradise within." There is, of course, some distance between Calidore's pastoral and the possibility of recovered paradise. It is a distance produced not so much by difference of kind as by elaboration and development, and they resemble one another in being set against a world of power that cannot accomplish permanent or real human good. I adduce Milton not to insist upon the "influence" of *The Faerie Queene* but simply to suggest that Spenser's stance in book 6 as Calidore and Colin had a moral plausibility that would press its claim against the humanist ethos of service to prince and nation. The shape of Spenser's meditation on his own age obliquely prophesies Milton's career as heroic poet.

𝓢 Epilogue

Escape from Mutability

What Spenser could not know was that he had predicted—with striking clarity—his own fate in the destruction of the pastoral world of book 6. Real-life brigands, Irish guerrillas, would drive him and his family from Kilcolman some two years after the publication of the second half of the poem. Whatever peace Spenser may have found before his death shortly thereafter had of necessity to come from his own mind, not from outward circumstances. For even allowing for exaggeration in Ben Jonson's assertion that he "died for want of bread in King Street," one cannot imagine much external satisfaction attending the death of a dispossessed colonial official, separated from his family and friends, whose very mission back to London bespoke the failure of policies of which he had been part. Without an inner defense, it would surely have seemed that the realities behind the Blatant Beast, Malengin, and Grantorto as well as the forces of mortal dissolution had triumphed over him.

And yet Spenser had in a sense anticipated the need to find permanence within destruction in the last part of *The Faerie Queene* he composed. While engaged in writing the *View of the Present State of Ireland*, he was also at work—defending himself psychologically and spiritually?—on the *Mutability Cantos*. In the cantos Spenser cautiously and obliquely brings together his two different senses of Ireland, and it must be for this reason that we feel here we are in the presence of some of his most personal and intimate poetry. The figure of Mutability personifies cosmic change, but as such she includes the change that operates in history and all the affairs of men and states. As a principle in the fallen world, she causes degeneration and decline in human polity:

Ne shee the lawes of Nature onely brake,
  But eke of Iustice, and of Policie;
And wrong of right, and bad of good did make,
  And death for life exchanged foolishlie:
Since which, all liuing wights haue learn'd to die,
  And all this world is woxen daily worse.
O pittious worke of MVTABILITIE!
  By which, we all are subiect to that curse,
And death in stead of life haue sucked from our Nurse.

[7. 6. 6]

Mutability is, moreover, a Titanness and a rebel, and as such she is a grander and more imposing version of the egalitarian giant. If we were to imagine Spenser writing a proem to a Legend of Constancy, we might suppose him tempted to contrast Mutability to the woman who chose *semper eadem* as her motto. In this vein Mutability is related to all those figures of impermanence, inconstancy, and mere appearance in *The Faerie Queene*. But in fact Mutability's realm includes Elizabeth and all her government and policies, and the alternative to Mutability cannot be a mortal queen but only an inward vision of the changeless realm of spirit. In book 1 Gloriana and her "city of glory" were assigned a participation in that unchanging realm, but now we hear nothing of such things. Spenser is not now concerned with his queen or her role in history; they have become irrelevant to his world of myth, things to be treated separately in a prose treatise.

Though the *Mutability Cantos* begin by treating mutability as an objective reality, we learn also of the poet's subjective experience of it. Toward the end of the first canto, Spenser interrupts the narrative to include an etiological fable for his own landscape. The tale of Faunus purports to explain why Arlo hill, "Beeing of old the best and fairest Hill," has become "the most vnpleasant and most ill." The whole tenor of the digressive fable, as indeed of most of canto 6, is comic and Ovidian, and because of the gentle comedy we scarcely notice that the tale is one of multiple betrayal: Faunus corrupts Molanna to betray Diana, Faunus betrays himself, then betrays Molanna. Diana, betrayed by the locale she had delighted in, leaves with a "heauy haplesse curse." The fable, which begins with emphasis on the beauty of Arlo hill and a loving description of the course of the stream personified as Molanna, ends with the content of the curse:

> *To weet, that Wolues, where she was wont to space,*
> *Should harbour'd be, and all those Woods deface,*
> *And Thieues should rob and spoile that Coast around.*
> *Since which, those Woods, and all that goodly Chase,*
> *Doth to this day with Wolues and Thieues abound:*
> *Which too-too true that lands in-dwellers since haue found.*
>
> [7. 6. 55]

With the last line we realize that the betrayal that lies in experience somewhere beyond the fiction is the poet's betrayal by a land he had become emotionally a part of. If it were not for the comic tone of the fable, we might say that the experience of Ireland that he thought to objectify in book 5 has been portrayed again in a more subjective mode. But the comedy cannot be denied, and we would surely be wrong to see the bitterness of the conclusions of book 5 or book 6 in the betrayal of Diana. The comedy implies a distancing from those emotions and an ability, in poetry at least, to see beyond the frustrations and angers that no doubt still beset him. A part of Spenser, the concerned colonial official, writes the *View of the Present State of Ireland*, while another part of him searches further within for alternatives to the mutable world of betrayal and injustice. Arlo hill may be cursed with wolves and thieves, but for the poet it is still a place of surpassing beauty and the setting in which the God of Nature displays the permanence beyond such manifestations of mutability.

It is probably an accident of poetic composition and circumstance that the last stanzas we have of *The Faerie Queene* are the two labeled "VIII Canto, vnperfite." But it is an accident like the incompletion of Mozart's Requiem at the serene final bars of the Recordare. The strange propriety of the two stanzas lies in their lyric mode as well as in their prayer for the permanence of an eternal Sabbath. For *The Faerie Queene* moves, especially in its final completed book and in these unfinished cantos, toward more personal expression of the poet's own inner experience. The poem, in content at least, was moving closer to the realm of lyric. As the poet's own response to his moral vision and as his personal plea for salvation, the two stanzas of the unperfected canto stand as a final reminder of this movement. They express how far we have come from the concerns of epic poetry and its preoccupation with history.

Spenser's loss of faith in the moral potential of political power —even as he writes of it in book 5—and his turn inward for poetic reassurance have an important implication when we consider *The Faerie Queene* as the preeminent example of what sixteenth-century humanism thought poetry ought to achieve. In so many ways the poem appears the embodiment of what Sidney in his *Apologie* envisioned poetry to be: a golden world, a "second nature," which expresses moral value with more precision than history and teaches it with an attraction and persuasiveness of which mere philosophy is incapable. The historical dimension I have been tracing in the poem is an important adjunct of this humanist conception of poetry, for it extends the poet's moral objectives to a concern for society. All through the sixteenth century, and beyond it, humanist schoolmasters taught that the true end of learning was not private delectation but service to the commonweal. Invariably this meant service to government or to religion. Spenser's increasing doubt in the ability of poetry to reach in any important way the possessors of political power thus represents significant modification of the humanist poetic. This is in fact the central irony of the historical dimension of *The Faerie Queene*: Spenser begins by insisting upon the public dimension of the essentially private virtue of holiness, and he ends in his last completed book with a vision of the inwardness of the social virtue of courtesy.

Seen this way, the poem itself encapsulates the change from the outward-looking, socially engaged aesthetic of the humanists to the introverted and private aesthetic of the poets in the first half of the seventeenth century. These poets do not all lose their conviction of the moral duty of the poet, but they enter gardens of private experience and generally avoid claims of a vatic role for the poet. Even Milton, as we noted, the most *engagé* and committed humanist poet of the century, finds his prophetic role not as the poet of national experience but as a celebrant of religious inwardness. Later in the century, of course, poetry will return to public concerns, but only after a retreat of some sixty years.

In the early 1590s Spenser would have been startled to suppose that his poem would be a harbinger of this retreat, for in the conscious shaping of his poetic career, he had seen himself as *vates*, the poet speaking to queen and nation. He was surprised not at receiving a pension from the crown but at all the trouble and delay he experienced in securing it. By the time he wrote the *Mutability Cantos*, whenever it was, he had adjusted his conception of heroic poetry. No longer need poetry be addressed to princes or concern public deeds to be properly termed heroic. The heroic includes inner experience as well, and in this unexpected introduction of the poet's personal identification with his epic vision, perhaps we catch another glimpse of the way *The Faerie Queene* predicts an aspect of Milton's epic.

But in Spenser's poem this turn inward was not planned or foreseen; it simply came as the poem evolved over some fifteen or twenty years. The *Mutability Cantos*, we recall, were discovered after the poet's death, and our "discovery" of them is something like Sir Calidore's happening upon the vision of the graces, a vision that concerns him but was not meant for him. For the conclusion seems inescapable that at this farthest verge of *The Faerie Queene* the heroic poet is addressing his lesson not primarily to his reader but to himself.

✨ Notes

Introduction

1. Donatus's life of Vergil can be consulted in the Loeb *Suetonius* 2. 464–83.
2. *Poeticarum Libri Tres*, 1. 208–9.
3. See Adam Parry, "The Two Voices of Virgil's *Aeneid*," and Kenneth Quinn, *Virgil's Aeneid*, pp. 51–58.
4. Although an extremely useful critical term, *mode* is seldom defined. In "Mode in Narrative Poetry," a lecture given at the Clark Library of UCLA, Paul Alpers made some acute suggestions about mode: "Critics resort to this term and use it in crucial places because it uniquely fuses formal and thematic considerations. It is the term to use when we want to suggest that the ethos of a work informs its technique and that techniques imply an ethos." He suggests this definition: "mode is the literary manifestation, in a given work, of the writer's and the putative reader's assumptions about man's nature and situation." I would amend his phrase "in a given work" to "in a given *part* of a literary work," for mode seems to me a flexible element in a complex narrative; a change of narrative perspective may signal important changes in the way a reader is to view man's nature and situation. Spenser gains much of his moral complexity, I believe, from variations, sometimes quite subtle, in mode.
5. Roy C. Strong, *Portraits of Queen Elizabeth I*, p. 82, pl. 21.
6. Ibid., pp. 75–76, 84–86, 102–5, 124–25; pl. 13, 15, 17.
7. An interesting discussion of this aspect of the *Calender* is to be found in Nancy Hoffman's dissertation, "The Landscape of Man," pp. 177–216. Paul E. McLane, in *Spenser's Shepheardes Calender*, identifies most (but not all) of the clerics to whom Spenser alludes in the ecclesiastical eclogues, but his study suffers from a naive understanding of Renaissance allegory and presents an unconvincing interpretation of the whole of the *Calender*.
8. William Pierce, ed., *The Marprelate Tracts*, pp. 42, 82, 170, passim. See also *Dictionary of National Biography*, s.v. "Perne, Andrew," and Harvey's "testimonial" of Perne in a letter to Spenser, in *Variorum*, 9:462.
9. That prototype was Richard Davies, the much-abused bishop of the Welsh diocese of St. David's. See McLane, *Calender*, pp. 216–34.
10. *Variorum*, 1:264.
11. *Studies in Spenser's Historical Allegory*, pp. 59–103.
12. See especially *Source and Meaning*, pp. 200–27. In a provocative attempt to reopen the question of history in *The Faerie Queene*, Frank Kermode also insisted upon the term historical allegory in "Spenser and the Allegorists" and in "*The Faerie Queene*, 1 and 5."
13. *The Structure of Allegory in The Faerie Queene*, pp. 9–10.
14. *Imagination and Power*, p. 58.

Chapter 1

1. See above, pp. 6–7, and the iconography noted by Roy C. Strong, *Portraits of Queen Elizabeth I*, pp. 75–76, 84–86, 102–5, 124–25.

2. See Edgar Wind, *Pagan Mysteries in the Renaissance*, pp. 1–25; Michael Murrin, *The Veil of Allegory*, pp. 3–20.

3. As Robert Durling has shown, the context of Ariosto's portrayals often qualifies the praises bestowed in them. *The Figure of the Poet in Renaissance Epic*, pp. 132–50.

4. Introduction to the second book of *The Reason of Church Government*, in *Complete Poems and Major Prose*, p. 669.

5. See, for example, Dryden's acute discussion of the contemporary political dimension of the *Aeneid* in the dedication of his translation (1697), in *The Poems of John Dryden*, 3:1011–21. On the more general topic of the relationship of a poet's fiction to history, see especially William Nelson, *Fact or Fiction*, in particular pp. 38–55.

6. As Homer wrote the *Iliad* to win the favor of his princes, Ronsard suggests, "Autant en faut estimer de Virgile, lequel lisant en Homere, qu'Aenée ne deuoit mourir à la guerre Troyenne, & que sa posterité releueroit le nom Phrygien, & voyant que les vieilles Annales de son temps portoyent qu'Aenée auoit fondé la ville d'Alba, où depuis fut Rome, pour gaigner la bonne grace des Cesars, qui se vantoyent estre sortis d'Iüle fils d'Aenée conceut cestre diuine Aeneide qu'aueq toute reuerence nous tenons encores auiord'huy entre les mains." Epistre au Lecteur to 1572 edition of *La Franciade*, in *Oeuvres Complètes*, 16:7.

7. "Saranno i veri historici molto al proposito intorno à gli auenimenti della guerra: & molte imprese porrano; le quali ò quanto al decoro, ò quanto alli stratagemi tanto del vago & del raro haurano, che senza biasimo pigliar le potremo ò in tutti ò in parte: col variare i luoghi, i tempi, le persone, & altre circonstanze: & col trasferirle ne nostri componimenti. Il che & la fatica dell'inuentione ci scemerà, & riputazione darà all'opera. Non disdirà anchora che à qualche cosa di nostri auenuta acceniamo, nel modo che Enea dinanzi à Didone nella sua partenza ad Augusto allude: che bassi tenne gli occhi al conspetto di Cleopatra, per non s'accender di lei. & Anchise morto con i giuochi, che fatti gli sono, à Giulio Cesare con i medisimi nella sua morte celebrato. & all'istesso Venulo di sella rapito da Tarchonte." *I Romanzi* (Venice, 1554), sig. M 2ʳ⁻ᵛ.

8. Although Renaissance writers mention such allusions, they are not inclined to see them as a significant element of the *Aeneid*. As Vladimiro Zabughin notes, "In Vergilio un cinquecentista apprezzava sommamente tre cose: l'organicità della struttura epica, il pathos, la sapiente economia degl'effetti, specie coloristici e decorativi," *Vergilio nel Rinascimento Italiano da Dante a Torquato Tasso*, 2:13. Perhaps the most striking negative evidence for this lack of appreciation of the historical side of the *Aeneid* in the Italian Renaissance is Vida's *Poeticarum Libri Tres* (1527). Although Vida's poem is an elegant treatise on the epic addressed to those who would write epic poetry and although Vergil is the explicit hero of his poem, he says nothing about Vergil's relation to history or his use of it in the *Aeneid*. Nor does Vida make any recommendations about history to the would-be epic poet. Tasso's precepts on the use of history in the *Discorsi dell'arte poetica* (1587) center upon the choice of a subject, for which he recommends history neither too recent nor too remote. When he mentions Vergil in this regard, he simply notes that Vergil did not follow history closely in his fiction, that the remoteness of that history allowed him to introduce the marvelous. But he says nothing of an historical design in the *Aeneid* or of the poem's relation to contemporary history.

9. *Giraldi Cintio on Romances*, p. 51.

10. Ibid., p. 45.

11. *Discorsi*, in *Opere di Torquato Tasso*, 1:667; subsequent citations of Tasso are to this edition.

12. Servius's commentary is believed to have been composed late in the fourth century. It exists in two versions, a shorter one that was known through the Middle Ages and was printed in fifteenth- and sixteenth-century editions of Vergil and a longer one (called Servius Auctus or Servius Danielis) first printed by Pierre Daniel in Paris in 1600. The latter was thought to be the more authentic version until the late nineteenth century when the edition of Thilo and Hagen found it to be an amalgamation of the shorter version with another commentary. It has been suggested that this second commentary in Servius Auctus may be the earlier work of Aelius Donatus (E. K. Rand, "Is Donatus' Commentary on Virgil Lost?"). Because of the different versions, I have quoted Servius from a sixteenth-century edition of Vergil (*P. Virgilii Maronis . . . Vniversum Poema*, Venice, 1562) but have located citations by reference to the Vergilian passage so that the glosses may also be found in Thilo and Hagen. Servius's commentary is chiefly valued by classicists now for its preservation of facts about Roman history, religion, customs, and language.

13. See Domenico Comparetti, *Vergil in the Middle Ages*, pp. 50–74, especially 57–60.

14. "Pompeij tangit historiam." Ad *Aeneidem* 2. 557.

15. "Namque qui bene considerant inueniunt omnem Romanam historiam ab Aeneae aduentu vsque ad sua tempora summatim celebrasse Virgilium. Quod ideo latet, quia confusus est ordo . . . Vnde etiam in antiquis inuenimus opus hoc appellatum esse non Aeneidem, sed gesta populi Romani." Ad *Aeneidem* 6. 752.

16. "Hoc loco per transitum tangit historiam, quam per legem artis poeticae aperte non potest ponere . . . Lucanus nanque ideo in numero poetarum esse non meruit, quia videtur historiam composuisse, non poema." Ad *Aeneidem* 1. 382.

17. "Vt verisimilem fugam faciat, circumstantijs vtitur. Notandum sane Virgilium sub aliorum persona causam exequi nobilium: vt hoc loco Marij. Item paullo post Pompeij." Ad *Aeneidem* 2. 135.

18. "De Historia est. nam Scipio Africanus, cum esset annorum vix decem & septem, patrem suum defendit in bello, nec cessit viginti septem confossus vulneribus." Ad *Aeneidem* 10. 800.

19. *Roman Vergil*, p. 302. J. W. Jones, concludes that "a goodly number" of the historical glosses have a degree of aptness that commends them to present-day scholars of Vergil, "Allegorical Interpretation in Servius," p. 225.

20. "Leucatae mons est altissimus in promontorio Epiri iuxta Ambraciam ciuitatem, quam Augustus Nicopolim appelauit victis illic Antonio & Cleopatra. Ibi & templum Actiaco Apolloni constituit, & ludos Actiacos. Vnde nunc Virgilius in honorem Augusti, qui ipse fecit, dat eius origini. Nam Aeneam illic dicit ludos celebrasse: & alibi inducit Aeneam promittentem templum Apolloni, quod fecisse constat Augustum." Ad *Aeneidem* 3. 274.

21. "Vt solet, miscet historiam. Nam hoc templum in palatino ab Augusto factum est, sed quia Augustus cohaeret Iulio, qui ab Aenea originem ducit, vult Augustum parentum vota soluisse." Ad *Aeneidem* 6. 69.

22. "Frequenter, vt diximus, ad opus suum Virgilius aliqua ex historia deriuat. Nam sic omnia inducit, quasi diuini honores soluantur Anchisae, quos constat Iulio Caseari tribuisse Augustum." Ad *Aeneidem* 5. 45.

23. "Bebius tamen Macer dicit à Caesare Augusto pueris qui luserant Troiam, donatas galeas, et bina hastilia: ad quod Virgilium constat adludere." Ad *Aeneidem* 5. 556.

24. *Virgil's Aeneid*, p. 54.

25. Jones, "Allegorical Interpretation," p. 217. Although Servius is sometimes spoken of as allegorical, in fact only a limited number of his notes, none of which concern history, can be so described (as, for example, his note on the golden bough, *Aeneid* 6. 186). A modern critic who wants to see the *Aeneid* as an historical allegory, in fact, faults Servius for turning away from allegorical traditions of interpretation (D. L. Drew, *The Allegory of the "Aeneid,"* pp. 98–101). Comparetti notes that Servius

gives certain lines or passages a philosophic meaning but that "there is no sign of any general and systematic theory of allegorical interpretation which would make all the incidents of the work tend in this direction," *Vergil in the Middle Ages*, p. 59.

26. Servius sees Augustus and Agrippa referred to in Jupiter's prophecy "Remo cum fratre Quirinus iura dabunt" (1. 292–93) and explains that Augustus was honored by the name Quirinus. As founder of Rome, Romulus too shadows Augustus, who restored Rome. Servius also suggests that the splendid palace of Latinus (8. 170–71) is a glancing allusion to the palace Augustus built on the Palatine.

27. See Durling, *Figure of the Poet*, pp. 138ff.

28. The translation is that of William Stewart Rose (1823–31).

29. *La Spositione . . . Sopra l'Orlando Furioso*. In the notes to his translation of the *Orlando Furioso* (1591), Sir John Harington often transmits these suggestions of Fornari under the heading "Allusions."

30. The translation is that of Edward Fairfax (1600).

31. The principal study of Spenser's debt to Vergil is that of Merritt Y. Hughes, *Virgil and Spenser*. The work suffers, however, from an incomplete understanding of the purpose of Renaissance imitation, and it does not mention Vergil's historical design. W. Stanford Webb, applying a more adequate idea of Renaissance imitation, gives some shrewd general consideration to Spenser's use of the historical dimension of the *Aeneid*, "Vergil in Spenser's Epic Theory."

Chapter 2

1. "Spenser and the Allegorists," p. 270.

2. See Norman Cohn, *The Pursuit of the Millennium*. On the early association of the Book of Revelation with chiliasm, see especially pp. 6–21.

3. See especially John Erskine Hankins, *Source and Meaning in Spenser's Allegory*, pp. 99–119.

4. Kermode, although pointing out the Vergilian origins of the historical dimension of book 1, does not pursue his insight far enough to see that Spenser's technique in creating that dimension also follows Vergil. In a subsequent essay, likewise learned and suggestive, Kermode insists that a detailed historical allegory "must" be present in book 1 ("The Faerie Queene I and V," p. 140). He accordingly supplies an allegory relating the early history of the English church to book 1. But I expect that Kermode would not insist that Vergil's serious treatment of history in the *Aeneid* necessitated historical allegory, and Spenser, I would contend, follows Vergil in method as well as in intent in book 1.

5. Besides Kermode, see *Variorum*, 1:449–95, and Hankins, *Source and Meaning*, pp. 205–27.

6. John Nichols, ed., *The Progresses and Public Processions of Queen Elizabeth*, 2:112.

7. "Queen Elizabeth as Astraea," pp. 37–65.

8. *Actes and Monuments*, sig. [I. v^v].

9. Ibid., sig. L. ii^{r-v}.

10. "Elizabeth as Astraea," p. 40.

11. See above, Introduction, pp. 6–7. In addition to the iconographic tradition, this association of Elizabeth with the sun breaking through a cloud was used politically in the tournament that expressed her decision not to marry Alençon ("The Fortress of Perfect Beauty," in Nichols, *Progresses*, 2:312–29, especially 319–22). But closest in meaning to Spenser's use of the image here is Joshuah Sylvester's interpolated memorial of Elizabeth in his translation of DuBartas. In the Third Day of the First Week, Sylvester "weaves" the lotos flower into DuBartas's garland of flowers and employs it as a symbol for Elizabeth's fortunes during the religious turmoil of mid-century. As the lotos sinks under water at night then rises at dawn, so "sacred Eliza" followed "th'eternall Sun of Peace and Righteousness." In her

sister's "superstitious Night" she sank beneath affliction but rose with the sun of returned truth: "So set our Sun; and yet no Night ensu'd: / So happily the Heav'ns our Light renu'd" (*Complete Works of Joshuah Sylvester*, 1:45–46). I am grateful to Norman Council for calling Sylvester's variation of this emblem to my attention.

12. *Actes and Monuments*, sig. [AAAAA. v^{v-r}]. In the homily of a prayer service of thanksgiving on Elizabeth's accession day, Edmund Bunny also emphasized the danger that surrounded her in Mary's reign: "In respect of her Maiesties owne good estate, the benefite is so much the greater, because that in those dayes her Maiestie was not onely imprisoned, but also almost (notwithstanding her innocencie) oppressed with death: but now she is not onely deliuered, but also reigneth to the glorie of God, and to the comfort of her people" (*Certaine prayers and other godly exercises for the seventeenth of November*, sig. [E. iv^v]).

13. For an account of the popularity and influence of Foxe, see William Haller, *The Elect Nation*, pp. 13–18; and Helen C. White, *Tudor Books of Saints and Martyrs*, pp. 167–68, 192–95. These two books offer complementary studies of Foxe; Haller concerns himself more with the historical development and importance of the *Actes and Monuments* and White with its literary merit and influence.

14. Graham Hough, ed., *The First Commentary on The Faerie Queene*, p. 5. Dixon made his annotations in a copy of the first edition of books 1 to 3 in about 1597. Dixon's commentary provides an important indication of how an educated, Protestant, but not particularly literary, Englishman read *The Faerie Queene* in the 1590s. He is very interested in the religious allegory (though he occasionally gets narrative details confused), is very perceptive of scriptural allusions, and provides some significant notes of historical allusions he felt to be present. He does not, however, note imitations of Ariosto or Vergil or show much interest in classical mythology. Although Dixon's notes on historical matters interest me most here, I have not dealt with all of them. In a note to the second stanza of the first canto, Dixon writes in cypher that Leicester is shadowed in Redcross, and in the same cypher he suggests Lord Cumberland is shadowed in Arthur (1. 10. 65). But Dixon mentions neither again, and the rest of his historical notes do not depend on these rather eccentric identifications. His various notes on Elizabeth show more conviction and insistence and seem to me of greater significance. On the provenance and subsequent history of the volume, see also Hough's article in the *TLS*, "The First Commentary on *The Faerie Queene.*"

15. Kermode makes this suggestion, "*Faerie Queene*, I and V," pp. 134–35.

16. *Actes and Monuments*, sig. [o. vi^r].

17. Ibid., sig. P. iiii^v.

18. D. Douglas Waters, *Duessa as Theological Satire*, suggests that Duessa is to be connected with the Catholic Mass by means of the "Mistress Missa" tradition of Protestant polemic. This adds an interesting dimension to her evident symbolism of Rome and the Catholic church. Less persuasive, however, is his assertion that this interpretation of Duessa is the "missing link" of criticism of book 1 (p. 121) and that the whole of the book must be reinterpreted from this point of view.

19. Lillian Winstanley and F. M. Padelford interpreted Duessa and Orgoglio as Mary and Philip, *Variorum*, 1:460, 470–71. Apart from the lack of indication in the text, an historical difficulty with such an interpretation is that it seems doubtful that the sensibilities of Elizabethans would have countenanced any explicit connection of Mary with the whore of Babylon. Though her rule had led England back to Rome, Mary was a Tudor, the daughter of Henry VIII, and the sister of Elizabeth, and even Foxe speaks of her, as Haller notes, "with a certain commiseration for her personal tragedy" (*Elect Nation*, pp. 195–96). In Elizabethan political symbolism, Mary's reign is silently ignored—as it was in Elizabeth's coronation procession (see Tottel's pamphlet in Nichols, *Progresses*, 1:41) and in Spenser's own ideal shadowing of Tudor rule in the Elfin emperors of Guyon's Faery chronicle (2. 10. 75–76). But this is not to deny an implicit hint of a dark and Antichristian royal marriage in the

liaison of Duessa and Orgoglio, especially in retrospect from Una's betrothal in the final canto.

20. *First Commentary*, p. 9.

21. Ibid., p. 11.

22. *Annals; or, The historie of the most renowned and victorious Princesse Elizabeth*, p. 16.

23. Printed in the *Harleian Miscellany*, 10 (1813), 260–62; quoted in part by E. C. Wilson, *England's Eliza*, pp. 4–6.

24. See Tottel's pamphlet in Nichols, *Progresses*, 1:38–60.

25. *First Commentary*, p. 10.

26. James E. Phillips, *Images of a Queen*, p. 19.

27. See Roy C. Strong, "The Popular Celebration of the Accession Day of Queen Elizabeth I."

28. *First Commentary*, p. 11.

29. *Allegorical Imagery*, p. 47.

30. The interpretation of the dragon as symbolic of death was first suggested in 1945 by Hankins, "Spenser and the Revelation of St. John," reprinted in *Source and Meaning*, pp. 99–119. Carol V. Kaske interprets the dragon of canto 11 as concupiscence, and the three-day battle as representative of the three stages of human nature in dealing with concupiscence: unregenerate man under the Law, baptized Christian man, and Christ the perfect man ("The Dragon's Spark and Sting and the Structure of Red Cross's Dragon-fight: *The Faerie Queene*, 1. xi–xii"). Kaske makes some useful suggestions, but the number of references to death and mortality in the narrative rhetoric of the episode makes me believe that Hankins's interpretation of the dragon was more nearly correct. Though an element of mortality, concupiscence is finally too narrow a term to embrace the Pauline concept of mortal weakness, which is what Redcross must overcome.

31. *The Prophetic Moment*, p. 45.

Chapter 3

1. *The Veil of Allegory*, pp. 75–97.

2. See Louis B. Wright, "The Utility of History," in *Middle-Class Culture in Elizabethan England*, pp. 297–338.

3. "Nanque qui bene considerat inuenit omnem Romanam historiam ab Aeneae aduentu vsque ad sua tempora summatim celebrasse Virgilium. Quod ideo latet, quia confusus est ordo," Ad *Aeneidem* 6. 752.

4. *The Sources of British Chronicle History in Spenser's Faerie Queene*, pp. 184–85. Harper concluded that Spenser follows Geoffrey of Monmouth in the main but draws also from Hardyng, Holinshed, Stow, and the *Mirror for Magistrates*; to these main sources he also adds material drawn from still other authorities. "In short, we see Spenser, not only as a poet, but also as a historian and chronicler and as an antiquarian" (p. 184).

5. To see the catalogues in books 2 and 3 as evocations of history and legend designed to call a reader's awareness of traditions into play, it is fortunately unnecessary to return to Phantastes' chamber to conjure up an "ideal sixteenth-century reader." John Dixon—our sixteenth-century, but scarcely ideal, reader—shows in his contemporary marginal annotations a keen interest in the historical catalogues. See Hough, *First Commentary*, pp. 11–14, 17–18. It is evident that the catalogues did evoke in Dixon a knowledge of history and legend obtained from chronicles; indeed it is apparent that Spenser sent Dixon back to his books (specifically Fabyan's *Chronicle*) to look up things he felt he needed to know about the matters briefly sketched in the poem. In general Dixon added more detailed information to Spenser's summaries or attempted (sometimes incorrectly, as in the note to 3. 3. 47) to solve the puzzles the poet had left.

6. *An Apologie for Poetrie,* in G. Gregory Smith, ed., *Elizabethan Critical Essays,* 1:157.

7. Ibid., pp. 169–70.

8. Harper found no source for the tradition of Debon and Canute (*Sources,* p. 50). T. D. Kendrick suggests that Spenser playfully added them on his own authority and that these and other fanciful additions were clues to his own skepticism about the British History which descended from Geoffrey of Monmouth (*British Antiquity,* pp. 128, 29).

9. *History of the Kings of Britain,* 1:16.

10. *The Allegorical Temper,* pp. 95–96.

11. Harper, *Sources,* pp. 117–20.

12. *Allegorical Temper,* p. 98.

13. See Edwin Greenlaw, *Studies in Spenser's Historical Allegory,* pp. 1–58; Charles B. Millican, *Spenser and the Table Round,* pp. 3–126; Kendrick, *British Antiquity,* pp. 34–44, 126–33.

14. Most discussions of the Faery chronicle have been concerned to decipher what was felt to be Spenser's elaborate code in the Elfin emperors; see Isabel E. Rathborne, *The Meaning of Spenser's Fairyland,* pp. 107–22, and the correspondence in the *Times Literary Supplement* of 1948, pp. 79, 233, 273, 345, 353, 373.

15. See Berger, "The Structure of Merlin's Chronicle in *The Faerie Queene* 3 (iii)."

16. Harper, *Sources,* p. 164; see also p. 184.

17. Cf. Thomas P. Roche, Jr., *The Kindly Flame,* p. 62.

18. Ibid., p. 65.

19. *Spenser's Faerie Queene,* pp. 140–41.

20. Spenser's source in this would appear to be Natilis Comes, who makes Proteus symbolize, among other things, the "force of the atmosphere": "Proteum Neptuni siue Oceani filium finxerunt, quem putarunt vim esse aeris, qui de Stoicorum sententia Iupiter fuit appellatus, ac per omnia pertransiret, & vbique esset, vt patuit superius, cum de Ioue loqueremur. nam aer proxime fit ex aqua in illum extenuata. Hunc naturam esse aeris, per quem temperatum omnia oriuntur, & vnde sit omnibus ortus principium & plantis & animalibus videtur significasse Homer. lib 4 Odyss." *Mythologiae,* 8. 8, sig. KKKᵛ. Somewhat inconsistently, Comes also goes on to interpret Proteus as prime matter, "materia omnis in intellectu forma prior." Hankins follows this latter interpretation of Comes, *Source and Meaning,* pp. 228–34.

21. H. G. Lotspeich notes that Spenser used a variety of material on Nereus brought together by Comes (*Mythologiae,* 8. 6), *Classical Mythology in the Poetry of Edmund Spenser,* p. 90.

22. *Kindly Flame,* p. 182.

23. *Variorum,* 4:269.

Chapter 4

1. *The Allegorical Temper,* p. 140.

2. On mythological "infolding" and "unfolding," especially of the Venus-Virgo, see Edgar Wind, *Pagan Mysteries in the Renaissance,* pp. 72–80.

3. Preface to *The Faerie Queene* (1758), 1:xxxi, quoted in *Variorum,* 2:206; see also W. B. C. Watkins, *Shakespeare and Spenser,* pp. 293–304.

4. This is essentially the point made, though not comically, in a tilt performed before the French in the spring of 1581. The "Four Foster Children of Desire" (among them Sidney and Greville) attempt to storm the "Fortress of Perfect Beauty" but learn that desire must not "destroie a common blessing for a privat benefit." It appears that the tilt was designed to announce, with delicate diplomacy, the queen's final decision on Alençon's suit. See Nichols, *Progresses,* 2:312–29.

5. Allan H. Gilbert, "Belphoebe's Misdeeming of Timias," 630; see also Paul J.

Alpers, *The Poetry of The Faerie Queene*, pp. 186–94, for a more complete discussion of Spenser's use of Ariosto here.

6. Roche links Belphoebe to the tradition of the Heavenly Venus, *The Kindly Flame*, pp. 96–149, especially p. 139.

7. *Queen Elizabeth I*, pp. 72–73; see also Leonard Forster, *The Icy Fire*, pp. 122–47, for an interesting discussion of Elizabeth's political use of Petrarchan conventions.

8. Walter Oakeshott notes that this passage is one marked by a penciled pointing hand in a copy of Spenser (1617 edition) that was owned by Raleigh's son, "Carew Ralegh's Copy of Spenser." Oakeshott believes that the penciled annotations are the work of Raleigh in the last year of his life. The copy also contains some annotations that Oakeshott assigns, on more certain grounds, to Raleigh's wife.

9. *Sir Walter Ralegh*, p. 55. Greenblatt sees in Raleigh "an intense histrionic sensibility constantly striving for a moving presentation of the self" (p. 23).

10. "Sir Walter Raleigh to the Qveen," in *The Poems of Sir Walter Raleigh*, p. 19.

11. The belief, of course, was that *aurum potabile* was good for the heart; see Burton, *The Anatomy of Melancholy*, pt. 2, sec. 4, mem. 1, subs. 4. The joke that gold might be "cordial" in another sense goes back at least as far as Chaucer, whose doctor of physic is especially fond of the metal: "For gold in phisik is cordial, / Therefore he lovede gold in special" (*General Prologue*, 443–44).

12. *Sir Walter Ralegh*, pp. 158–69; my account of the affair follows Rowse.

13. Neale, *Elizabeth*, pp. 327–28.

14. *Poems*, p. 37; see also line 271 (p. 34) and the introduction, p. xxxvii, for Latham's opinion that the poem, which she entitled "The 11th and last Booke of the Ocean to Scinthia," was written while Raleigh was in the Tower in 1592. Both Greenblatt (p. 76) and Rowse (pp. 164–65) agree with this judgment.

15. See Greenblatt, *Ralegh*, pp. 57–98.

16. *Poems*, p. 11.

17. *Kindly Flame*, p. 137n.

Chapter 5

1. T. K. Dunseath, *Spenser's Allegory of Justice in Book Five of The Faerie Queene*; Jane Aptekar, *Icons of Justice*; Judith H. Anderson, " 'Nor Man It Is': The Knight of Justice in Book V of Spenser's *Faerie Queene*."

2. *The Prophetic Moment*, p. 45.

3. *Spenser's Image of Nature*, p. 150.

4. The origins of the detective novel, significantly, are British, and those of the western, of course, American. Most of the exceptions that can be adduced to my brief and general description of the detective fiction are American and reflect the introduction of the concerns of the western into the genre. This fact, one supposes, indicates something about the relative trust in law in the two countries.

5. *Variorum*, 9:46.

6. *Prophetic Moment*, pp. 146ff.

7. On the relationship of the sheriff to the assize court, see Wallace Notestein, *The English People on the Eve of Colonization*, p. 207; Artegall also functions at times like that workhorse of Elizabethan justice, the justice of the peace. See Notestein, *English People*, pp. 211–27; and F. W. Maitland, *The Constitutional History of England*, pp. 207–19, 232–33.

8. *The Dyaloges in Englishe betwene a Doctour of Diuinitie and a Student in the lawes of Englande*; St. German's work was reprinted eleven times between the first English edition of 1530 and 1593.

9. Ibid., sig. B. i^r.

10. Ibid., sig. B. i^{r-v}; St. German says that the "lawe of secondarie reason general" is called so because the law of property is kept in all countries; he adds that the "lawe of reason secondary particuler" is derived from customs and "of diuers maximes and statutes ordeined in this realme." It may be that the settlement of the

Amidas vs. Bracidas case is meant as an illustration of this second part of the law of property, since it depends upon a maxim of law.

11. Herbert B. Nelson, "Amidas v. Bracidas." Nelson found that Bracidas had no case either in common law or in admiralty court law. This fact, along with several others, presents some difficulty for Douglas Northrop's argument ("Spenser's Defence of Elizabeth") that Spenser is allegorizing the workings of the six high courts of justice in the first half of book 5. Since Spenser was a layman whose knowledge of even common law appears more general than exact, one must suppose that his allegory of law is more concerned with general principles than with the particular workings of various courts.

12. *Prophetic Moment*, p. 163.

13. Recognizing the arbitrariness of the conclusion, Keats composed a stanza that brought the episode into line with the intervening two centuries and copied it into his own much-used copy of Spenser at the end of canto 2:

> In after-time, a sage of mickle lore
>> Yclep'd Typographus, the Giant took
>> And did refit his limbs as heretofore,
>> And made him read in many a learned book
>> And into many a lively legend look;
>> Thereby in goodly themes so training him,
>> That all his brutishness he quite forsook,
>> When, meeting Artegall and Talus grim.
> The one he struck stone-blind, the other's eyes wox dim.
>
> *Keats' Poetical Works*, p. 393.

14. Duncan B. Heriot, "Anabaptism in England during the 16th and 17th Centuries." Nashe satirizes John of Leyden and his followers quite savagely in *The Unfortunate Traveller* (1594) and describes, with scarcely a modicum of pity, the slaughter of Munster as their inevitable and merited end.

15. See James E. Phillips, *Images of a Queen*, pp. 44, 66, 82–84, 129, 162–69.

16. See Gough, *Variorum*, 5:201.

17. In choosing Egyptian symbolism for the "allegorical core" of his consideration of English justice, Spenser may have been influenced by Sir John Fortescue's fifteenth-century dialogue on English law, translated by Robert Mulcaster as *A learned commendation of the politique lawes of Englande* (1567). Fortescue contrasts England's "politic law," that is, common law, with the Roman or civil law in use on the continent and praises the English system for restraining its monarchs from tyrannical absolutism. He tells the son of Henry VI that in civil law "the princeis pleasure hath ye force of a lawe." But the king of England "can neither chaunge lawes without the consent of his subiects, not yet charge them with straunge imposicions agaynst their wylles" (sigs. D. ii^v–iii^r). Fortescue then cites Diodorus Siculus, considered one of Spenser's chief sources for the Isis and Osiris material, for his account of the subiection to law of the ancient Egyptian kings: "The Egiptien kings liued first not after ye licentious maner of other rulers, whose will & pleasure is in steede of law, but they kept themselves as private persones in subiection of the lawes. And this did they willingly, beeing perswaded that by obeyinge the laws thei should be blessed" (sig. E. ii^r).

18. *Nicomachean Ethics*, 5. 10, in *Basic Works of Aristotle*, p. 1020.

19. See Stuart E. Prall, "The Development of Equity in Tudor England." St. German, *Dyaloges*, sig. D. iiii^v, discusses this aspect of equity; Edward Hake, *Epieikeia*, devotes the second and largest section of his dialogue on equity to "the Equity of the Common lawes of England." Hake's work was written in the late 1590s.

20. "*The Faerie Queene*, I and V," pp. 123–50, esp. 143–45.

21. Quoted by J. E. Neale, *Elizabeth I and Her Parliaments, 1584–1601*, pp. 118–19.

22. Dolon, living a "little wide by West" and being "well shot in yeares," alludes to Philip II, especially in his capacity as the author of plots against Elizabeth.

"Guizor," his son, suggests the French family of Guise and points to the close political relationship between the Guise and their powerful Spanish associates (A. B. Gough and C. G. Osgood, *Variorum*, 5:211–12). René Graziani has suggested that the specifics of Dolon's treachery refer to a supposed plot to blow up Elizabeth's bedchamber about the time she was deciding about Mary's death warrant ("Elizabeth at Isis Church"). Archimago, of course, shadows similar treachery on the part of the papacy.

23. Northrop details the points of agreement—and disagreement—between the episodes in the last five cantos and the theoretical norms of international justice discussed in the Renaissance ("Spenser's Defence of Elizabeth").

24. René Graziani, "Philip II's *Impresa* and Spenser's *Souldan*." Aptekar reproduces the *impresa* from Ruscelli's *Imprese illustri* (1566), *Icons of Justice*, p. 82.

25. *Icons of Justice*, p. 108; cf. pp. 58–69.

26. William Nelson, "Queen Elizabeth, Spenser's Mercilla, and a Rusty Sword."

27. *The Poetry of Edmund Spenser*, p. 268. If Spenser's "principall" is read as principle, then the terms are reversed for what he obviously means to say.

28. Roger Sale, *Reading Spenser*, p. 175.

29. Mercilla/Elizabeth has been defended by the suggestion that mercy is indeed being shown—but toward her subjects, whose safety Duessa/Mary threatens: James E. Phillips, "Renaissance Concepts of Justice and the Structure of *The Faerie Queene*, Book 5"; Graziani, "Elizabeth at Isis Church." The argument, however, is specious, and Spenser does not make any such claim. It is rather as if Isabella in the last scene of *Measure for Measure* should announce that she will indeed show mercy, not to Angelo, but to the people of Vienna whom he has wronged. The most rigorous and uncompromising legal justice is always "mercy" in this sense, but this is not what a man expects when he throws himself on "the mercy of the court."

30. Josephine Waters Bennett suggested this conflation of Grey and Norris in the Artegall of canto 12 (*The Evolution of the Faerie Queene*, pp. 194–95).

31. Alexander C. Judson, *Life of Spenser*, in *Variorum*, 11:132–35, 162–63.

32. *The Allegory of Love*, p. 349.

33. Judson, *Life*, in *Variorum*, 11:198–99.

Chapter 6

1. See Donald Cheney, *Spenser's Image of Nature*, pp. 176–96.

2. See *Variorum*, 6:349–64. It was such a supposition that led earlier critics to identify Calidore with Sidney or the Earl of Essex. But the inconclusiveness of the debate between the critical partisans of each was telling: there is no evidence in the poem that Spenser wanted us to connect Calidore with either man, and the scholars' arguments were based mainly on the contemporary reputations of Sidney and Essex.

3. *Spenser's Image of Nature*, p. 195.

4. "The Prospect of the Imagination," p. 94.

5. *Spenser's Faerie Queene*, pp. 208–9.

6. *The Allegorical Temper*, pp. 120–60.

7. "I have, God woot, a large feeld to ere, / And wayke been the oxen in my plough." *Canterbury Tales*, A 886–87.

8. *Spenser's Image of Nature*, p. 192.

9. E.g., Berger, "A Secret Discipline" and "The Prospect of Imagination"; Richard Neuse, "Book 6 as Conclusion to *The Faerie Queene*."

10. *Spenser's Image of Nature*, pp. 223–25.

11. "Nemo nostrum per Deos immortales qui Paridem suo iudicio non damnet: nemo propè rursus est, qui tam turpe Paridis iudicium, non imitetur." *Mythologiae*, 6.22, sig. Yy ^r.

12. "Consultante uidelicet Paride secum, qua è tribus potissimam ad felicitatem uiam eligeret, eligit denique uoluptatem, cum uerò sapientiam spreuerit, & potentiam, meritò imprudenter felicitatem sperans, incidit in miseriam. Duae tantum occurrisse traduntur Herculi, Venus scilicet, atque Iuno. Hercules neglecta Venere, animosam sub Ionone uirtutem est secutus, neque tamen inter mortales propterea felix, perpetuò certaminum labore uexatus, sed hunc tandem exequat uictoria coelo, huic denique superata tellus sydera donat. Duae quoque Philebo cuidam obuiae, uoluptas, atque sapientia, de uictoria contenderunt, atque eo iudice, Venus Palladem superauisse uisa est. Sed paulò pòst Socrate rectius decernente, Minerua uictoriam reportauit. Spreta uerò Venus simul atque Iuno Socratem tandem sub falsis iudicibus agitatum, morte damnarunt. Laurentius denique noster Apollinis oraculo doctus, nullem posthabuit superiorum. Tres enim uidit, tres quoque pro meritis adorauit. Quamobrem & à Pallade sapientam & à Iunone potentiam & à Venere gratias poesimque, & Musicam reportauit." *Marsilii Ficini Florentini . . . Opera*, sig. Mmm4^v. Paul Oskar Kristeller discusses the passage and Ficino's interpretation of the choice of Paris in *The Philosophy of Marsilio Ficino*, pp. 357–59.

13. *The Tempest*, act 3, sc. 1, lines 2–4.

14. "DICUNTUR Gratiae filiae esse Iouis & Eurynomes, quod nihil aliud significat, quàm fertilitatem agrorum, frugumque abundantiam: nam ευρὺ latè significat, at νόμος, legem, haec nimirum agrorum vbertas non nisi pacis beneficio prouenit, quod ipsum significat etiam Eunomia. Vbi enim leges & aequitas dominantur, cessatque vis, & latrocinia, & direptiones alienarum rerum; tunc agri rident, domus laetantur, templa Deorum immortalium iucunda sunt, omnibusque rerum ornamentum accedit." *Mythologiae*, 4.15, sig. Ee4 ^{r}.

15. *The Allegory of Love*, p. 351.

16. Lotspeich, *Classical Mythology in the Poetry of Spenser*, p. 39.

17. *Spenser's Image of Nature*, p. 235.

18. "Nam in tam prodigiosa corporis forma, quae humanitas, quae iustitia, quae temperantia, quae pietas esse potuit? aut qui dimidium sui belua teterrima exsisterit, quo pacto non in maximas difficultates ob sua flagitia illabatur, patriamque & per summam turpitudinem relinquere cogatur?" *Mythologiae*, 7.4, sig. Bbb2 ^{r}.

19. *Spenser's Faerie Queene*, p. 222.

◆ Works Cited

Alpers, Paul J. "Mode in Narrative Poetry." In *To Tell a Story: Narrative Theory and Practice*. Los Angeles: William Andrews Clark Library, University of California at Los Angeles, 1973.

_____. *The Poetry of The Faerie Queene*. Princeton: Princeton University Press, 1967.

Anderson, Judith H. " 'Nor Man It Is': the Knight of Justice in Book 5 of Spenser's *Faerie Queene*." *PMLA* 85 (1970): 65–77.

Aptekar, Jane. *Icons of Justice: Iconography and Thematic Imagery in Book 5 of the Faerie Queene*. New York: Columbia University Press, 1969.

Ariosto, Ludovico. *Orlando Furioso*. Edited by Remo Ceserani. Turin: Unione tipografico editrice torinese, 1966.

_____. *Orlando Furioso*. Translated by William Stewart Rose. Edited by Stewart A. Baker and A. Bartlett Giamatti. New York: Bobbs-Merrill, 1968.

Aristotle. *Basic Works of Aristotle*. Edited by Richard McKeon. New York: Random House, 1941.

Bennett, Josephine Waters. *The Evolution of The Faerie Queene*. Chicago: University of Chicago Press, 1942.

Berger, Harry, Jr. *The Allegorical Temper: Vision and Reality in Book 2 of Spenser's Faerie Queene*. New Haven: Yale University Press, 1957.

_____. "The Prospect of Imagination: Spenser and the Limits of Poetry." *Studies in English Literature* 1 (1961): 94–120.

_____. "A Secret Discipline: *The Faerie Queene*, Book 6." In *Form and Convention in the Poetry of Edmund Spenser*. English Institute Essays. Edited by William Nelson. New York: Columbia University Press, 1961.

_____. "The Structure of Merlin's Chronicle in *The Faerie Queene* 3 (iii)." *Studies in English Literature* 9 (1969): 39–51.

Bunny, Edmund. *Certaine prayers and other godly exercises for the seuenteenth of Nouember*. London, 1585.

Burton, Robert. *The Anatomy of Melancholy*. 3 vols. London: J. M. Dent, 1932.

Camden, William. *Annals; or, The historie of the most renowned and victorious Princesse Elizabeth*. 1615. Translated by R. Norton. London, 1635.

Chaucer, Geoffrey. *The Works of Geoffrey Chaucer*. Edited by F. N. Robinson. 2d ed. Boston: Houghton Mifflin, 1957.

Cheney, Donald. *Spenser's Image of Nature: Wild Man and Shepherd in "The Faerie Queene."* New Haven: Yale University Press, 1966.

Cohn, Norman. *The Pursuit of the Millennium.* London: Secker and Warburg, 1957.

Comes, Natalis [Conti, Natale]. *Mythologiae sive Explicationis fabularum libri decem.* Padua, 1616.

Comparetti, Domenico. *Vergil in the Middle Ages.* Translated by E. T. M. Benecke. 1908. Reprint. Hamden, Conn.: Archon Books, 1966.

Dictionary of National Biography. Edited by Sir Leslie Stephen and Sir Sidney Lee. London: Oxford University Press, 1908–9.

Dixon, John. See Hough, Graham, *First Commentary.*

Drew, D. L. *The Allegory of the Aeneid.* Oxford: Basil Blackwell, 1927.

Dryden, John. *The Poems of John Dryden.* Edited by James Kinsley. 4 vols. Oxford: Clarendon Press, 1958.

Dunseath, T. K. *Spenser's Allegory of Justice in Book Five of The Faerie Queene.* Princeton: Princeton University Press, 1968.

Durling, Robert M. *The Figure of the Poet in Renaissance Epic.* Cambridge, Mass.: Harvard University Press, 1965.

Edwards, Thomas R. *Imagination and Power: A Study of Poetry on Public Themes.* New York: Oxford University Press, 1971.

Ficino, Marsilio. *Marsilii Ficini Florentini . . . Opera.* Basil, 1576. Reprint. Turin: Bottega d'Erasmo, 1962.

Fletcher, Angus. *The Prophetic Moment: An Essay on Spenser.* Chicago: University of Chicago Press, 1971.

Fornari, Simon. *La Spositione . . . Sopra l'Orlando Furioso.* Florence, 1549.

Forster, Leonard. *The Icy Fire: Five Studies of European Petrarchism.* Cambridge: Cambridge University Press, 1969.

Fortescue, Sir John. *A learned commendation of the politique lawes of Englande.* Translated by Robert Mulcaster. London, 1567.

Foxe, John. *Actes and Monuments of matters most speciall and Memorable, happenyng in the Church, with an vniuersal history of the same.* London, 1583.

Geoffrey of Monmouth. *History of the Kings of Britain.* Translated by Sebastian Evans. London: J. M. Dent, 1912.

Gilbert, Allan H. "Belphoebe's Misdeeming of Timias." *PMLA* 62 (1947): 622–43.

Giraldi Cintio, Giovanni Battista. *Giraldi Cintio on Romances: being a translation of the Discorsi intorno al comporre dei romanzi.* Translated by Henry L. Snuggs. Lexington, Ky.: University of Kentucky Press, 1968.

Graziani, René. "Elizabeth at Isis Church." *PMLA* 79 (1964): 376–89.

————. "Philip II's *Impresa* and Spenser's Souldan." *Journal of the Warburg and Courtauld Institutes* 27 (1964): 322–42.

Greenblatt, Stephen J. *Sir Walter Ralegh: The Renaissance Man and His Roles.* New Haven: Yale University Press, 1973.

Greenlaw, Edwin. *Studies in Spenser's Historical Allegory.* Baltimore: Johns Hopkins University Press, 1932.

Hake, Edward. *Epieikeia: A Dialogue on Equity in Three Parts.* Edited by D. E. C. Yale. New Haven: Yale University Press for the Yale Law Library, 1953.

Haller, William. *The Elect Nation: The Meaning and Relevance of Foxe's Book of Martyrs.* New York: Harper and Row, 1963.

Hankins, John Erskine. *Source and Meaning in Spenser's Allegory.* Oxford: Clarendon Press, 1971.

Hamilton, A. C. *The Structure of Allegory in The Faerie Queene.* Oxford: Clarendon Press, 1961.

Harington, Sir John, trans. *Orlando Furioso: Translated into English Heroical Verse by Sir John Harrington.* Edited by Robert McNulty. Oxford: Clarendon Press, 1972.

Harper, Carrie A. *The Sources of British Chronicle History in Spenser's Faerie Queene.* Philadelphia: John C. Winston. 1910.

Heriot, Duncan B. "Anabaptism in England during the 16th and 17th Centuries." *Transactions of the Congregational Historical Society* 12 (1933–36): 256–77, 312–20; 13 (1937–39): 22–40.

Hoffman, Nancy. "The Landscape of Man." Ph.D. dissertation, University of California at Berkeley, 1971.

Hough, Graham, ed. *The First Commentary on The Faerie Queene.* 1964. Reprint. Folcroft, Pa.: Folcroft Press, 1969.

————. "The First Commentary on *The Faerie Queene.*" *Times Literary Supplement* 63 (1964): 294.

Hughes, Merritt Y. *Virgil and Spenser.* University of California Publications in English, vol. 2, no. 3. Berkeley: University of California Press, 1929.

Jones, J. W. "Allegorical Interpretation in Servius." *Classical Journal* 56 (1961): 217–26.

Kaske, Carol V. "The Dragon's Spark and Sting and the Structure of Red Cross's Dragon Fight: *The Faerie Queene*, 1. 11–12." *Studies in Philology* 66 (1969): 609–38.

Keats, John. *Poetical Works.* Edited by H. W. Garrod. London: Oxford University Press, 1956.

Kendrick, T. D. *British Antiquity.* 1950. Reprint. New York: Barnes and Noble, 1970.

Kermode, Frank. "*The Faerie Queene*, 1 and 5." *Bulletin of the John Rylands Library* 47 (1964): 123–50.

————. "Spenser and the Allegorists." *Proceedings of the British Academy* 48 (1962): 261–79.

[Both essays reprinted in *Shakespeare, Spenser, Donne: Renaissance Essays* by Frank Kermode. London: Routledge and Kegan Paul, 1971.]

Knight, W. F. Jackson. *Roman Vergil.* London: Faber and Faber, 1944.

Kristeller, Paul Oskar. *The Philosophy of Marsilio Ficino.* Translated by Virginia Conant. 1943. Reprint. Gloucester, Mass.: Peter Smith, 1965.

Lewis, C. S. *The Allegory of Love.* 1936. Reprint. New York: Oxford University Press Galaxy Book, 1958.

Lotspeich, Henry Gibbons. *Classical Mythology in the Poetry of Edmund Spenser*. 1932. Reprint. New York: Octagon Books, 1965.

Maitland, F. W. *The Constitutional History of England*. Cambridge: Cambridge University Press, 1908.

McLane, Paul E. *Spenser's Shepheardes Calender: A Study in Elizabethan Allegory*. Notre Dame, Ind.: Notre Dame University Press, 1961.

Millican, Charles B. *Spenser and the Table Round: A Study of the Contemporaneous Background for Spenser's Use of the Arthurian Legend*. Cambridge, Mass.: Harvard University Press, 1932.

Milton, John. *Complete Poems and Major Prose*. Edited by Merritt Y. Hughes. New York: Odyssey Press, 1957.

Murrin, Michael. *The Veil of Allegory: Some Notes toward a Theory of Allegorical Rhetoric in the Renaissance*. Chicago: University of Chicago Press, 1969.

Neale, J. E. *Elizabeth I and Her Parliaments, 1584–1601*. London: Jonathan Cape, 1957.

———. *Queen Elizabeth I: A Biography*. London: Jonathan Cape, 1934.

Nelson, Herbert B. "Amidas v. Bracidas." *Modern Language Quarterly* 1 (1940): 393–99.

Nelson, William. *Fact or Fiction: The Dilemma of the Renaissance Storyteller*. Cambridge, Mass.: Harvard University Press, 1973.

———. *The Poetry of Edmund Spenser*. New York: Columbia University Press, 1963.

———. "Queen Elizabeth, Spenser's Mercilla, and a Rusty Sword." *Renaissance News* 18 (1965): 113–17.

Neuse, Richard. "Book 6 as Conclusion to *The Faerie Queene*." *ELH* 35 (1968): 329–53. Reprinted in *Critical Essays on Spenser from ELH*. Baltimore: Johns Hopkins University Press, 1970.

Nichols, John, ed. *The Progresses and Public Processions of Queen Elizabeth*. 3 vols. 1823. Reprint. New York: Burt Franklin, 1966.

Northrop, Douglas. "Spenser's Defence of Elizabeth." *University of Toronto Quarterly* 38 (1969), 277–94.

Notestein, Wallace. *The English People on the Eve of Colonization*. New ed. New York: Harper and Row Torchbook, 1962.

Oakeshott, Walter. "Carew Ralegh's Copy of Spenser." *The Library* 5th series, 26 (1971): 1–21.

Parry, Adam. "The Two Voices of Virgil's *Aeneid*." *Arion* 2 (1963): 66–78. Reprinted in *Virgil: A Collection of Critical Essays*. Edited by Steele Commager. Englewood Cliffs, N. J.: Prentice Hall, 1966.

Phillips, James E. *Images of a Queen: Mary Stuart in Sixteenth-Century Literature*. Berkeley: University of California Press, 1964.

———. "Renaissance Concepts of Justice and the Structure of *The Faerie Queene*, Book 5." *Huntington Library Quarterly* 33 (1970): 103–20.

Pierce, William, ed. *The Marprelate Tracts, 1588–89*. London: J. Clarke, 1911.

Pigna, Giambattista. *I Romanzi*. Venice, 1554.

Prall, Stuart E. "The Development of Equity in Tudor England." *American Journal of Legal History* 8 (1964): 1–19.

Quinn, Kenneth. *Vergil's Aeneid: A Critical Description*. Ann Arbor: University of Michigan Press, 1968.

Ralegh, Sir Walter. *The Poems of Sir Walter Ralegh*. Edited by Agnes M. C. Latham. London: Routledge and Kegan Paul, 1951.

Rand, E. K. "Is Donatus's Commentary on Virgil Lost?" *Classical Quarterly* 10 (1916): 158–64.

Rathborne, Isabel E. *The Meaning of Spenser's Fairyland*. New York: Columbia University Press, 1937.

Roche, Thomas P., Jr. *The Kindly Flame: A Study of the Third and Fourth Books of Spenser's Faerie Queene*. Princeton: Princeton University Press, 1964.

Ronsard, Pierre de. *Oeuvres Complètes*. 20 vols. Edited by Paul Laumonier. Paris: Didier, 1937–75.

Rowse, A. L. *Sir Walter Ralegh: His Family and Private Life*. New York: Harper and Row, 1962.

St. German, Christopher. *The Dyalogues in Englishe betwene a Doctour of Diuinitie and a Student in the lawes of Englande*. London, 1554.

Sale, Roger. *Reading Spenser: An Introduction to The Faerie Queene*. New York: Random House, 1968.

Servius Grammaticus. Commentary in *P. Virgilli Maronis, poetae Mantuani, Vniuersum Poema*. Venice, 1562.

_____. *Servii Grammatici qui feruntur in Vergilii Carmina Commentarii*. Edited by G. Thilo and H. Hagen. 3 vols. 1881–87. Reprint. Hildesheim: G. Olms, 1961.

Shakespeare, William. *The Riverside Shakespeare*. Edited by G. Blakemore Evans. Boston: Houghton Mifflin, 1974.

Smith, G. Gregory, ed. *Elizabethan Critical Essays*. 2 vols. London: Oxford University Press, 1904.

Spenser, Edmund. *The Works of Edmund Spenser: A Variorum Edition*. Edited by Edwin Greenlaw, C. G. Osgood, F. M. Padelford. 9 vols. Baltimore: Johns Hopkins University Press, 1932–49.

Strong, Roy C. "The Popular Celebration of the Accession Day of Queen Elizabeth I." *Journal of the Warburg and Courtauld Institutes* 21 (1958): 86–103.

_____. *Portraits of Queen Elizabeth I*. Oxford: Clarendon Press, 1963.

Suetonius. *Suetonius*. Loeb Classical Library. Edited and translated by J. C. Rolfe. 2 vols. Cambridge, Mass.: Harvard University Press, 1914.

Sylvester, Joshuah. *Complete Works of Joshuah Sylvester*. Edited by Rev. Alexander Grosart. 2 vols. 1880. Reprint. New York: AMS Press, 1967.

Tasso, Torquato. *Jerusalem Delivered*. Translated by Edward Fairfax. Reprint. Carbondale, Ill.: University of Southern Illinois Press, 1962.

_____. *Opere di Torquato Tasso*. 2 vols. Edited by Bortolo Tommaso Sozzi. Rev. ed. Turin: Unione tipografico editrice torinese, 1968.

Tuve, Rosemond. *Allegorical Imagery: Some Medieval Books and Their Posterity.* Princeton: Princeton University Press, 1966.

Vida, Marco Girolamo. *Poeticarum Libri Tres.* In *The Art of Poetry: the Poetical Treatises of Horace, Vida, and Boileau.* Edited by Albert S. Cook. 1892. Reprint. New York: G. E. Stechert, 1926.

Virgil. *Virgil.* Loeb Classical Library. Edited and translated by H. Rushton Fairclough. 1916. Rev. ed. Cambridge, Mass.: Harvard University Press, 1935.

Waters, D. Douglas. *Duessa as Theological Satire.* Columbia, Mo.: University of Missouri Press, 1970.

Watkins, W. B. C. *Shakespeare and Spenser.* Princeton: Princeton University Press, 1950.

Webb, William Stanford. "Vergil in Spenser's Epic Theory." *ELH* 4 (1937): 62–84. Reprinted in *Critical Essays on Spenser from ELH.* Baltimore: Johns Hopkins University Press, 1970.

White, Helen C. *Tudor Books of Saints and Martyrs.* Madison, Wis.: University of Wisconsin Press, 1963.

Williams, Kathleen. *Spenser's Faerie Queene: The World of Glass.* London: Routledge and Kegan Paul, 1966.

Wilson, Elkin Calhoun. *England's Eliza.* 1939. Reprint. New York: Octagon Books, 1966.

Wind, Edgar. *Pagan Mysteries in the Renaissance.* 1958. Rev. ed. New York: W. W. Norton, 1968.

Wright, Louis B. *Middle-Class Culture in Elizabethan England.* Chapel Hill, N.C.: University of North Carolina Press, 1935.

Yates, Frances A. "Queen Elizabeth as Astraea." *Journal of the Warburg and Courtauld Institutes* 10 (1947): 27–82. Reprinted in *Astraea: The Imperial Theme in the Sixteenth Century.* London: Routledge and Kegan Paul, 1975.

Zabughin, Vladimiro. *Vergilio nel Rinascimento Italiano da Dante a Torquato Tasso.* 2 vols. Bologna: N. Zanichelli, 1921–23.

Index to The Faerie Queene

(General Index Follows)

Characters and Places in The Faerie Queene

✖ General Index